Bert Roebben

# Seeking Sense in the City

# Dortmunder Beiträge zu Theologie und Religionspädagogik

herausgegeben von

Prof. Dr. Gerhard Büttner

und

Prof. Dr. Thomas Pola

Band 7

LIT

Bert Roebben

# Seeking Sense in the City
European Perspectives on Religious Education

LIT

**Bibliographic information published by the Deutsche Nationalbibliothek**
The Deutsche Nationalbibliothek lists this publication in the Deutsche
Nationalbibliografie; detailed bibliographic data are available in the Internet at
http://dnb.d-nb.de.

ISBN 978-3-643-10321-5

A catalogue record for this book is available from the British Library

©LIT VERLAG Dr. W. Hopf Berlin 2009
Fresnostr. 2    D-48159 Münster
Tel. +49 (0) 2 51-620 32 22    Fax +49 (0) 2 51-922 60 99
e-Mail: lit@lit-verlag.de    http://www.lit-verlag.de

**Distribution:**
In Germany: LIT Verlag Fresnostr. 2, D-48159 Münster
Tel. +49 (0) 2 51-620 32 22, Fax +49 (0) 2 51-922 60 99, e-Mail: vertrieb@lit-verlag.de

In Austria: Medienlogistik Pichler-ÖBZ GmbH & Co KG
IZ-NÖ, Süd, Straße 1, Objekt 34, A-2355 Wiener Neudorf
Tel. +43 (0) 22 36-63 53 52 90, Fax +43 (0) 22 36-63 53 52 43, e-Mail: mlo@medien-logistik.at

In Switzerland: B + M Buch- und Medienvertriebs AG
Hochstr. 357, CH-8200 Schaffhausen
Tel. +41 (0) 52-643 54 30, Fax +41 (0) 52-643 54 35, e-Mail: order@buch-medien.ch

Distributed in the UK by: Global Book Marketing, 99B Wallis Rd, London, E9 5LN
Phone: +44 (0) 20 8533 5800 – Fax: +44 (0) 1600 775 663
http://www.centralbooks.co.uk/html

Distributed in North America by:

**Transaction Publishers**
New Brunswick (U.S.A.) and London (U.K.)

Transaction Publishers
Rutgers University
35 Berrue Circle
Piscataway, NJ 08854

Phone: +1 (732) 445 - 2280
Fax: + 1 (732) 445 - 3138
for orders (U. S. only):
toll free (888) 999 - 6778
e-mail: orders@transactionpub.com

# Foreword to the Second Edition

The first edition of this book was published in 2009. The positive reviews in respected international journals and the helpful feedback of many readers inside and outside Europe encouraged me to apply for a second edition of the book within the series of Dortmund contributions to theology and religious education. I thank my colleagues Michael Basse, Gerhard Büttner and Thomas Pola for allowing me to do so. In comparison to the 2009 edition the book in front of you contains three more chapters. They were written and partly published after 2009 and are fitting well into the overall concept of the book. At the back a new index is added and on several places corrections have been made. The book is now presented in hard cover.

The corporate design of my research program "Seeking Sense in the City" is added on the cover as a head line. The artist who created this, is my brother Anton Roebben, production designer, creative advisor and co-founder of the independent animation studio "Walking the Dog" in Brussels. The image of the road sign is rather surprising: many ways are open for driving and interpreting. It is up to the young learner to decide which path to choose. But he/she is not left alone in that discernment, in that "sense seeking" in the midst of the complexity of the city. Others are sharing the learning space: friends, parents, teachers, ministers. They all can become "meaningful" others in that quest, when they show the courage of their convictions and point to promising landscapes. I wish you as a reader a pleasant journey too. Please send me a postcard with your views, visions and comments on the road. My address can be found on www.seekingsense.be.

Bert Roebben
Leuven, Spring 2013

# Table of contents

Foreword to the second edition — 5

Table of contents — 7

Introduction — 11

## PART 1 – EDUCATION, RELIGION AND VALUES

Chapter 1 – To initiate into a world of difference
Design for a dynamic-integral values education — 29

Chapter 2 – Responsible imagination
Moral education and cultural change — 43

Chapter 3 – Religious communication in modern culture
The case of young adults — 65

Chapter 4 – The vulnerability of the post-modern educator
Raising children as *locus theologicus* — 93

## PART 2 – EDUCATION, RELIGION AND SCHOOL

Chapter 5 – Narthical religious learning
Redefining religious education in terms of pilgrimage — 111

Chapter 6 – Children's theology
Concepts and contexts, problems and horizons — 127

Chapter 7 – Learning in difference
Inter-religious learning in the secondary school 143

Chapter 8 – Modern narrative identities and the Bible
A subversive concept of religious education 167

Chapter 9 – Between professionalism and spirituality
The education of teachers in religion 185

Chapter 10 – Kenosis, human flourishing and solidarity
Re-thinking the goal of education 201


PART 3 – EDUCATION, RELIGION AND THE CITY

Chapter 11 – Shaping a playground for transcendence
Youth and young adult ministry in the global era 213

Chapter 12 – Reading the signs of the times
Prolegomena for a theology of youth ministry 227

Chapter 13 – The mirror effect
Youth ministry and theological education 245

Chapter 14 – International developments in youth ministry
research. A comparative review 259

| | |
|---|---|
| Epilogue | 275 |
| References | 279 |
| Acknowledgments | 299 |
| Index | 301 |

# Introduction

Education is an act of faith: an act of believing in the future. Whoever undertakes the task of caring for children and youngsters is showing a boundless faith in what is yet to come. In caring for children one gives attention to the awakening possibilities that are in full development. One imagines the invisible, based on the assumption that all will be well for this particular child, this particular youngster. There is a future for this child's unique life destination. The fruits of this development are ripening, silently, but irreversibly. Education is an act of faith: one gives his best to something that is bigger than oneself and bigger than the best of oneself. In the act of educating giving is receiving, to act is to set children free. In education the ultimate paradox of what it means to be human comes powerful to the fore: to live life to the fullest is to set free.

This book about religious education is anchored in this idea of boundless faith. It aspires to be a 'literacy of hope' (in German: *Alphabetisierung der Hoffnung*, see Balderman 1996, 15-23) written on every day's lifelines and points to the direction in which that life reproduces new life when one sets children free. This book aims to give insight in the learning processes that take place between the generations when people show each other their most intimate 'burning inside', namely that of faith. Religious education does not differ from general education. In everyday education children's questions are taken seriously by means of undertaking the task of beginning to formulate an answer together. The educator is attempting to do so in a conscious manner, trying to keep as much as possible in agreement with the norms and values as he has planned. By attempting to formulate an answer, the question itself gets perpetuity value. The question has been heard, the child has been seen and the world is becoming a better place. Strictly taken one does not need religious faith when educating children. Just a good amount of common sense suffices. The opposite is true though: to educate children 'in faith' one has to have faith in education.

**Project developer or hope generator?**

In education nowadays the question is often heard whether or not there is an alternative for the human being as a 'project developer'. Children and youngsters obviously cannot be perceived as projects. They are not moldable, adaptable and cannot be domesticated (in the double meaning of to tame and to bring home). They are uncompromisingly themselves, on their way to full maturity, to the fulfillment of their own life destination. In their protest, cry for attention, longing for protection and in the provocative question 'is this the future yet?' lies the denial of the ideal of feasibility of our days. In each and every child the future presents itself in a surprising and unique manner. That is a fact that no one, not even the best equipped and most professional educator, can undo or manipulate. In these late modern times, where also the master narratives about education have disappeared, one is confronted in a completely new way with the irreducible uniqueness of children and youngsters. Never before the 'big questions' about the meaning of life have been so eminent as today, and never before the need for 'worthy dreams' was felt so explicitly as in our days (Daloz Parks 2000). The honest and powerful handling of fragility and uniqueness cannot rely on the old religious or humanistic answers anymore, inasmuch as they are occupied with their own institutional self-preservation.

The first goal of this book is to give religious educators a pat on the back, to enable them to do their jobs with truthfulness and inspired professionalism, whether they are school teachers, parish catechists or religious educators in the congregation, youth ministers, religious counselors or parents. The big challenge for education lies in the designing of a new and liberating perspective on being human, together with actual children and youngsters, in order to generate hope for the future of this world. Educators who set themselves the task of teaching morality and spirituality to future adults are called upon to fulfill the role of 'hope generator'. In my perspective this is needed now more than ever. In my 1994 doctoral dissertation I described our era as experiencing a 'call for education', an era in which adults are more conscious of their task to help young people to be truly human and to support them with counter pressure and ideals (Roebben 1995a). Today, fourteen years later, I dare to speak of a time which is ready to take up the dialogue with the big religious movements of our culture. The pedagogical question has become a theological one. Perhaps, the hope which our day and age so desperately longs for can be enhanced by this dialogue. At least on the condition that educators learn to set children and youngsters free in their *religious* education ...

Which expertise is needed for this cultural turnaround? Undoubtedly domain specific knowledge on the terrain of ethics and religion. Undoubtedly didactical skills to explain things clearly. Undoubtedly communicative competencies to stimulate the dialogue between young people with each other and internally as well. But what is needed the most is pedagogical concern, the willingness to be interested in them and to be among them (in Latin: *inter-esse*), in the 'in between' of youth and culture, of past and future, of already and not yet, of experience and revelation. The generator of hope is a person with a soul in his body. Someone who knows what it means to go through life being a moral and/or religious person. Someone who dares to wrestle with the complexity of modern existence, who lets his own values, norms and meanings be challenged by everyday life, who brings his own spiritual sources in movement, enabling them to endure this quest and give it meaning. Such a person is truly inspired. Hopeful education brings this inspiration and care for the concrete quest of (young) people permanently under attention. Their little stories are given space in order to be seen and told in relation to the big movements of our culture that are happening in depth (historical), in breadth (socially) and in the distance (with respect to the wellbeing of future generations). In hopeful education everything is kept together, not torn apart. Life stories and story traditions can of course fall to pieces on the floor, but in modern and hopeful education one is able to pick up the pieces and go on. According to Herman Servotte, who during his lifetime as priest-professor was an intellectual leader to many young people in Leuven (Belgium), this is the characteristic of the moderns: they keep having faith that one can pick up the pieces and that they even can be bound together into new syntheses. Radical post-modernists have decided for themselves not to pick up the pieces any more, let alone bind them together. Education in a modern and hopeful (religious) teaching perspective invites the youth to learn to formulate and experience a holistic view on life, to bind themselves with and to each other.

**Vision and discernment**

The educator of the future is fascinated by a vision for which he wants to be held responsible. He has heard the calling for life enrichment that arises out of the belly of society and more particular out of the lives of youngsters. He does not speak, nor act, on his own accord, but entrusts himself to the ultimate meaningfulness of this magnificent 'young' reality that surrounds him. He sees the desire of young people to be of worth. He senses their creativity and lets this come to light. He recognizes their impatience and understands their outcry for attention. All this is experiential knowledge to him. Without this vision he feels empty and meaningless. Whenever a society as a whole decides not to see and articulate the vision of hope expressed in their children, the youth starts to run wild (freely translated from *Proverbs* 29:18). The modern West-European society is well on its way realizing this: the outcry of the youth for ideals is not heard anymore, the call for inspiration is nipped in the bud. Can we then really be surprised that some youngsters indulge in excessive violence, brought upon themselves and others – in an attempt to be seen or heard?

Religious education can play a meaningful part in invoking the vision and the experiential learning of the practice of discernment, because it hands over a destination for the thinking and acting of the learner. As previously stated, religion teaches one to look at reality from an alternative perspective, not for the gain of oneself, but from the view of the other. Religion de-centers, it points away from the narrow-mindedness of the own truth, to a direction of broader orientations. Religion sensitizes for the non-constructible, indefinable, unforeseeable in a human person's life, which transcends humanity. Especially in the experience of transcendence new life is possible – fresh, authentic and completely immanent new life. Whoever has been introduced to that vision is challenged to educate in a completely new way and is able to distinguish what is important in everyday education.

In the splendid novel *The gift of Asher Lev* by Chaim Potok (1990) the main character struggles with his place in creation. He experiences the vocation to develop his qualities as an artist no longer to be in conflict with the strict religious community in New York City to which he belongs, but in accordance with it and with respect to the artistic shine of it. This is an enormous stretch from the conflict of the early years of his career as an artist, when he, because of his offensive religious paintings, was banned from the same community. This ban is described in the earlier novel by Potok, *My name is Asher Lev* (1972).

Asher Lev realizes that he has been fighting for the ideals of his youth and that his vocation slowly but surely gained its place in his own religious community. He stays at a safe but rewarding distance. In the second novel he finds himself for the choice: can he be open to the future of his children that choose to live again in the community of New York or does he act in the same excluding manner as his parents did? This is a dilemma he is constantly struggling with and he is summoned regularly by the Rabbi to exchange views on that matter. In one of the conversations the Rabbi shares with him an idea that beautifully demonstrates what I mean with vision and ability to discern. According to the Rabbi, the spiritual leader as well as the artist, participate in that vision. They are not opponents of each other, but are able to express, each in their own way, the dynamics of a society and the call to act. In a fundamental way it all boils down to the ability to see in a new way: not with eyes that only see the temporary, but from a holistic perspective. Not with eyes that only see the fragmented, but out of a perspective of wholeness and salvation. "Man sees only between the blinks of his eyes. He does not know what the world is like during his blinks. He sees the world in pieces and fragments. But the master of the universe sees the world whole, unbroken. That world is good. Our seeing is broken, Asher Lev. Can we make it like the seeing of God? Is it possible?" (Potok 1990).

This new way of seeing, this new vision, lies at the root of the vision of a modern way of educating. It releases energy for enhancing a sharper sight, for the ability to discern, for inspiration – to do the thing that must be done today. Whoever had such an experience is not able to keep silent about it. To see and to inspire – care and encouragement – are the two big stimuli of education in general and religious education in particular. They are the starting point of this book.

## Longing and perspective

In this book I work with a 'narthical model' of religious communication and education (see especially Chapter 5). With this I mean the following. In order to see more clearly one's life destination, the religious educator leads the young person on a quest within the narthex, the passageway between outside and inside, between already and not yet, between longing and perspective. Narthex literally means: the entrance of a church building. In this book narthex is used metaphorically: as an image for the religious learning process. The student experiences himself as being on his way in his own existence, longing for life fulfillment. By being initiated in the narthical space, he can catch his breath, as to, precisely in that moment of inner peace, be confronted with stories from 'elsewhere' which shed a new light on that longing. This new light is a pedagogical light (images and stories that enable me to renew my own narrative identity), but also a theological light (images and stories that remind me of the carrying ground of my existence). The narthex is not meant as a stepping stone as to be lured into the Christian experience which is reserved for the *intimi* of the inner circle. The narthex is a space for anyone who is tempted to give his own life (temporarily) out of hands, to look at it from a completely different perspective and who is willing to be addressed by something completely new. The latter is never alienating: it requires a minimum of recognition, of awareness that what is shown is strange and provocatively new. The narthex invites the learner to enter the space of 'productive otherness'.

Therefore a thick description of religious communication and education should be used. They offer more than just a 'bloodless' informative and communicative circle of knowledge and insight about a certain religious theme. It not only shows the way in which people in cultures and traditions deal with the religious and how the student can use this opportunity as a 'religious tourist' to build his own religious identity. It challenges the student to become a 'pilgrim', to be touched deep within and become reborn as a new person who resources himself in the dynamics of life of immanence and transcendence. The person on the quest can decide to go on based on his own strength, not caring about an ultimate concern. But he cannot withdraw himself of the 'lingering questions' which are placed upon him by life itself, when he is led into the narthex and is persuaded to contemplate about that existence. My approach with regard to religious communication and education is an attempt to offer *soul food*. To a person who is hungry one does not explain how the digestive tract works (*Den religiösen Hunger stillen* 1998), one puts soul food on the table of learning!

Whoever undertakes this learning process is becoming vulnerable and remains somewhat distant to *instant* religious education which collects *fast food* answers and represents the idea that one can be religiously *self made*. Narthical religious education takes the person on the quest seriously in his unfulfilled longing and the awareness of the limitations of his own fulfillment, helps that person in formulating lingering questions and leaves space for 'living in dedication', for temporality and not-knowing. And precisely there a new light can come into existence, a new destination for his own life story. Than the person on the quest realizes: 'I have been seen already, I don't have to attempt being noticed. I am grounded already, I don't have to ground myself. In my quest I have already been found. And when I fall, I will never fall into ultimate meaninglessness'. *Faith* occurs here: belief, devotion, trust. This differs completely from *submission*: humiliation, subjection, self-denial. There are many forms of religious communication that do not end up with 'faith'. Under the cloak of being visionary they do injustice to the vision, because they disconnect the person from his ability to discern critically what needs to be done in the holy space of *his* life.

## Cities and theologians

The post-modern city forms the broader context for these reflections. In this book, meant to be a practical-theological re-imagination of the work of the religious educator, the city is the *root metaphor* for a postmodern society on the move. The city is symbolizing the complexity and plurality of organizational principles of contemporaries to live a meaningful and happy life. It is also symbolizing the clashes in this process of meaning giving. People can fundamentally agree but also disagree with one another in their search for a meaningful sense of direction. They can stand in the way of the other: morally and religiously. In a globalizing society the perspectives of promise and brokenness, hope for fulfillment and despair, are eminently present in daily life. The critical theologian who is present in society, is aware of these situations, is able to make them explicit and to formulate learning perspectives, relying on his knowledge, wisdom and engagement in a religious tradition of hope. He is legitimating his position by using a theological frame of reference that is anchored in his own critically interpreted religious experience.

The culture of young people, radically rooted in the experience of real and virtual cities, open for renewal and new horizons, is a challenge to modern theology to reframe its knowledge of, wisdom about and engagement with the living God. In line with this argument I will address in this book also the issue of theological education in seminaries and university departments of theology (see Chapters 6, 9 and 13). Three central goals should be on the agenda of a contextualized theological education: a) to enter in hopeful dialogues with the emerging issues and shifting grounds on which contemporaries are working, living and loving; b) to be proactive in theological reflection and in asking questions such as 'What are the theological criteria for assessing new experiences, new ideas and fragments of tradition-in-the-making?' 'What is the frame of reference for reading the signs of the times?'; and c) to take part as (future) theologians in actual religious disclosing practices in our society. European developments and scholarly discussions in religious education praxis, theory and research form the greater part of this book. It was my explicit intention to make the different voices of European research in religious education (in Dutch, English, French and German) accessible to the English speaking world. Standing on the crossroads of cities and contexts, listening to the multi-lingual voices and vibes, I consider this book to be a modest mirror of what is going on in the *kosmopolis* Europe, this 'minimum space with its maximum diversity' (Kundera 2007, 28) of (religious-educational) ideas and practices.

**Summary and acknowledgments**

This book contains fourteen chapters, grouped in three sections, namely a) education, religion and values; b) education, religion and school;

and c) education, religion and the city. The first part brings together basic elements for a contemporary discussion on education, morality and religion in a post-modern culture. Chapter 1 and 2 are dealing with a comprehensive view on moral education. Through a historical and systematic lens the need for moral authenticity and creativity in contemporary education and society is described and evaluated. Human dignity is in this respect not only the goal of moral education, but also its central value and virtue. The quest for human dignity in society and the relationship with the warm spiritual undercurrent in that same society urge us to speak of moral education as cultivating 're-sponsible imagination'. Chapter 3 deals with the dynamics of religion in the public sphere, with its individualized quests for meaning and with the idea of *kairos* (Greek for the good moment) to respond to this situation with the rich legacy of churches and religious communities. In Chapter 4 the pedagogical justification of (young) parents in daily education is explored and theologically reflected.

In the second part the emphasis lies on religious education in schools. This learning area I take pre-eminently as a quest. Youngsters are taken by the hand in an attempt to 'discover' meaning in their own life and the lives that surround them. They are confronted with insights that are not theirs, but which can be an inspiration to "re-define and re-dignify" (Chapter 7 § 7) themselves and their environment in a completely new way. The 'narthical' learning model in Chapter 5 connects to this perspective of going on a quest in religious education. The ability to critically enter into 'detours' sharpens the openness for the unexpected, the surprising, for the meaning that does not disclose itself automatically. Chapter 6 discusses the German approach of *Kindertheologie*, theologizing with children, as an exciting tool in supporting and empowering children in raising vital questions and exploring meaningful answers. In Chapter 7, inter-religious learning is presented as one of the most appropriate models for the subject of religious education in the modern West-European secondary school. Youngsters learn to document different religious beliefs and to communicate with people about these differences, often concretely present in their classmates. I describe the recent developments of this approach, but also take it a step further. Whoever lets himself be touched by the otherness of the other in the classroom cannot remain unaffected and has to be able to formulate the beginning of a religious position by him self. My estimate is that young people, because of their religious frankness, are capable of the inter-spiritual meeting with the other. Good education stimulates this possibility. In Chapter 8, I take the view that there is a positive attitude among youngsters to quench themselves at the great stories. The Bible is a book that can stimulate and uncover the narrative identity quest of the youth, on the terms that the religious educators are willing to give testimony of the struggle that this invokes in them selves. Chapter 9 is an attempt to reframe the theological preparation of future teachers of Roman-Catholic religious education within the boundaries of canon law at the one hand and practical 'culture theology' at the other hand. In the final chapter of the second part the goal of education is conceived as "growing in shared humanity". Becoming a flourishing human being, aware of one's vulnerability and uniqueness – and therefore radically in relationship with others – is theologically reframed as incarnation.

The final part of the book is focusing on religious communication with young people outside the school, in the broader context of the city, as a metaphor for growing urbanization, globalization and (moral and religious) diversification. In Chapter 11 an exploration of different approaches to youth ministry is undertaken, in the context of ongoing globalization. In Chapter 12 a comprehensive model for ministry with youth and young adults is developed, in which seeing, judging and acting are complemented by dreaming and remembering. Youth theology evolving out of this ministry is a strong reminder to academic theologies to remain life-related and rooted in actual religious practices. Chapter 13 underlines this idea by reporting on a concrete experience with young adults during two summer camps. The lived theology that I could discover there mirrors the idea that solidarity with human beings is risky and that Gods unconditional love comes to us as 'risky revelation', in the vulnerable heart of people who are careful and considerate. The final contribution to the book in Chapter 14 discusses international developments beyond Europe in youth ministry research: con-texts, themes and textures are unraveled as challenges for future research in practical theology.

Most of the chapters in this book have been previously published as articles (see the list of acknowledgments at the end), but have been adjusted to the overall perspective of the book. The narthical approach has played a central part in this, by which I want to show that religious education and youth ministry have been revitalized by the concept of *religious experience*. I describe and empower this tendency and reinterpret recent developments within this framework. As such this collection reflects the contemplative process that has occurred in the author as well.

**Retrospective and vision**

This book offers the reader a retrospective of almost twenty years of teaching and research in the field of religious education. Since the defense of my thesis, *Een tijd van opvoeden. Moraalpedagogiek in christelijk perspectief* [A time to educate. Moral education in Christian perspective] at the faculty of theology of the Katholieke Universiteit Leuven in June 1994 (for the published edition, see Roebben 1995a) and during my teaching and research in Leuven (Belgium, 1995-2000), Tilburg (the Netherlands, 1995-2007) and Dortmund (Germany, since 2007) I focused mainly on the study of religious education in and out of schools. This resulted in the publication of my Dutch book *Godsdienstpedagogiek van de hoop. Grondlijnen voor religieuze educatie* (published in Leuven by Acco in three editions, namely 2007, 2008 and 2012). In this book – and in the underlying English version of it – the theological considerations gained more and more the upper hand in spite of the pedagogical, didactical and social theoretical ones. It is my contention that religious education in theory, research and praxis has realized the interests of recent didactical developments. Numerous insights from the 'new learning movement' have been integrated. Mainly the theologians have been the first to implement these new perspectives on their own didactics. It goes without saying that a lot of work remains to be done in this field. But I have the strong impression that out of the grassroots of religious education and resulting from the theoretical reflection on this subject, a new language game announces itself, a language game that is more theological in its nature.

People in the workplace are eager to know 'what' they will tell the youth, not so much 'how' they will tell this – which didactics or methods they need to do this. They mainly ask themselves 'why' they tell the things they tell, from which principles and stories these things originate, and if they are authentic and future-able. It is my solemn conviction that the future wellbeing of the youth in a globalizing society should be the centre of interpretation for these origins. Whoever did not envision this clearly, will not be heard by youngsters because he is considered as someone who has nothing meaningful to say. The implications of this perspective on (religious) education for theology, for the systematic reflection on the origins of faith, are immense. Tradition is the ongoing process of resourcing of a religious community that wants to be transparent on behalf of the future of next generations. In this process I would like to invite my readers. This book is meant for the study and reflection in higher education, in the training of religious educators, catechists or pastoral ministers, at universities, institutes of higher education and seminaries, but it can also be used in the living room, at school, in a parish or congregation by people who want to know more about religious education in changing contexts.

I am deeply grateful to all my students and colleagues in Leuven and Antwerpen (B), Utrecht and Tilburg (NL), Pittsburgh and Boston (USA), Stellenbosch (RSA), Dortmund (D) and Wien (A), for their critical voices and helpful insights in the reflective process that gave birth to the chapters of this book. Moreover, I had the chance to meet with great people on the road, during the conferences of the 'Religious Education Association' in the United States (REA), the 'Coordinating Group for Religion in Education in Europe' (CoGREE), the 'European Forum for Teachers of Religious Education' (EFTRE), the Dutch Association for the study of religious education (NGPG), the 'International Association for the Study of Youth Ministry' (IASYM), and during the workshops of the Council of Europe in Georgia, the Russian Federation and Ukraine. I have learned so much about the common and global questions to religious education and youth work, precisely by getting involved in the very local and particular answers to these questions. I am particularly grateful to Andrea van Dijk and Eveline van der Ham (Tilburg University) and to Kim de Wildt (Dortmund University) for their enormous help with editing the text. I acknowledge with appreciation my Protestant colleagues in Dortmund Michael Basse, Gerhard Büttner and Thomas Pola and *Chef Lektor* Michael J. Rainer of Lit-Verlag in Münster, for allowing me to publish this book in a second edition in the 'Dortmunder Beiträge zu Theologie und Religionspädagogik'.

One image is particularly inspiring for my work as a religious education scholar and teacher. It is called the 'Sternenweg', the way of the stars, a forty meter long piece of art made of steel and stone, erected at the French banks of the Rhine in Neuf-Brisach, at the level of the German town of Breisach. Here the Black Forest and the Elzas meet each other. The artist Helmut Lutz (° Freiburg-im-Breisgau, 1941) designed this piece of art with the intention to function as a stage of communication for people who cross natural and spiritual boundaries and want to communicate with each other on this subject. The colossus has traveled along the great rivers of Europe and has been exposed in Rome, Santiago de Compostela and Jerusalem. In the summer of 2006 it was erected in Sarajevo where it served as a stage for a contemporary mystery play (www.sternenweg.de).

When one observes the picture carefully three elements come to the fore: the 'Sternenweg', the Rhine and the Roman church, the *Sankt Stephansmünster*, highly elevated above Breisach, at the other side of the river. They represent respectively dialogue, border and perspective. Upon visiting this site in 2003 the interplay of these elements inspired me to reflect on religious education. Whoever wants to educate young people spiritually makes them aware of the borders of life and opposite side of the narrow-mindedness of the own truth. In doing so he shows perspectives and panoramas in all their diversity. Without the specification in a concrete tradition one cannot speak of religious experience or religious education. Therefore he needs the vivid connection to a spiritual tradition, a church, a community, etc. And last but not least he offers a communicative stage where people exchange what they have seen and heard – where they 'learn in the presence of the other'. The teacher thus encourages the dialogue on what is ultimately ineffable but real. In winter time the 'Sternenweg' is mostly covered up with snow and fog. Silence has then descended on the borderland of the Rhine. Religious education can then ultimately not realize its own goal as religious communication. Only silence remains.

# Part 1

# Education, Religion and Values

# Chapter 1

# To Initiate into a World of Difference
# Design for a Dynamic-Integral Values Education

The passing on of moral values can be described as the natural consequence of the love that parents and teachers have for their children. They set a moral example because they believe this will enhance the happiness and well-being of their children. They are not indifferent to values in education because these make a genuine difference to the adult the child will one day become. The objective of the educational process is crucial. If you ask parents what they are seeking to achieve, many will respond: we want 'the best' for our children. In this sense, parents are not engaging in moral education, but simply loving their offspring. In the words of the British philosopher Donald Winnicot: "This is the first principle of moral education, that moral education is no substitute for love" (1963, 102). This desire on the part of parents is common to all ages and cultures. One might thus conclude at first sight that we ought to leave them alone – it is a 'good thing' that parents want 'the best' for their children.

However, when we pause to examine the practical educational actions of contemporaries we realize that there is no longer a clear definition of what is 'best'. How do we define well-being and happiness of children these days, what are the goals of education? We want the best for our children, but what does that mean in concrete terms? Views are no longer unanimous. There seem to be many different ways of achieving happiness, ranging from hedonism to asceticism, from cynicism to dogmatism, with the narrow path of personal development in solidarity running somewhere between. An educational paradox has arisen: the love and care felt by parents makes them desperately eager to make their children happy, but they no longer know how to shape that eagerness in concrete terms. Things are no longer set out for them, the Grand Narratives which once held out ideals for living and educating are no longer 'working', are no longer considered relevant by many people. Parents and teachers must now discover for themselves what they consider to be worthwhile. The context in which we live and raise our children today is one of profound educational goodwill accompanied by great moral uncertainty.

I continue this chapter by focusing attention on this educational dilemma, and by suggesting that the challenge facing values education in the near future is chiefly a social one. I will then present a design for values education that particularly addresses the tasks and responsibilities of the educator. The design seeks to be integral, in that it deals with the mind, the emotions and the will, and dynamic, in that it takes account of the child's development, from dependency to moral independence. I will conclude with a few brief thoughts on the spirituality of parents and teachers.

## 1. Values education as a challenge to a pluralistic society

The dilemma currently facing parents and teachers – characterized above as the tension between educational goodwill and moral uncertainty – is an entirely new one. Things were very different up until the 1960s, prior to which education could be characterized as a one-way street. Parents showed their children a straight and unambiguous path towards a good life. That is no longer the case in our own time, when parents and teachers share the lack of direction suffered by society as a whole. Adults have lost their monopoly on knowledge and understanding of values, and it is no longer a foregone conclusion that they will be the only ones to convey these things. We might respond by writing this development off as the decline of education and start looking for scapegoats: parents no longer have time to bring up their children properly, schools are only interested in passing on dry facts and the media is fomenting moral decline.

I prefer to view this state of 'educational uncertainty' as a positive challenge. Parents and teachers must be encouraged to express what motivates them and what they value; they must be persuaded to enter into a dialogue on these matters with other parties. There is no shortage of sociological treatises dealing with our changing times, but the most important question regarding the near future is how we ought to deal with these developments in practice? In other words, how can we mobilize sufficient utopian will and imagination to design a viable future for our young people? It can be done, provided that people come together and combine their creative energies in a new future-oriented project.

Theodor W. Adorno once argued, in the skeptical period following the Second World War, that it is the task of the educator to teach the awareness to the 'cold' situations of injustice and oppression (1970). That is certainly the case. But we ought not to forget that simply identifying what is 'cold' is not enough for education. We must also seek to create small, powerful nuclei of social 'warmth', places where meaning and engagement are once again pursued, where young and old regain their taste for innovation through education, and where teachers can again contribute "very actively and without diffidence (...) to the restoration of a social project" (*De school staat niet alleen* 1994, 102). This is the kind of project I would like to describe here. We see it burgeoning in the real world, amongst the grass-roots, real parents and teachers who are prepared to take responsibility for their educational actions, who are willing to speak about the values they adhere to in education *because* they do the same with their children. Educators will be able to justify themselves to some third party, because their education is based on addressing the children *as if* they were already individuals. The educators are basically engaging in a simulated conversation with the children or a conversation with themselves (Mollenhauer & Rittelmeyer 1978, 85). There is, in my view, only one way of tackling educational uncertainty, and that is to enter into a dialogue on it with fellow educators, to encourage one another and, overcoming our differences, together to pursue those things that are worth pursuing for the well-being of us all.

Consequently, this chapter is concerned primarily with the responsibilities of the educator. It is crucially important to the success of values education that parents and teachers are prepared to make the first move by explaining their most profound motivations, what inspires them, the nature of their life's project and how they wish to express these things in the education they give. In a sense, therefore, values education is identical with explaining/justifying education in general (van Haaften 1988). This is not merely a question of 'putting it into words' for oneself, but also of 'justifying' as part of the dialogue with others who might hold different views – a dialogue in which the validity of one's claims has to be proven, corrected and harmonized with the common good. The key notion is thus 'communication' – negotiation and the quest for consensus as to what is fundamentally worth pursuing in order to achieve our common well-being: the *bonum commune.*

It is only when this willingness has been found and educators are prepared to face the world with an open mind that a new awareness of values in child-rearing and education will be unlocked. Only when people show themselves willing once again to communicate with one another about the 'future of the future', they will be able to bring young people up to genuine responsibility and participation in a morally 'healthy' environment. The ancient realization that credibility is a vital ingredient of education is no less valid today.

This may be clearly illustrated using an example. The city of Leuven in which I live, has an extensive network of public transportation that is also used by children on their way to school. However, because of poor traffic regulation, the buses spend a great deal of time during peak periods blocked in traffic jams. This makes the drivers nervous and causes them to drive very aggressively. In this way, young people are thrown unwillingly into a spiral of physical and verbal violence. If this *'Brutalisierung des Alltags'* on the journey to and from school becomes the tacit norm, how can we blame young people any longer for all the violence and vandalism on the streets? And how are we to teach young people in such a context to perceive the value of a non-violent and understanding society? The illustration shows that values education is basically a social question for which everyone is jointly responsible (Vriens 1998). The beginnings of a solution will be provided by parents and teachers setting a responsible example. I will now outline how this educational responsibility may be given a new foundation. Through the dynamic-integral design an effective framework is provided for an approach to values education that is both justifiable in contemporary terms and normative in a fundamental educational sense.

## 2. A dynamic-integral view of values education

The famous German religious education professor, Adolf Exeler, once argued that solid values education rested on three pillars: exercising good habits, learning how to experience appropriate moral emotions and an understanding of the rational justification of moral behavior. Acting, feeling and thinking – or moral virtues, emotions and reasonning – are the three components of integral values education (Exeler 1984, 239). None of the three may be neglected.

It was amply demonstrated above that values education can only succeed if parents and teachers are prepared to learn to justify their educational actions and the values and standards on which these are founded. They also do this *de facto* – indeed, they cannot do otherwise. Education asks this from them, to declare themselves, to justify their lifestyle and the values for which they stand. In the confrontation with their parents, young people want to know what is so precious about the values and standards to which they adhere. In discussions of music and literature, for example, youngsters do not simply wish adults to agree with them, but are looking for a sounding board on which to test whether their value judgment is meaningful and sound. In a sense, therefore, young people themselves are asking for a grounded opinion on the part of the educator, as a confrontation and a foundation for the design and justification of their own moral judgment. Education thus reveals its own objective, namely the moral independence of the child. Morally well-educated people are capable of an autonomous value judgment on the way in which they organize their lives. As their development continues, growing youngsters are increasingly capable of this chiefly cognitive skill. As pointed out already, justification and communication are key concepts in this task.

Cognitive justification is crucial to our suggestion that values education must be considered to be a social issue. There are, incidentally, solid academic foundations for such a view. We will briefly cite two of them. The first is the well known 'Values Development Theory' postulated by the American moral psychologist Lawrence Kohlberg. This researcher came to the conclusion that a kind of transcultural development process can be detected with regard to moral judgment (Kohlberg 1981; 1984). People develop in an ideal-typical process from a pre-conventional moral judgment ('I behave morally to avoid punishment or because I respect the personal interests of the other person'), through a conventional moral judgment ('I behave morally because that is socially acceptable or because I am doing my duty') to a post-conventional moral judgment ('I behave morally because I fulfill my undertakings and because I can justify my behavior to my own conscience'). The hope of parents is the achievement of the post-conventional behavior of the child. He will then be able as a morally well-educated person to justify himself, and capable of making moral judgments in as adequate and proportionate a manner as possible in the given circumstances.

Such justification of one's own behavior must necessarily take place through communication with others. Reference ought to be made at this point to a second cognitive approach to moral education, namely the 'Values Communication' approach as set out by the Dutch practical theologian Johannes A. van der Ven (1985; 1998). This scholar describes moral education in terms mainly of ethical and argumentative competence. Young persons learn in a step-by-step way to participate in communication on values and standards and to justify their views to conversation partners who dispute, supplement, reject and/or integrate their claims. The objective of values communication is to achieve consensus between those participating in the dialogue regarding the values that are worth pursuing. Themes from school life might be drawn upon (bullying, pressure of study, attitudes, punishments, etc.), but social issues like the environment, a tolerant society, a just world order, and so forth, also belong to the realm of values communication.

We accept the insights that have been provided by the primarily cognitive approach to moral education, given the present social context in which we seek to construct a new social project. The ability to use communication to justify oneself morally is the objective of moral education. Yet we are firmly convinced that this cognitive approach alone is not sufficient, that the general objective of values education cannot be achieved solely through exercises in post-conventional judgment and communicative action. Morality is not simply a cognitive matter. Good habits and moral sensitivity are as important as cognition. Moral action and moral awareness are as important as the facility to understand the reasons for one's behavior and whether these reasons are valid – i.e. whether they can be justified in communication with others without the discussion itself being rendered impossible. Moral maturity implies moral judgment, but also action and feelings. There is a significant danger that a purely cognitive approach will result in an intellectualism whereby people are perfectly capable of analyzing and remedying the ethical problems of a particular period, but are not motivated to actually do the right thing "from the inside of morality" (Richard Peters). Furthermore, history repeatedly shows us that people who are convinced of their so called moral mandate – think of the Nazi's – are capable of the most horrific evil, while all the time retaining a so called 'clear conscience'.

I therefore propose a dual correction to the purely cognitive values education approaches of Kohlberg and Van der Ven. The goal is indeed the post-conventional stage – as Kohlberg rightly argues –, but the conventional stage ought not to be overlooked in the process. Before children are capable of offering reasons for particular behavior they first have to learn that behavior as an *insider,* as a member of a specific moral community. Post-conventionality presupposes the existence of conventions. Habit-formation and values initiation into what parents consider to be of virtue regarding the ability to live meaningfully with others precede critical reflections upon those habits and virtues. The British educational philosopher Richard Peters expresses this very concisely: "The palace of reason has to be entered by the courtyard of habit" (Peters 1978, 314). This is embodied in the child's own development. Before children are capable of weighing values against one another to determine which ought to prevail in a particular situation, they first have to familiarize themselves with the actual content of those values. This content is embodied in virtues, in virtuous attitudes held by real people. This explains the importance of setting an example of what is good, true and beautiful, so that the child may identify these things. Such an example cannot, admittedly, be counted on. It is merely tentative, with the parent or teacher 'trying' to live up to a particular virtue. At least he should be aware of the fact that education cannot be value free: even in the smallest things of daily life, in the rituals of keeping house, participating in traffic, shopping or community life, etc. values are at stake. It is chiefly during this tentative (and therefore justifiable) stage of moral education, in the quest for authenticity in example-setting, that the spark will be carried over. Children do not learn actual values at first but rather the way in which adults 'appreciate' or 'value' these values, how they deal with them and how they reveal what such values truly mean to them. In this sense, adults lead children into the courtyard of habit, but do not imprison them in that stage, nor do they indoctrinate them. Now and again they offer children a glimpse of the palace of reason and nurture an awareness of the ultimate riches of moral life. They learn them the practices, the rules behind the practices and the reasons behind the rules – but always gradually.

The second correction I would propose to a merely cognitive view on values education is an affective one, and in response to Van der Ven's 'Values Communication' approach. The objective of moral education is indeed to enable young people to arrive at an adult moral judgment that they can justify in the dialogue with others. However, the human person does not communicate in a void. He is constantly engaged with real, fellow human beings. From the moment I ask myself as an adult moral agent: 'What ought I to do?', I have already admitted into my discourse conversation partners (at least notional ones), to whom I wish and am able to justify myself. I am always involved in the dialogue as a flesh-and-blood person. This emotional engagement with the 'communio' is a necessary precondition for successful communication. For why should I feel any moral obligation to explain myself through communication unless the community has in some way questioned me and called upon me to justify myself? Ideal communication that leads directly to consensus does not exist. Every community in which communication takes place is a 'real' community that constantly moves along the path of conflict and reconciliation. Therefore, children also have to learn how to relate to other persons in a variety of situations and together come to a concept of what is good for every person, for every 'conversation partners' in the moral community. For example, they have to learn that the feeling of indignation or shame can be appropriate in certain conditions (e.g. when a friend is excluded) and that guilt can sometimes be inappropriate (for instance when a supposed rule is infringed) (Roebben 1995b).

An integral design for moral education comprises the following: making judgments that can be justified, acting virtuously and being sensitive to the well-being of others. Thinking, acting and feeling belong together. The objective of values education is to achieve post-conventional and communicative moral judgment and action. But post-conventional morality presupposes the existence of conventions and virtues, while values communication presupposes perceptive involvement in a community of real conversation partners. It is evident that this 'extended' view on values education can also help those young people who are cognitively less developed than others to come to a personal commitment to the moral realm. Furthermore, this view can guard us from giving too much attention to the development of the so called cognitive abilities of the human person. Ethics is first of all a matter of sensitivity and practice of the good.

## 3. Values education as a dynamic process

Actually doing good (virtue component) and learning to perceive situations of good and evil in the discourse with others (emotional component) are primarily learned in the early stages of education. This is schematically termed the 'values initiation' period. The expression of an appropriate moral judgment (cognitive component) belongs chiefly to the final stage of education, that of 'values communication'. The first stage mainly occurs in the context of the family, and the second at school. Yet both stages of moral education presuppose the existence of the other because of a constant interactive process. They invoke one another during the practice of education. Virtues and emotions are learned with a view to the later acquisition of an adult moral personality. And the reverse is also true: moral insight implies engagement with conventions learned earlier and emotional commitment to the partners in the dialogue. This dynamic or dialectic is essentially embodied in the actual process of education. The human being develops from relationship to social commitment and from symbiosis to interdependence, with values education forming part of this dynamic. Initiation is geared towards communication, while communication presupposes earlier initiation.

Consequently, initiation and communication ought both to be pursued as part of values education. One can refer here to the double etymological root of the word 'education'. Education always has a large element of *educare* (Latin for 'kneading' or 'molding', 'leading in'), in the sense that it is about teaching the youngster to perceive concrete achievements of good, truth and beauty. It is education in the sense of cultural initiation. But values education is also about communication with that culture, dealing with the examples, criticism and differences to be found there, or education in the sense of the Latin *e-ducere,* 'to see someone off'. This is the key to moral education: gradually letting a child go, seeing him off into a 'world of difference', but only after first introducing him to the 'difference of worlds'. We might express the dynamic between these two more effectively by stating that values education is 'introducing a child into a world of difference'.

This dynamic view allows us to avoid two potential pitfalls in education: cynicism and dogmatism. Cynicism arises when adults positively refuse to initiate the child into a well-defined concrete ethos, because they constantly criticize any ethos, including their own. Educators of this type believe they can skip the initiation stage and move directly to so-called communication with children. It is an illusion to argue that children can cope with this. What is more, writes the Dutch Jewish educationalist Lea Dasberg, "by withholding tradition, we deny our sons, daughters and pupils the opportunity to be novices, we deny them the right to a pedagogical relationship and we deny them the right to their share of history" (1980, 31, translation BR). The extreme opposite of this cynicism is equally damaging. Educational dogmatism occurs when educators hold children hostage in the initiation stage and indoctrinate them in such a way that they are unable to move on to judgments based on personal conscience during the stage of values communication. It should be stressed that indoctrination need not always occur consciously. It is critically important to ask whether any room is left for free initiative, youthful authenticity, creativity and moral experimentation in the highly commercialized world that is the social context of today's young people. To put it more provocatively, are young people still allowed to be 'young'? Our society is in fact irresponsible to young people when she forces them into a straitjacket of consumption, triviality and obsession with performance, before condemning them to the wilderness as scapegoats, laden with the evils for which adults them selves are unable to find any remedy.

Education is impossible where an attitude of dogmatism or cynicism prevails. The cynical educator believes that nothing is valuable and everything is relative, while the dogmatic educator has lost a sense of perspective and sees only absolutes. A dynamic-integral design of values education can deflate such extreme cynicism and dogmatism. It takes the process of educational development seriously, as it does not skip the stage of initiation. But it also gives due consideration to the goal of education – it does not stop at initiation but proceeds to a post-conventional, ethical attitude that transcends the level of conventions and private ethical structures, and enables children to adopt an individual lifestyle freely and with full awareness. Parents can thus provide their children with a solid initiation into what they believe to be valuable, provided that they are prepared to explain themselves and to teach the child to understand their justification.

## Conclusion

I would like to conclude by returning briefly to the social context in which we nowadays are obliged to carry out values education. The temptation to succumb to educational cynicism or dogmatism is powerful. It is tempting in the given circumstances to say to young people 'Work it out for yourself, I'm keeping my head down', or

'Here is a clear moral code to which you must adhere unconditionally'. But such attitudes are immoral and unworthy of the teacher. It ultimately boils down to the question whether or not we still want to educate? Do we still have the will or 'guts' to educate?

I am of the opinion that the fundamental question is how we will interact in the near future with the 'other': will we trivialize the other by assimilating them into an easy-going but concomitantly indifferent post-modern lifestyle? Will we exclude the other as someone who threatens our identity and as someone who in the most extreme case has to be exterminated? Can we freely and with impunity choose between cynicism and dogmatism? Are we really authentic as educators if we are afraid for an open discussion on what is worth while for every person, not only for the next of kin, for our good friends and relatives, but for every human person living on this planet. The final question is, I think, whether we will come to accept the 'other in ourselves', as a call for ethical vigilance, as a challenge to finally learn to live together as human beings in unity and diversity?

# Chapter 2

# Responsible Imagination
# Moral Education and Cultural Change

"Talk to me, read to me, play with me. That's how I learn. Let's talk. It makes a difference". This text on a bus stop poster which I came across in Boston in 2007, perfectly illustrates both the complexity and the challenge of contemporary education. Children and adolescents are desperately craving for responsible educators. They need biographical advice from their parents and teachers, they need responses to their quest for meaning, they provoke to response-ability. "When you are there for me wholeheartedly, we could both make a difference." Moral education of children and young people is first of all an issue of morally sensitive parents and teachers. They have to be aware of the hidden moral and spiritual call coming from children today and they need to be responsive to this call. Young people in modern Western societies are faced with two radical and intertwining challenges: finding a meaningful life perspective that can count as their own and learning to cope with moral and religious diversity while searching for this life perspective. Successful humanization of society will imply that future generations are provided with rich opportunities for their quest for meaning and with insight in the both enriching and conflicting dimensions of moral and religious diversity.

This pedagogical chapter is explicitly embedded in this social discourse. Many parents and educators have become educationally shy. They do not dare to speak out loud, because they are uncertain about what should be said and done. This "malaise of modernity", according to Charles Taylor, this being delivered to one's own moral and spiritual solitude, is deep and sometimes coming to the surface as a shock wave, when the ordinary range of things is interrupted. People feel then extremely insecure in the actual realization of norms, values and meaning, but at the same time common sense makes them aware of what the good life *could* be, where just and unjust *can* be distinguished, where the dividing line between good and evil *can* be found. This warm undercurrent of consciousness, present in post-modern culture, deserves to be made more explicit. All too extreme answer schemes do not do justice to the complexity of our culture and society. Clarification is required as to what could be good, true and beautiful, *in the midst* of people's lives. The vulnerable situation of ethics (of norms, values and meaning in an overheated and disoriented society) demands an ethics of vulnerability, an actual involvement in daily practices of the good life. This demands "responsible imagination" (Sharon Daloz Parks, quoted by Hess 2003, 136-138), the engaged and critical surrender to dialogue, to a process of communal discovery and realization of truth. This societal option for vision and discernment demands for a new comprehensive view on education.

The dynamic-integral view on values education in Chapter 1 needs to be evaluated against this societal background. It is my contention that since the publication of my doctoral dissertation in 1994 (of which Chapter 1 can be considered to be a summary) many things have changed, which have 'accelerated' this view (Roebben 1998b; 1998c; 2001d). Three events have made me aware, *post factum*, of these shifts: the civil war in the Balkan in the early 1990s, the Dutroux affair of child abuse in Belgium in the mid 1990s, and 9/11 at the beginning of the new millennium. In editing this chapter I thought that the outline could refer to these three events: respectively the lack of moral autonomy in keeping the different post-modern fragments together (identified as 'Balkanization'), the vulnerable situation of children in education, and the need for a new vision on humanity in the midst of moral and religious diversity. In what follows, I will focus on these three elements. I will conclude with five recommendations for educational leadership today.

## 1. Towards a comprehensive approach to moral education

How to deal with the moral complexity of contemporary society? How to educate children and young people into this complexity? How can we comfort them with a more general sense of direction? In what follows, I will show how the dynamic-integral model of values education (in Chapter 1) implies a more holistic or comprehensive view on education. Moral values refer to what is valuable and precious, what is considered to be not only interesting but also radically indispensable to be handed over to the next generation. Moral values are encompassing the vision on the good live of concrete human beings. Mothers and fathers, teachers and ministers show the courage of their convictions, because they have found something so valuable they cannot but talk about it and show it. They want the 'best' for their children and youngsters, in the way they are convinced this is the best. They feel challenged to do so by the mere presence of the future generation. Moral values are not just objective entities. They are always relational: they are embodied (or not) in the life of concrete human beings.

It is my contention that in the last fifty years this task has become extremely difficult. The traditional family values have been destroyed according to some, or have been totally reframed according to others (for a critical appraisal, see Dillen 2006). The least one can say is that the beacons of meaningfulness have disappeared and that one needs quite some social-ethical and educational flexibility to 'survive' the jungle of daily life. This journey of the last fifty years is reflected in the theoretical development of moral pedagogy, just like in a mirror. Education and society are reflected in theory. The different practical approaches can also be found in theory: from 'values transfer' to 'values clarification' and 'values development' in the 1970s, and from there to 'values communication' and 'values orientation' in the 1980s, and back to 'character education' as a form of values transfer in the 1990s (for an overview, see Van der Ven 1998 and Ziebertz 2003,

128-136). In what follows I will look back on the oppositions in the theory building and will evaluate them as 'unfruitful' – this is partly possible because of my standpoint today. The analysis will culminate in a comprehensive or holistic view on moral education that can face the contemporary challenges. The importance of the life span, of development and growth of moral competence and moral identity in the human person (considered as an autonomous moral agent) are key concepts in this view.

## 1.1. Unfruitful oppositions

Theoretical constructions of the last fifty years have developed in a permanent state of opposition to one another. One model of moral education could set itself up as the opponent of the other with the justification that something important had been forgotten and needed to be reinstituted. The anti-authoritarian model could reap success in the 1970s on the basis of its critique of the traditional inculcation of values. A powerful form of character education was successful in the 1980s and 1990s as a response to and a rejection of the former models as biased. What were these contextually biased oppositions precisely that made the road of moral education so bumpy?

First, the opposition 'cognitive versus affective-conative' (or reason versus feeling and will) is remarkable. The liberal models of the seventies critiqued indoctrination, affective moralization and character formation according to the traditional transfer model. They argued that moral education should not be an unreasoned acceptance or imitation of a 'bag of virtues' (Lawrence Kohlberg), but must be a personally considered and worked out moral judgment that can enable the person even to reject what he learned in education. Moral education is 'critical thinking', an appeal to the faculty of reason. Thomas Lickona in turn disputes this, along with Sidney Callahan. Creative moral judgment happens on the basis of "emotionally laden experience" (Lickona 1991, 51), since conscience is rather an affective than a cognitive category.

Another distinction is 'normative versus instrumental'. The original meaning of moral education, to become authentically oneself in line with the demands of one's own conscience, is in some models "sacrificed to its technical perfection. The search for the optimalization of the means gets the upper hand. The broader perspective of intrinsic responsibility disappears behind the horizon. The goal can only be attained in an effective and efficient application of instruments and means" (Nijhuis 1996, 33; translation BR). It does indeed occur that in the long run "a set of methods was in search of a theory", as Lickona argues in his critique to the values clarification model of the seventies (1991, 239).

Yet another opposition is made between 'authoritarian versus anti-authoritarian', or 'paternalistic versus liberal' (Carr 1996, 9-12). The adult needs to set an example in moral education or should, in contrast, only be a facilitator in the conversation. He remains as a distant equal or engages himself as a superior – beforehand by posing the rules, or *ad interim* by coming between two parties when a conflict of values arises.

Another often voiced opposition is that of *führen* versus *wachsen laßen*, leading versus growing (Bucher 1995, 66-68). Is moral education a biological growth process that, subject to the presence of some minimal conditions will lead spontaneously to moral independence? Or is formal training needed, coupled with conditioning and modeling? Where can one find the boundary between self-discovery and formalistic example learning?

Is moral education primarily procedural in nature or orientated towards content? Should it help to acquire formal procedures and thought strategies or transfer reproducible knowledge contents? Is the student expected to be able to systematically describe a new situation and judge it on its moral content, or should he learn the (historical and systematic) basics of human morality? This distinction, that can be found in different positions on the school subject 'ethics', is often a controversial topic of discussion as well.

A distinction that makes deep inroads on moral education further sharpening the preceding bipolarities is 'initiation versus communication'. Is moral education purely an introduction into the values of the moral life as it is lived in a concrete setting, or does it also strive for the formulation of an 'appreciation' of this life in dialogue with others? How is the tension between socialization and critique to be resolved?

And finally, in moral educational literature there is the often-used distinction between the liberal and the communitarian model of education. Liberal moral educators especially stress autonomy as the goal of education, a rational autonomy that is able to emancipate itself from the tutelage of moral traditions speaking for it. The communitarians then again point to the limits of this approach. Eventually, the so called rational judgment of liberal ethicists would be nothing other than the articulation of a specific modernist opinion with regard to a moral problem. Communitarians at the contrary advance a plea for the restoration of isolated, homogeneous moral communities with high profiled virtues in order to be able to resist liberal emotivism.

## 1.2. Development as a bridge from initiation to communication

The most important characteristic of the new integral-dynamic model of moral education (see Chapter 1) is the concept of 'development'. Seen from the life span of the person, biases are relativized and integrated by this concept. Moral educational researchers have troubled themselves with endless discussions on model preference (in general: transfer versus self-agency or heteronomy versus autonomy), argues Howard Kirschenbaum, an eminent adherent of the values clarification approach. Avoided, however, is the most important question, namely: "*When* is each approach appropriate?" (Kirschenbaum 1991-92). What is the right moment in the life span of the child, the youngster, the young adult, etc. for a specific modus to be implemented?

Just like morality, moral education is a multifaceted phenomenon. The communitarian and liberal views, for instance, should not be considered as two contradictory camps in the moral educational field, but rather as complementary conceptualizations that involve different dimensions or moments in the moral development of the child. Moral education must be viewed from a pluralistic or multi-dimensional perspective (Snik 1992-93). The young child has a right to adults who introduce him to good habits and rules; the growing youngster deserves the space in order to gradually discover his own perspective on the world and himself and to draw conclusions regarding values and norms. The other polarities above can also be seen in this perspective. The different poles, therefore, need not exclude each other; they can rather include each other. They are stages in a developmental process, and can in time be isolated from each other. The art is in determining when which mode of conceptualization is under consideration in education, or better still, when it is not!

With regard to the communitarian intuition in moral education, which is prominently present and influential in moral educational research and praxis since the end of the previous millennium, the following can be observed. In a pluralistic society difficult ethical decisions have to be made daily that require practical reasoning, democratic discussion and solid argumentation. Many voices are present in this debate and no one participates in it as a *tabula rasa*. The articulation and justification of perspectives in dialogue are thus in a pluralistic society a *conditio sine qua non* for the growth and flourishing of the human person. The communitarian intuition should not be a "leere Pathosformel" (Lesch 1995, 122), an empty expression of mere passion, that helps to deal with the so-called post-modern failure of a universal ethical perspective and/or of democracy. It must rather be seen as an historical broadening of our hermeneutical perspective, something that makes us aware of the vulnerability of every communication of values, even in education. The communication of values presupposes concrete discussion partners and communities of concrete persons who do not surrender their own tradition of values but feel the commitment to cultivate these values. The aim is the realization and enrichment of a 'pluralistic' discourse. Moreover, values-initiation into a specific tradition of the good life (including specific moral virtues) should always happen in such a way that the child is challenged to gradually (according to his own course of development) learn to articulate and justify the reasons that this tradition deems valuable for itself and which can stand the test of validity in dialogue. At bottom, it is matter of initiating and communicating in doses according to the personal growth of the child (Roebben 1995a, 207-273).

## 1.3. Moral identity and moral competence

In recent moral pedagogy, the multi-dimensional human person and his 'moral identity' have been radically stressed. Morality is anchored in a global life-project that assures, among other things, that "a person is not torn, but finds balance in his existence", that by means of his personally integrated ideals into his narrative identity, he can prevent that "certain values are forgotten", and finally that he does not have to be crushed beneath the tragic circumstances of life, like suffering, misfortune and injustice (Nijhuis 1996, 74; translation BR). It is only in the framework of a meaningful life-project, in terms of the personally integrated and shared experience of the distinction between good and evil, that one can make mention of persons with "a strong propensity to act according to their moral judgments" (Damon and Gregory 1997, 117), persons whose actions are in accordance with their insights.

Young people have a right to a comprehensive view on morality wherein their developing moral subjectivity is taken into serious consideration. If this is not so there can be no place for any moral approachability and growth at all. In that case adolescents are considered to be *pre-moral* beings. And still more: without this possibility of responsiveness of the youngster, education would become meaningless and would finally collapse. For how should one, for instance, responsibly teach young people to deal with sexual intimacy while one argues that they do not yet have a (feeling of a) personal moral identity, more so, while one ignores their conviction that their personal identity is constituted, among others, by the sexual encounter (Roebben 1998b)? In this regards, the most fruitful way of moral identity formation is perhaps an invitation to the young to maintain contact with themselves, to counter self-deceit (closing themselves off from the judgment of others or immersing themselves in a group ethos), to build up social defenses and resilience, and to learn from mistakes. This presupposes educators who challenge youngsters to gain back their breathing space, to express for themselves the reasons for their behavior and convictions (Tappan and Brown 1996, 106). What is needed is a 'mental playground' provided by adults, wherein youngsters (always provisionally) can become able to sort themselves out (see also Chapter 11).

A second concept that is recently linked to a comprehensive approach of moral education is 'moral competence'. A person is considered to be morally competent when he is capable of an inter-subjectively mediated perception of reality, through togetherness with others. The moral appeal emerging from reality is, as already mentioned, a dialogue. As Jürgen Habermas has shown, even in the most closed communitarian, authoritarian or doctrinally directed moral community the same concepts are inter-subjectively accounted for, like truth, rationality and justification, and are at play as in a democratic setting (Lesch 1995, 128). For instance, that someone who is a member of a sectarian movement is capable of doubting what he adheres to, points to the possibility of communication (he wants to do away with this doubt at least with a virtual dialogue partner) and to the inter-subjective perception of reality (Apel 1986). Moral solipsism does not exist, except as a psychological aberration. Theoreticians of moral competence want to link up precisely with this fundamental experience of inter-subjectivity. Moral competence is training in social competence and risking perspective change or adopting the standpoint of the other. This can be exercised in school, by making the otherness of the other a theme in literature, film, media education, intercultural projects, or just simply in classroom discussions, for instance by perceiving and evaluating an event at school or in society from a moral perspective (see also Chapter 1 and the 'just community' approach in the later work of Lawrence Kohlberg, see Bucher 1995, 69-71). The religious dimension of inter-subjective encounter will be discussed in Chapter 7.

Learning morality 'by doing' is reflected concretely in good practices, such as the social learning project 'Compassion' (Riegger 2003) or the awareness raising project 'Living Values Education'. According to the Dutch educationalist and theologian Thom Geurts (2003), the whole school is a permanent moral learning community. Its moral learning should not be restricted to specific extra-curricular activities. The school is in itself a 'values community' *(waardegemeenschap)*. Learning in the classroom is always a moral activity *(waardegericht leren)*. The school can be a splendid provider of 'rough material' for moral education and it can be a good trainer to polish this material (Haers 2004). Here as well the concept 'mental playground' is at stake: the teacher must take care that a minimum of trust prevails among the youngsters; he is entrusted with the task of making the classroom "safe for diversity" (Lickona 1991, 276-278).

Both dimensions, moral competence and moral identity, start with the presupposition that an important part of moral education is self-education. This is an old piece of wisdom that is again gaining currency. Education is self-discipline, namely gathering a courageous openness to new experiences confronting them with the life-project that one has constructed thus far. It is the possibility of social mobility to open oneself to the surprising foreignness of a situation or encounter, and through this come to a new phase of integration. As such, the goal is the path: transformations change and shape the structures of content (Bucher 1995, 68). Paying attention to the young person's narrative will also contribute to a more comprehensive view on moral education. Let it be clear that the recent and polarized methods are taken up in this whole: initiation and communication, linked by the concept of development, and confirmed by the self-clarification of the person who is prepared gradually to discover and justify what he stands for, are mutually included and reinforce each other.

Such a comprehensive concept of moral education (see also Mustakova-Possardt 2004) challenges the educator to give plenty of room to children and adolescents to become truly themselves as moral agents, as the narrators of their own story, at home in their own lives. In what follows this comprehensive view on morality and moral education, to respond critically and imaginatively (with vision and discernment) to the complexity of post-modern times, needs further elaboration. The concepts of vulnerability (paragraph 2) and human dignity and spirituality (paragraph 3) will play a central role in this debate.

## 2. Moral education and vulnerability

Moral education, understood as the critical, sensible and competent appraisal of values at stake in a specific situation – this always in dialogue with other critical, sensible and competent human beings –, is by its nature involved with the future. The distinction between good and evil, to be evaluated and applied by responsible persons – young and old –, will challenge us today and tomorrow. However, this future is vulnerable, because people live scattered lives, in the midst of the overwhelming ethos of market and media. Will they stay in tune with them selves and 'each' other? Will they be able to deal with the ambiguous task of combining the search for a meaningful life with the need for social cohesion?

### 2.1. The moral pedagogical relevance of the White March

This question was raised fundamentally during the protests against child abusers in Belgium in the midst of the 1990s. People came on the street and claimed not only punishment for the perpetrators and justice for the family of the victims, but also a new climate of social justice and human dignity. This was truly a moral claim: to save the lives of vulnerable people (first of all: of children) and to rediscover vulnerability as a main characteristic of morality in society. On the 20$^{th}$ of October 1996, three hundred thousand people took the streets of Brussels to protest in the so called 'White March' against the brutal facts of child abuse (committed by Marc Dutroux and his accomplices) and against the juridical system that failed to defend the rights of citizens, especially children, and left these matters unpunished (in order to veil the possible involvement of politicians and other respected members of the Belgian society). In those days a number of social-ethical speculations were made regarding the legal and humanitarian quality of our society. I take up this movement to present acutely the context wherein, in my judgment, the future of moral education will have to take place. Young people were at the forefront in this movement. They asked for authentic justice and for jurisprudence, which is consequent to this movement.

An important guiding principle in the analysis of the moral pedagogical relevance of the White March seems to be the distinction made by Charles Taylor between an ontological analysis that gauges the underlying motives of social and cultural phenomena, and an action analysis that proceeds along the line of factual value and norm orientations (Taylor 1996). The criticism of the White March against a corrupted state policy and juridical structures should not only be assessed on the action level, it should be pushed through to the ontological level. In my judgment and in the line of Taylor's argument this criticism contains two elements: a) People took to the streets to indict the loss of credibility of modern democracy. In recent years politicians trampled on the legal rules and laws that were previously accepted loyally by citizens as a reflection, reinforcement, and in a certain sense an extension of their dignity as citizens. b) In the White March the fragmentation of the contemporary life world was indicted: solidarity as well as the social safety net is disappearing because the internal cohesion in daily life – work, recreation and family – is scattered. People grow away from one another and from themselves. As a result, they can no longer rely on democracy that binds forces together. Actual democratic decision-making is itself marked by crumbling into personal wishes, interest groups, social services, and political favoritism, to name but a few.

The silence surrounding the movement of the White March a couple of years later likewise reveals that politics has especially functioned on the action level (reorganization of the court and police structure, revision of the system of political arrangements, etc.), but has paid little or no attention to the more deep-seated ontological level (new political culture, the demand for more humanity and less fragmentation of work, family and leisure time, etc.). It was especially this ontological disinterest for the demands of (mostly young) people that was indicted by the White March. It is this "hermeneutical awareness" (Haste 1996, 53), this very practical and actual sensibility for questions of humanity and solidarity, that stood central in this protest movement. It can be interpreted as a communitarian element in the societal discussion today that is ready to justify itself rationally, thus within the framework of a liberal discourse.

## 2.2. Moral sensibility based on an ethics of vulnerability

People want to feel at home somewhere, to be accepted and to be respected in their moral subjectivity, to be someone. Only when addressed personally, one can also be responsive and be held responseable. Moral sensibility is a concept that renders both aspects well. Morality implies not only 'being touched' by the joy and pain of others, but equally a 'touch-ableness', that trustful coping with reality and with others that convinces us of the fact that fragments of answers to moral questions can precisely be found in this interaction. The experience of good and evil can only be mediated and understood on the basis of a culture of vulnerability or mental openness for these phenomena. In the White March this was present as a pertinent question: what is the state of affairs of our culture of vulnerability, what is the state of affairs of a society wherein children disappear in the circuit of crime and corruption, or expressed more 'innocently', wherein children have to conform to the demands of the market, consumption, performance and perfection (Mercer 2005; Mette 2007, 109-119; White 2005, 35-62)? In a hectic society there seems to be no place for 'childlike virtues' like vulnerability, provisionality, growth and experimentation. "May our children still be children?", asks one of the slogans of the White March.

How can moral sensibility or approachableness in education be restored? In my opinion this can happen along two very concrete paths (Roebben 1998c): by contact with peers and friction with adults. Young people are in need of opportunities for interaction with their peers. They can only learn to understand moral claims by entering into the action themselves, by being allowed to undertake something, by being responsible for something (see above, paragraph 1.3). Contact with adults who are able show the courage of their convictions (not, by definition, verbally or with impressive arguments, but rather by their lifestyle) and against whom youngsters are allowed to clash forms a second possibility for sharpening moral sensibility. Friction in education is at first sight a negative reality: it is a matter of conflict. But this conflict can also be fruitful: out of friction follow warmth, involvement, presence and interest. In the protest or the indifference of the young a demand for interest often resounds. Moral education is a lost cause when adults require from youngsters a conscientious and sensible behavior towards others, while these adults themselves do not display this behavior towards the young. In some schools excellent mission statements are drawn up and imposed as moral norms on the young without them ever being concretely addressed to participate in the decision-making of the contents therein (Taylor 1996, 140-141). Whoever does not feel involved accordingly cannot display any behavior of sincere involvement in moral judgments and actions. This experience is still strengthened by the impression of young that the noble values they are expected to actualize form a part of a utilitarian and calculative moral technology (Eid 1995, 155), based on money and power, as the superstructure for a neo-capitalistic society (Hull 1996; Copley 2005). Or in the way I heard it once expressed in the hallways of an American university campus: "We are expensive, so we must be good".

## 3. Moral education, human dignity and spiritual leadership

### 3.1. The perspective of ultimate reality in moral education

When people ask themselves – often with regard to dramatic events like the Dutroux-affair in Belgium – "What in heaven's name is going on?" the 'what' or the ultimate meaning of education is evoked. In a number of boundary experiences, when the moral faculties of the person seem to break down, which also seems to appear in the vulnerable undertaking of education (understood as a permanent taking leave of the child), the question of ultimate reality comes to the fore. In a secularized society like ours, traditional religious institutions that have thematized and cultivated this perspective since time immemorial have lost their plausibility. But this does not restrain people from searching for fundamental explanations for the big questions of life.

This is, however, a vulnerable undertaking. The moral community, in which the societal and educational dialogue takes place, is fragile. People are 'delivered' to themselves and to one another. They are confronted with their dark side in the light of the greatness or limitation of others; people can make life sour for one another, even with the best intentions for that matter, which can harden to irreconcilability; people can loose their vitality and resilience in the hard struggle for a good life, etc. In my judgment, moral education or ethical formation can only become a vital force in the process of restoring the social cohesion of a society when it takes up images, concepts, narratives and experiences of the 'trans-ethical' in its own rationale. By 'trans-ethical' I mean the affirmation of the finality of the human person and the relativizing of the own possibilities of ethics, within ethics itself and as a special dimension of the moral competence of the person. This affirmation is not added extrinsically (via religion or a philosophical worldview) but belongs intrinsically to the reality of morality and ethics itself. "Everything is ethics, but ethics is not everything". Whoever doubts this sinks into 'ethicism'.

This trans-ethical dimension in ethics can be fleshed out, though not necessarily, in a religious way. Essentially it concerns the basic trust in the ultimate meaningfulness of reality, on the basis of which people make moral decisions. The argumentation goes as follows: I am drawn to the good life, to the distinction between good and evil, because I am convinced that reality ultimately bears in itself sufficient meaningfulness in order to be able to make and address this distinction. The advantage (initially, at least) of a non-religious articulation of this basic trust is this: in the inter-cultural and inter-religious encounter people can help one another to articulate and to integrate this trans-ethical moment. No one is excluded, because religion or worldview is not a necessary element. One only needs to be 'human'. A second advantage is that this articulation can take place amidst one's professional life. People can anchor their moral decisions within their professions (as doctor, manager, politician, teacher, etc.), in order to describe the borders of their profession's ethical discourse and together they can strive for a new moral sensibility. Once again, I am convinced that in this way ethics can more strongly realize its own project, namely as a relative-autonomous undertaking that is liberated from suffocating pretensions to absoluteness. The religious domain as well is then restored. It is no longer some "elite rest-category" (Bucher 1995, 64; translation BR) that comes into force when human morality can go no further, but it fulfills precisely the critical function that is needed to enervate the absoluteness of other functional dimensions of human life, such as ethics and education, or moral education (see for this perspective also Chapter 4)!

## 3.2. Human dignity and spirituality

Indifference is incompatible with education. Brutal indifference causes cynicism and in the long run even fundamentalism. These are very bad guys in the company of children, adolescents and young adults (and not only for them!). The opposite of indifference, namely being aware of the difference of life options at stake in daily life and education, open the space for commitment and responsibility. As human beings we share this same experience of difference. Moreover we are invited to cherish our uniqueness, in order to creatively participate in the mutual nourishment of our human existence. This 'shared humanity' – being one in diversity – seems to be the ultimate spiritual project of our times and can connect us to each other in a new way.

With this approach people learn how to deal authentically and creatively with issues of ultimate meaning in the midst of a secularized society, no longer on the basis of traditional religious institutions, but based on the common and universal experience of humanity, relying on the warm undercurrent of meaningfulness. This universal stream of conscience is like a bosom: it carries and cares for the differences and enables them to flourish for the common good of every individual. In the encounter I step forward and I step out of myself, and become aware of the other. In his vulnerability the other teaches me to get rid of the exclusivity of myself and to become involved in the life project of the other: 'The centre of gravity is lying outside myself, I am not the centre of the universe.' Moreover this spiritual experience can liberate me from moral and religious self-liberation: 'In my searching I have already been found. I do not have to attract attention of others to myself, I have already been seen in my deepest self. I do not have to justify myself, I am already fundamentally accepted the way I am here and now. And if I might fall, that will never happen in ultimate meaninglessness.'

This spiritual project is anchored in the personal quest for meaning of contemporaries and not exclusively connected anymore to the ministry of churches and religious movements. The German philosopher Hans Joas (2004) is referring to post-modern experiences of 'self-transcendence' and of being caught ("Ergriffensein") by another reality that transcends my own daily reality. He refers to a basic trust, a conviction that one is accepted, loved and carried; it is all about life in dedication, living with open hands. For the North-American theologian Sandra Schneiders, spirituality is "the conscious involvement in the project of life-integration through *self-transcendence* toward the ultimate value one perceives" (2003, 166). By way of example: the same sort of trust can be found when parents trust their children to the hands of the leadership at the beginning of a summer camp. At that very moment they express their confidence in the ultimate reasonableness of reality, that things will not be harmful, that God is looking over their shoulders – to put it in a religious way – and is taking care. Religious faith is related to this basic attitude of existential faith, of 'basic trust'.

As human beings we share this original position with each other. It is the basic structure of humanity. This kind of spirituality, radical openness to and trust in a reality that never definitively collapses but that remains open for the future, is actually calling for responsible people – people who are prepared to transcend themselves, people who remain in contact with their deepest longings, with their soul, in the basic structure of humanity within their own existence. They are aware of the light that is shining in and through them. They are able to accumulate that light and to reflect it to other human beings, as a light house. True friendship is the deepening and intensification of this original human disposition. As friends people can reach the ultimate depth of existence, as they are sharing their lives *as human beings who care.*

Undoubtedly, the same issues can be found in every human being's story. It all depends on how far one can and will go in carefully exploring, explicating and sharing them with other fellow human beings. I believe that friendship is an excellent place for this exchange. Two souls can meet there on the deepest level of humanity.

### 3.3. Courageous leadership

This difficult process of humanization of post-modern culture demands courageous leaders. People are needed who are *in actu* able to show what it means to live meaningfully in a complex era. Such people are both enthusiastically and wisely able to express what is really needed to become a happy human being. And, based on a 'exemplary' path of life they are able to show how such happiness can actually be realized, simply and authentically. By 'example' I mean the critical-reflective way of dealing with one's own tradition of meaning: bearing witness to one's own struggle with the project of life that one is given.

This leadership has spiritual roots. Leading the way in the good life implies internal familiarity with the traditions of meaning, with the discourse communities that shed light on the ancient questions on life. In the complexity of a dazzling post-modern culture these questions are more acute that ever before, because the master narratives that bring about meaning and hold possible answers are no longer available. People have to rely much more on themselves, either alone or in small groups. Yet many intrinsically sense the value and preciousness of such ancient (moral and religious) answers. I am of the opinion that not a lack but rather an abundance of fragments of meaning giving can be found, and that people are not aware of the grounds on which they are able to make conscious and well-considered choices. They lack beacons of meaningfulness and freedom in a culture without orientation. Competent leaders provide insight without indoctrination. They give a glimpse of the meaningfulness of a particular project of life, and they invite contemporaries to share their observations.

## 4. Conclusion

Educational leadership is spiritual leadership (Alexander 2001). The little, vulnerable flame of the child should be cherished and fed, so that it can be ablaze and can enlighten fellow human beings in their search for meaning. Educators should set priorities so that this 'warm' comprehensive view on education can become reality. Children have the right to such thoughtful educators. By way of conclusion I present a list of five educational priorities or values. Educating *for* some value implies educating *with* this value. What you do as educator, is what you get. You can only reap what you have sown. The list goes as follows:

| Educating for contemplation | Contemplative education |
| --- | --- |
| Educating for responsibility | Responsible education |
| Educating for imagination | Imaginative education |
| Educating for sensibility | Sensible education |
| Educating for passion | Passionate education |

*Contemplative* education means to respect the given time in education, to slow down or un-hasten, if necessary, the learning process. It warns for the idea that education is all about getting a better instrumental grip on chaos. It makes room for silence and meditation, for what transcends the immediate perception. *Responsible* education refers, as argued, to the capacity of the adult of being responsive and open to the situation of the learner, as well as to the preparedness to tell ones own story, to enrich or to shade the situation. *Imaginative* education is an invitation to children and adolescents to become the storyteller of their own life, to practice the virtue of moral and spiritual imagination and to cultivate the taste for humor! *Sensible* education makes children aware of the different positions and people at stake, helps them to see that the good life is all about honoring and celebrating these differences, and that indifference is a bad guide for the exploration of the good life. *Passionate* education means to show the courage of one's convictions as an adult, to show where the passion and the energy comes from, to resonate with the great longings of our times.

These five qualifications of comprehensive education form the acronym *crisp* and lead to the idea of 'crispy education'. Such an education is fresh, resolute, positive, direct, stimulating, alive and kicking. In the same Boston area to which I referred in the introduction of this chapter, I could read on a subway tram advertisement: "Make a difference. Become a teacher". This comes close to the truth, I believe. I would say, to make it still more salient: become a 'crispy' teacher!

# Chapter 3

# Religious Communication in Modern Culture
# The Case of Young Adults

Theology is moored in time and space. Roman-Catholic theology in the Netherlands and Flanders is trying to find its way in today's culture, forty five years after the Second Vatican Council. Much of what was considered to be the promise of a new and grown-up church and in which especially the Netherlands served as a model for these dynamics of renewal, has stranded on the resistance of conservative forces in the church. This is painful for many who are active in the church. This pain is, however, of no concern to young adult students in theology departments. The struggle of the church with her self-understanding ever since the Second Vatican Council has passed them by simply because they are less than forty five years old. The disappointment of unfulfilled promises, the 'blues' of the eighties and early nineties ("things should be different in the church, but they can't be") (Michiels & Roebben 1994) is wasted on them. They would rather like to know what is driving religiously convinced people, i.c. Christians, to experience and answer present-day questions in their own specific way. Moreover Christian churches are confronted for the first time in their history with a generation of young adults who have been hardly religiously socialized at home. Young theologians are voicing this experience of their contemporaries. This situation is food for thought.

What Jan Bluyssen, former bishop of 's-Hertogenbosch (Netherlands) already wrote in the eighties 'after the great church abandonment', is applicable more than ever to religious communication in modern culture. From an pastoral-educational concern he writes in the late eighties: "We are not in the need of believers who worry day in day out about how for heaven's sake they can go on with *this* church. Nor do we need believers who fearfully mourn the losses of the church. Young people who see their educators deal with their Christianity in such a strained manner, or see them struggle so painfully with the questions of our times, will hardly be tempted to join the Lord and his church. What we need first and foremost are people who give evidence of a well-tested and deep-seated faith in God" (Bluyssen 1989, 195, translation BR). Practical theology can reinforce this question, place it in a new time frame ("joining the Lord and his church" might have meant something different in the eighties than it does in 2009) and reflect on it theologically. In any case the request for authentic religious communication in our society and for the presence of the Christian tradition is prominent. Theologically educated young adults (between 16 and 25 years old) in Belgium, the Netherlands and Germany, engaged in higher education, intermediary relations in church and society and in all sorts of volunteering, show these dynamics.

In this chapter I would like to systematize these dynamics as follows. In the first section (problem definition) I will indicate in what manner traditional religious institutions try to deal with the pressure of modernization in society. The point that I am making is that churches do not know how to deal with these developments. They appear to be unable to convey their traditions of meaningful life to future generations. In the second section (analysis) I attempt to go beyond the perspective of the crisis of tradition and I opt to corroborate the creative powers in a modern society in its search for meaning from a religious perspective. I analyze the process of 'interactive search for meaning' of contemporaries and offer some critical notes in the margin. As a practical theologian I would like to offer insight in the ways churches might react, now that they are confronted with new challenges. This will be done in the third section (perspective). I believe that churches should set themselves up as mature dialogue partners 'in religiosis'. They should dare to bring their language of meaningful life in a critical interrelationship with the way life is experienced nowadays. This assumes new priorities where religious socialization, communication and leadership are concerned. At the end of this contribution (section four: strategy) I make a plea for religious education of young adults. More than ever before, religious socialization of children assumes educating young adults as future parents in matters of religious communication.

## 1. Society under the pressure of modernization, churches under the pressure of tradition

Present-day society is pressured to modernize. This is a development with deep-seated historical roots. Its analysis is complex. Karl Gabriel, the German sociologist of religion, interprets this as follows: de-traditionalization concerning frameworks of values and meaning causes people to fall back on themselves to give meaning to their lives (Gabriel 1991, 69-88). The supply at the 'meaning-seeking-market' is overwhelming, there is no shortage of religiosity and spirituality. People have to steer by their own compass to make responsible choices from this supply. Ever since Enlightenment traditional religious institutions have lost more and more of their function of orientation in moral and religious symbolization. A systematic approach of this situation by re-confessionalization and denominational segregation (or 'pillarization') in the Netherlands and Flanders (especially in the educational and health care sector in the $19^{th}$ and $20^{th}$ century) has not been able to turn the tide (Roebben & de Wildt 2010). Also the Netherlands and Flanders became more and more secularized. Research of sociology of religion has confirmed this trend (Dekker, de Hart & Peters 1997; Dobbelaere, Elchardus & Kerkhofs 2000).

Along with this de-confessionalization the de-traditionalization has progressed even further and faster than before. At many levels of society institutionalized religious traditions have lost their "good grounds" to find acceptance for a religious stance concerning existential questions and the transfer of faith. There is a crisis of tradition. The process of religious 'tradere' (Latin for passing on) itself has become problematic, sometimes even lost. The relation faith-life is characterized by correlation weakness, or even a breach in correlation. Young people wonder pityingly: "What is it that religious people talk about? What are they getting upset about?" Attempts by theology to reestablish the plausibility of a religious perspective on every day life deal with the same crisis that institutionalized religions are experiencing. The tradition crisis is to be felt deep into the reflexive layers of religious institutions. In this section I proceed as follows. First I define four problem areas concerning religious communication (two ecclesiological and two religious educational ones) that offer insight in the given that churches nowadays do not know how to offer a meaningful learning route 'in religiosis'. Subsequently I refer to two explanation models for this situation out of the sociology of religion. Finally I indicate what concrete actions churches undertake nowadays in order to deal with the given circumstances.

**1.1. Four problem areas**

First of all, it is true that virtually no *substratum of experience* corresponds to the traditional religious socialization of the church anymore. People do not identify with the church anymore, they do not understand its language anymore, do not know what it wants to express with its symbols and sacraments. If young people, for example, do not know of the effectiveness of salvation (*opus operatum*), how can they be expected to engage in the sacrament of confirmation out of a personal involvement (*opus operantis*) (Roebben 1999b). When this religious mooring disappears, so does the social relevance of faith. People continue to belong to the church by means of baptism, but (virtually) no religious praxis, experience or practical insight in the liberating dynamics of the gospel corresponds with it. The official church finds its influence in the life of believers shrinking and attempts to win them back by entrusting religious socialization to the family in a gesture of generosity. It no longer claims to be the originator, but positions the center in the 'home church' and its permanent religious initiation. The former secretary of the Council for Family Ministry in Flanders, Paul Deleu, has seriously criticized this development: "The greater the established secularism, the greater the expectation of the churches with respect to the family. As if secularism has stopped at the threshold of the home church. By thinking about the family in this manner one does not really approach it for its own worth, but as the carrier of frustrated church expectations". And this leads to the paradox: "One can proclaim that the family is an in-between that can evangelize and be evangelized, and still ignore the specific experience of the evangelizing family" (Deleu 1988, 52 – translation BR). On the face of it, the attention is shifted from occasional catechesis in church towards a permanent evangelization in the home church, from church initiative towards support of religious education at home, but the concern remains the same: to close the gap between church and world and to strive for the highest possible degree of participation in the life of the church.

Secondly and in line with the above, German authors like Erich Feifel and Walter Kasper (1987), Karl Gabriel (1991) and Volker Drehsen (1994) have phrased interesting thoughts about the *crisis of credibility of the church* in a post-modern society. The church stands in its own way if it makes people responsible for personal belief on the one hand, but does not permit the development of dissenting views or praxis on the other hand. People are leaving the church while they are kept in their place because of a traditional socialization idea (Drehsen 1994, 48-55). The church is faced with an immense educational dilemma, according to Drehsen: either it persists in its infertile attitude of being in the right until it has become totally unworldly and sectarian, or it takes up the challenge of the 'Tradierungskrise' and turns it into the focus of mature religious communication itself. In another analysis Drehsen states that as a result of this situation the church is no longer capable of formulating the true religious questions of modern people. Ever since the process of secularization has started, it has not taken advantage of the return of religion in many new colors. That is its ultimate tragedy: people cannot find their way in church, it conveys little to them, because it conveys little 'about' them. They do not feel heard in their quest for religious self-clarification, in their efforts to deal with the contingency of life in a meaningful way. The church is struggling in its heart of hearts with its "religiöse Integrationsfähigkeit" (Drehsen 1994, 8), with the question of how to 'authenticate and communicate' its religious message within a modern world that is confused and self-confident at the same time. Friedrich Schweitzer and Rick Osmer have called this the 'education gap' of the church vis-à-vis the world (2003, xvi).

A third element in the explanation of the absence of successful religious socialization by the church is of a socio-pedagogical nature and has to do with the *educational uncertainty* of parents and educators (see Chapters 1 and 4). They hesitate to continue to raise their children within a Christian perspective. Either they have dropped out in the opinion that the message of the church has lost its credibility in their eyes or they lack the nerve to point out the religious dimension of life to their children altogether. Many parents do not have their children baptized in the opinion that they should leave them free to make the decision themselves later in their lives. They assume that an education devoid of value judgments and religion is possible, or in other words that the perspectives of life and faith are completely incompatible. The church and its message do not appeal to them, they do not arouse their interest. Other parents are all too happy to see their child initiated in the full life of the church by way of the first communion or confirmation without realizing that this implies engagement. They shrink from questions about this half-heartedness, stay away from catechetic introductions for parents but drift along on the flow of what is socio-culturally taken for granted. If children are no longer aware of the scope of, for example, confirmation and only concentrate on the festivities and presents and parents cannot or dare not voice an alternative (not even a generally sacral, a religious or non-materialistic perspective), then it is to be expected that this process only enlarges the educational embarrassment of parents. The youthful perception of reality (being in fashion, on top of the latest trends, flexible) becomes the norm. Parents are unable to deny their children the celebration annex festivities surrounding confirmation, because it would make them lose face with their friends. In these confusing times children frequently lack grown up 'biographical advisors', adults who have in mind something other than a certain degree of material habituation and a lukewarm identity.

A final explanation arises from the radically *different experience of being young* nowadays. Adolescence differs structurally from the way it was some forty years ago. It is no longer viewed as a storm-free transition period from childhood to adulthood (between the age of 12 and 18), but as a turbulent and independent period in which adolescents create their own biography and attempt to gain insight into the dynamics of their own story, identity and person (Schweitzer 1993; 1996; 2004). Nowadays being young means that one has to learn to deal with the fact that as a future (young) adult one will have to live continually in a situation of transition. One will have to take an honest and integrated standpoint in the postmodern experience of 'social mobility'. In addition to that, the onset of adolescence has been accelerated (earlier than 12) and the period of schooling prolonged, so that the entrance into the world of adulthood, employment, partner choice and raising a family has been postponed. This definition of young adulthood (caught in the paradox between personal and professional insecurity and huge societal expectations) will later in this essay function as a starting point for a renewed reflection on religious communication with young adults. Many of them are dwelling in an existential vacuum after their experiences with congregational catechesis and religious education at school. The challenge of working with young adults is huge. All this, according to Friedrich Schweitzer, has drastic consequences for religious socialization, for example for confirmation. This no longer serves to demarcate the passage into adulthood, but has lost its social impact as a moment of initiation (Schweitzer

1993, 77-79). The sacrament of confirmation can therefore no longer be legitimized theologically from this viewpoint. Furthermore, the prolonged biography of youth entails that those who join in children's and family services become progressively younger (Schweitzer 1993, 80) and that the young adult (or post-adolescent) parents with small children of today feel that they belong to that generation segment of 'youth' with its typical experience of life. This new situation implies an important task for youth ministry that in this context has to work with young people mainly on 'moral/religious self-clarification' and building of identity against the background of a blurred society (Roebben 1999b).

**1.2. Two models of explanation**

In sociology of religion in the past forty years at least two models of explanation have been developed (Ebertz 1999; Ziebertz 1999). One speaks of the *secularization thesis*: religion in general and the churches in particular are no longer the overarching 'meaning-providers' for culture and society. They have lost their impact in several domains of human life. Nowadays people self-confidently search for meaning. The term 'functional differentiation' applies here: within the complexity of life its domains have become disconnected. They have grown apart more and more and have started to lead their own life. Religion is but one of those domains, conveniently next to and apart from the others, just like for example relationships, raising children, education, work, leisure, sports, etc. Additionally, in sociology of religion one speaks of the *modernization thesis*. Traditional religious institutions have indeed lost their influence; however, at the same time former churchgoers and their contemporaries are freely and unrestrainedly searching for meaning in their lives. Individualization is the keyword of modern culture and this carries over into the area of religion. De-traditionalization has the effect that people no longer find inspiration for their own way in life in traditions as passed on by religious institutions. Living authentically means that one can and dares to steer by his or her own internal compass. Pluralization is the result of this development: numerous religious options that can be combined indefinitely (syncretism) are available in modern culture. One can speak of a 'reli-market' – where a person can offer his own life project as ware and where the customer can get a bargain and determine whether and how much religion one takes home. "Could you make that a little more, please?"

Because of the disappearance of the great narratives that build a context of meaningfulness, people have been left to their own devices. They are in each other's charge, but at each other's mercy as well. After all, individualization can also pressure people: "I *have* to be free and authentic". It carries the risk of being lived, because the task of making choices time and again is felt as too much of a burden. Paradoxically our freedom becomes a constraint. "I determine" becomes equal to "I am determined". The building blocks of freedom have become nothing other than monoliths, organically fitted into what the market requires. Added to this can be the fact that the promise of modernization of culture as a project of meaning seeking is often not fulfilled. The 'meaning-seeker-without-external-compass', the person who has freed himself from enslaving traditions, often enough chokes on the experience of contingency and ambiguity, an experience that not only characterized human life in the old days, but still does today. The promise of life as a self-directed project, which is what modernity is all about, often dead-ends in itself. Since no one can direct the contingent circumstances of his or her own life, especially not the last circumstance: death. The core of the human self is 'not available'. And that is disturbing to modern people. The French sociologist of religion, Danièle Hervieu-Léger argues as follows: "The structural tension in the experience of modernity stems from the fact that it simultaneously produces the expectations it is supposed to satisfy and the feeling of helplessness arising from the awareness that it provokes of the world's opaqueness. The affirmation of the reign of man [sic], his autonomism, his all-powerfulness, breaks down at the very moment and in the very mechanism through which it was made" (1990, 24).

Religion can serve the purpose of contingency management. People can experiment with alternative medicine and meditation. They join eagerly groups that offer the opportunity of contact with what goes beyond everyday reality. After abandoning the church, they knock on the doors of private caregivers who design religious rituals for key moments in life. Popular religion is booming. In the overheated sorry-culture confession is called upon again. The 'new-religious longing', according to the Dutch systematic theologian Anton van Harskamp (2000) is developing in many ways in the tension between the individualization of meaning and the awareness of its ultimate unavailability.

## 1.3. Three possible reactions

This situation could be a temptation for churches to welcome the 'new receptivity' with open arms and to functionalize it in view of new membership. They could focus exclusively on the new and new-religious longing to undo their own anemia and to adapt to what is marketable. This option has a variation that is milder: that of re-profiling what is typically Christian, in view of a more forceful testimony in the world of meaning-seekers. The German sociologist of religion, Michael Ebertz, distinguishes three possible reactions: the option of self-complacency (with the corresponding strategy of closing rank – since the world is in the wrong), the option of self-regulation (with the adaptation strategy – since we have to get through these difficult times) and the option of self-direction (with the development strategy – which are the opportunities for learning and change in this situation?) (Ebertz 1999, 140-141). He makes a plea for the third option and strategy. Only then churches can become sacrament of salvation for the world, since that is what they are meant to be, according to Ebertz.

There is much uncertainty in church circles about how to deal with religiosity outside the church. One thing is for sure: the dynamics *ad intra* (what does modernization of religion mean for a community of believers?) and the dynamics *ad extra* (what can churches mean to modernized contemporaries?) need to remain connected. Self-absorption of the church on the one hand or its clearance sale to culture on the other hand does not serve any purpose. In the research project 'God in the Netherlands' this ambivalence is recognized, but at the same time one remarks that it is not easy, from a church political point of view, to keep these two motions together. Choices have to be made, according to this paper (Dekker, de Hart & Peters 1997, 117-123). This process of prioritizing calls for profound analysis.

## 2. The longing for religious orientation in modern culture

For a modernized perspective of religion 'creative perception' is necessary. In the analysis one needs to be courageous in order to look at reality differently. The present-day crisis of faith might be an optical illusion: maybe churches are so focused on certain developments that they are unable to see the new ones (Tieleman 1995). What is happening to a modern community of faith is comparable to the sinking of the Titanic, a fortress of power that is perishing and desperately casting life-boats from where one wistfully looks back at what is gone forever. Or is it perhaps something else: is today's culture more like a sea of meaning on which many drift about without any sense of orientation, in search of a perspective of meaningful life; as an open space of discovery of meaning out of whose depths the Christian story emerges next to other fragmented frames of reference; as a collection of disparate pieces of wreckage, that remind us of a rich and dynamic past, to which the meaning-seeker can cling?

## 2.1. Kairologic analysis

The first scenario, a disaster scenario, refers to the secularization thesis of the former paragraph, the second scenario, an emergence scenario, refers to the modernization thesis. Emergence points at the positive act of coming up for air, of recovering one's breath. At the same time it points at the urgent nature (*emergency*) of this analysis: who spends too much time mourning the lost glory will be unable to see through the tears that people in their vitality are already busy looking for a new *modus vivendi*. Modern theology should keep an open mind for this development and should be open to the signals of the young who have no experience of the struggle that the church has gone through in its Titanic-stage. Schematically both scenarios yield the following ways of being-church. For the time being they help to look at religiously loaded reality in a clear and original way.

| Disaster scenario | Emergency scenario |
| --- | --- |
| Ideological | Spiritual |
| Moralistic | Enthusiastic |
| Imposed | Self-directed |
| Top down | Contextual |
| Retrospective | Innovative |
| Self-glorifying | Self-criticizing |

In practical theology a kairologic awareness is present: the practical theologian can choose a hopeful perspective for assessing a situation, because he or she is convinced that it concerns a *kairos*, an inspired moment for a new and critical praxis (Englert 1992). This *kairos* is founded in the conviction that reality does not shut tight once and for all, but remains open as a meaningful and humanizing event that can be assented to and interpreted by people. Viewing the current situation as a 'crisis' and considering practical theology as some sort of 'science of crisis' does little justice to the search for truth of people today and to the freedom of the coming of God in the middle of this process.

The term 'crisis' presumes a deficiency, something that is lost. It sounds wistful and threatens to play down what is new and trying to break through in time. The term *kairos,* on the contrary, has a positive meaning. It refers to the trust in the fullness of reality, as it is intrinsically comprehensible for contemporaries and contains opportunities to learn and change.

## 2.2. Interactive search for meaning

Every person searches for meaning, develops dynamics for his or her life, consciously or subconsciously. Whenever those dynamics are interpreted as a finality with an origin and a goal, one speaks of a philosophy of life; this in its turn can be filled in an explicitly religious or profane way. As is argued above, search for meaning is a syncretic event nowadays. Young people are dealing flexibly and unrestrainedly with what is pre-given, with whatever they happen upon. The pleasure of *surfing* (exploring), *fiddling* (taking apart) and *sampling* (mixing) of moral and religious convictions and life patterns often in different settings at the same time, is more important than the final result. The latter is difficult for young people to envision as a matter of fact, because things were not thought out or planned in advance. Two Dutch youth researchers, Jacques Janssen and Maarten Prins, speak of the primacy of action over reflection and of annexing religious traditions as a 'toolkit of symbols' (2000, 12) in that process. And especially: "the building-schemes can only be made after their buildings have been completed" (2000, 11). Older people tend to feel insecure with such a 'balancing identity'; but the young feel like fish in the water. Cell phones and chat-boxes on the internet are favorite media for them to undertake action, to develop patterns and ways of thinking on the go – in and through the interaction with peers, without building-schemes, purely for the pleasure of exchange. Action to them is interaction, dynamics and involvement.

Also religious language games do not escape this enthusiastic process of annexation. Young people are abundantly experimenting with religion. The attraction of crossing the boundaries of reality, the utopia and the relationality of religion appeals to them. Older people can be shocked by this annexation of religion in youth culture and view it as a lack of respect. But in the mean time it is really happening: "the irreverent spiritual quest of generation X" (Beaudoin 1998). Numerous music clips contain religious connotations and artifacts. There are sites on the internet that offer an alternative (Christian) worship. Youth channels are deliberately taking a religious stance and are aiming at some kind of democratization of religion. Examples of this development abound. One of them is especially eloquent. It was picked from the program Republica on Studio Brussels, a Flemish youth station. It has a section *'Van god los'* (cut off from god) in which the reporter Peter Derie addresses young people in the street and asks their opinion about a variety of religious topics. Lieven Vandenhaute, the host of *Republica*, motivates his decision to tackle religion as follows: "Religion is no nonsense. It is an essential part of human beings. In our radio program we have fun talking about everything that makes life worth living: theater, books, sports, fitness, fashion – only religion we safely ignore. Why would I stay away from it, when it is truly fascinating? Religion is one of the major realizations of human beings – I am not the only one who thinks that way – and post-modern people are slowly realizing that they should not throw away the child with the bathwater, that if we push religion out of our daily thinking, it surfaces elsewhere in the form of an addiction to shopping, for example. A credit card becomes heaven on earth. But religion is always there. You show it out of your house by the front door and it sneaks back in through the back" (Hens 2001 – translation BR).

What functions as a general principle in construction of culture, functions in the construction of religious meaning as well. "No matter how fast the young can run, their elders will catch up with them" (Jacques Janssen). Retro-socialization or the fact that adults often imitate the disrespectful behavior, options and patterns of youngsters, is also the case here. In the *main stream* culture religious elements resurface. God and religion are allowed to be topics again in popular radio and television programs, if coming from unexpected sources. The internet is crowded with religious sites. After eroticism, religion is the most popular topic. After the 11$^{th}$ of September 2001 the interest in religious information has leapt forward. People want objective information about other religions, but more profound than that, there is a need for a language to tackle one's confusion at the level of religious orientation.

An important aspect in the development of the interactive search for meaning is its commercialization. The 'dissemination' (Ebertz 1998, 148-149) and democratization of religious matters in modern culture is of interest to salesmen. They are always looking for new trends that can be marketed. Just like commercials play with the ecological and ethical sensitivity of potential buyers (think of 'green products', the 'clean clothes'-campaign and cars with 'controlled performance') (Van Gerwen 1995), the market goes along with the present-day longing for religious orientation in the search for meaning. Coca-Cola is a terrific example of this. In its clips it makes use of young people who have mock religious experiences in nature and in friendship. This company employs a dazzling and contemporary *styling* to voice the more profound longing of young people to launch its message ... "Enjoy Coca-Cola". A deep longing for community, for a firm basis, etc. is picked from the collective memory of modern young people, thematized, pictured seductively and subsequently neatly filled in materially. I suspect this multinational of having the know-how of professional theologians at its disposal in the marketing-department!

## 2.3. Critical evaluation

It is true that our contemporaries are looking for firm ground, an existential mooring for their search for authenticity. They are able to find this in religion. It is true that the plurality of life makes people long for fulfillment and wholeness, something that can already be found in religious encounters and communities of all sorts (Van Harskamp 2000). It is true that young people are making a challenging track in this process: the development of their identity is taking place in a culture that is searching for an identity itself (Mette 2001). However, should we not place some critical notes in the margin concerning this development? Three aspects require our attention – because they illicit criticism from a Christian-theological perspective, and because they are food for thought to explore new horizons of religious communication at the same time.

The first comment has to do with the aspect of esthetical use or 'glamorization' of religion. Everything gets linked to everything. Elements picked from different religions, are gathered and collected in a patchwork quilt. Nothing is holy in itself. The attraction of religion lies only in the attraction of this process of taking into use. Therefore it cannot be claimed that young people are totally isolated from religious language games. On the contrary, in their search they rearrange old frames of reference. They fall back on chunks of religious socialization from the old days. The question that surfaces, however, is the following: Does it go any further than just attribution? Does the basic religious experience underneath those terms mean anything to young people (Roebben 2001a, 100-102)? In other words, is it only the functional aspect of religion that remains (attribution), religion aimed at making the contingency of life tolerable and exciting, and not the substantial meaning of religion (experience)? And is the substantial role of religion at all possible without being anchored in a community of faith? Or even: is a new type of religion developing, one that is completely self-directed, a new type of religious self-awareness, making use of the affirmative language of religions, but reworded in a completely individualized re-composition?

A second problem is linked with this: assuming that religion is designed for search, in which the experience of searching itself takes priority over finding, how can the aspect of action of such a venture be studied? If it is true that "the building-schemes are made after their buildings have been completed" (Janssen & Prins 2000, 11), how can the designers be approached? Young people want action, rather than reflection. They do not ask for the meaning of things, they use the meaning. They recreate a chaotic and confused jumble of impulses into a livable whole. Do the young handy-men know what they are doing, what they are getting into? May we speak of a new habitat, one that is held together by shoestring, but viewed more closely a source of inspiration for the young themselves? And could this be a rich experience to them, beyond traditional religious substances?

Next comes the question: is it true religion that is involved here? True religion articulates the relationship between the life of human beings that is visible and what transcends it. It takes a position in the tension between existential self-management and ultimate perspective, or the tension between individualization of meaning and the awareness of its ultimate non-availability. However, the new religious longing threatens to continue the myth of self-realization that is so characteristic for our day and age. It leads people to expect that they will be able to escape the ruthlessness of time by following a merciful alternative under one's own steam. This already hard existence becomes even more burdened: one has to realize his or her own salvation. In true religion a person is urged to be guided by the wisdom of predecessors, who struggled in their own way with the same questions and were able to find parts of answers. Religion leads people into a symbolic order that can liberate them as a person. Here one could also remark: is religion taking on a fundamentally new appearance? Is the substantial element abandoned in preference of the merely functional aspect? Is the break in culture complete in the sense that people can only be approached as far as the profane aspect of religion is concerned? Will there be a religion without God before long? The Dutch theologian Anton van

Harskamp claims that in the mean time we should wait for God – now that He is 'out of the picture'. His colleague, Erik Borgman, wonders if God will reveal himself in a new shape or that God will never be okay again (2000). Apparently theologians admit that there is no way around these difficult questions any longer. Religion is being used by people (for their own salvation) – and that is contrary to an important characteristic of religion in general and Christianity in particular: religion will not be used, that is not what it is for. Religion is gratuitous, something that indeed confirms human deliberations, but transcends, questions and challenges them as well.

## 3. Churches as dialogue partners 'in religiosis'

An embankment of the longing for religious orientation in our present-day culture can be discerned. People do not stay impassive in their quest for meaning in complex times. This longing is ambivalent and calls for clarification. For the practical theologian who considers it his/her job to perceive culture in an intensified theological perspective, this means a challenge to open up new horizons of religious communication. The questions are numerous: How will believers evaluate this situation theologically? How do they view themselves? And how will the theological tradition be revitalized? Which role do churches claim in this process? In this section I will indicate several crucial dimensions of a church community that is at the same time critically questioning and recognizably involved in daily life, a church that neither turns away from nor gets lost in this epoch.

### 3.1. Reading the 'signs of the times': beyond crisis technology

With the kairologic perspective I have chosen for the hopeful analysis, averse to pastoral panic and hectic. I assume that the future of traditional religious institutions lies in a day to day willingness to be open to the culture and to trust culture to be a place of religious confrontation and deepening. Too much pastoral activity shuts off this possibility and suffers of self-complacency, of the illusion that nothing is wrong and that everything should continue along the old and familiar tracks, embellished with the newest tricks of 'pastoral crisis technology'. However, when the deeper and supportive layers of ministry are barely touched upon in the work itself, people who are searching for religious orientation will turn away from it. Since ministry can give the impression of ruthlessness: full of itself, disconnected from the deep longing in culture, and even worse, cut off from the source of life that inspires it.

If, however, the ministry knows how to master the art of listening at the new-religious longing and wording it in the language in which it is anchored itself, the opportunity for new things will arise. This tension between inside and outside, refreshing itself at its own sources of faith in view of a better understanding of religious revitalization of culture, this mutual transformation of Christian tradition and cultural context, is pre-eminently the task of Christianity today. The "critical interrelationship" of text and context, of theological tradition and present-day culture, on the basis of the story of grace of Christianity (in a nutshell: God who cares about the well-being of people, who declares his solidarity in the person of the living Jesus, to make people become fully human, united and merciful towards each other and their world) is the task of Christians today: as study and as engagement. This calls for a fundamental choice of openness of the churches towards the signs of the times. The metaphor of the 'inn' could be helpful: the church could be an inn where people can find rest and friendship, where they can jump in to be part of the table community (Hendriks 2000). The table is the central source of this happening, but not for members only. It is an attractive source for many people who enter the tavern. The table is connected to the stream of grace inside the house, on the basis of which the management of the tavern decides to open up its doors every day and decides to be responsive for the quest for meaning in contemporary culture.

## 3.2. Support for religious socialization in families

Religious socialization in a post-modern context can no longer be viewed as an offer that is already defined in time and space, but it will rather have to be considered as a *lengthy and interactive process* in which the critical education of the young, the skill to find their way independently in a dynamic environment and to word their own point of view, should be the focus. The fact that the young go a different direction from what their predecessors had hoped for in the beginning is inherent to the possible outcome of that process of socialization. The crux of the matter is that acquiring one's own identity can be viewed as a religious process and can therefore be the content of religious education. The initial religious sensibility is then no longer the starting-point of a systematic explanation of religion and faith, but the theme itself of this learning process.

How will this process remain sufficiently socially coherent? In my opinion this will imply a permanent communication among all parties involved. Erik Vossen, a Dutch religious educationalist, has eminently proved before how this communicative view of religious socialization can take place within the family. First of all it presumes sufficient attention for the initiation aspect of the socialization: "The religious development of children is to a large degree a social learning process, in which learning goals and content are determined by the parents (either consciously or subconsciously) and in which they supply the actual 'learning material' by way of the examples set by their own practice. Those parents who truly want to guide their children towards a personal deliberation of their religious orientation and thereby offer their own believes and praxis as a starting point, will have to concretely initiate their children" (Vossen 1989, 128-129).

This is not indoctrination, according to Vossen, this an aspect of development: "(Since) we have no other choice than to follow a strategy of transmission and making-familiar for young children, if we want to hand them enough material in order to make their own critical choice later on. What matters is, how we handle this already laid foundation later in the religious education" (124 – translation BR). Of great importance is how religious practices (like evening prayer and regular talks about faith – practices with a highly socializing value) are framed in a general openness for the life of parents and children. What sticks in the experience of young people is the willingness of adults to justify what they do and do not do. The best way to learn is the confrontation with adults who are not yet 'finished' or have 'been there', but who want to learn and grow, and who want to involve their children in this learning process. This 'communicative initiation' within the family seems to be a major challenge for vigorous communities of faith. Here the religious socialization of children acquires new dynamics, namely from the religious communication with young adults. This way a new meaning can arise, as a self-discovered 'horizon' of meaningful and authentic life, that is worth passing on, communicatively to fellow travelers and intergenerationally to one's own children. This way a new language will originate, anchored in private life experience and mastered in personal involvement (Maas & Ziebertz 1997).

## 3.3. Religious communication in a language concerned with life

How can such a language come into existence and be confirmed? How can the social stratum in which the request for religious orientation is made, grow into a new language experience for communities of faith? The need is great and many immediate 'Ersatz' solutions can be thought of. For example the churches could present the Christian faith as a radical anti-story, represented as a leap into the dark, as an option – as 'go swim by yourself in the abysmal deep of the deposit of faith'. Churches could charm people to take the step towards full identification with Christian faith. One could speed up the process of joining by skipping the cultivation of the longing. One could aim for a uniformly accelerated motion in the direction of the creed. The tender societal stratum, like a vulnerable river bed, however, would not be able to handle this. The water is hardly deep enough to catch all those who might jump. And modern people will not be persuaded to let their life story be determined by the comments of others. They want to be the architect of their life story themselves. What they cannot appropriate will never become clear to them.

The Flemish dogmatic theologian Peter Schmidt has made an impressive analysis of the loss of meaning of religious language, when it is no longer sufficiently supported by contemporary human experience. The problem of the comprehensibility of faith in the church can be avoided perfectly well, according to Schmidt, "by curving back on oneself mentally". That is the way it often happens. Spiritual leaders are friendly, cooperative where others are concerned, but avoid expressing the "truth of faith" (Schmidt 1993, 87 – translation BR). "A lot of attention is paid to the interior decoration of the fortress of faith. The fact, however, that the drawbridges have been drawn, thus keeping anyone from entering, is a problem that one would rather not pay attention to" (90). And Schmidt continues by saying: "If the communicated content of faith is true in a totally different way than the way it is expressed, why should it be expressed that way? The language game used, cannot be converted into another anymore" (97). All that can still be done, is soulless repetition and imitation. In other words: a religious language game that ignores the religious longing in which it could be embedded, becomes esoteric and devoid of meaning. Those who lead in church no longer understand themselves what it is they believe and in which they feel obliged to guide others. That is the worst that can happen to a community of faith – that it has nothing left to say, not *ad extra*, not *ad intra*.

### 3.4. Towards new forms of religious leadership

"After the Second Vatican Council one has paid too little attention to education of the public", Mgr. Alfred Daelemans, former director-general of the Flemish Secretariat of Catholic Education once confided to me in the early nineties. I think that indeed a major part of the depression in the Roman-Catholic church in particular has to do with this. Laymen feel attracted to the *aggiornamento* of the council. Attention was paid to their active participation in church, liturgy, catechesis and ministry, but too little was invested in educating and encouraging them at the intersection of faith and culture. There were some good initiatives; but no lay theology. For concrete questions from everyday life (intimate relationships, raising children, work relations, tension family-work, etc.) a normative way of speaking of the church was available, but that was miles away from the actual experience and words of regular searching believers (Luther 1992). The Canadian Dominican Jean-Marie Tillard thinks that, with regard to searching contemporaries, the church has adapted or hidden itself too much – as it were "entre le magistère des mass media et le magistère de la chair ecclésiale." No real confrontation has taken place with the intelligence of the faith in daily life, the church has not been able to show younger generations what the authority of faith means to those who are in tune with their own experience, according to Tillard (1997, 14 passim).

In this context the importance of new forms of religious leadership should be mentioned. In a complex society like ours, in which many alternatives are present (par. 2), a need for authentic identification figures exists, people of flesh and blood who live the 'Verbindlichkeit' or engagement of a religiously inspired life project in the double sense of the German word: they feel obliged to live it and they feel connected with it. Erik Vossen has pointed out before that "current culture [makes] Christianity insufficiently explicit to enable young people to make sense of religious-Christian examples" (Vossen 1986, 250). Many examples and ideals are shown, but they are often so exalted and idealized (think of Mother Theresa, Oscar Romero, etc.), that a critical confrontation frequently leads to frustration. There is a need for a real life and 'semantically explicit' religious leadership that is 'food for thought', which can be disputed, questioned and tested. This can also be an inspiration to concrete spiritual leaders such as parents and educators; they can be pioneers and maybe heralds of a new and realistic justification of faith. All of this presupposes guidance, education and support of parents and educators, since in confrontation with their children their own questions, lamentations and inability surface. Religious socialization of children can, as stated before, no longer leave out a critical retrospective view of the story of faith of the adults themselves. Religious socialization and its justification (from a meta-perspective) in religious communication are interwoven, just the way moral socialization and its justification in moral communication are interwoven (see Chapters 1 and 2).

**4. The option of religious education with young adults**

A new generation of young adults is lining up, who have had no or hardly any religious socialization. Moreover this generation is an easy prey to the current pressure of modernization. The idea of the self-managing of life, work and love is imprinted in them in many different ways. They are the primary targets of advertising and marketing. In addition to that they are expected as young employees or managers, as young lovers, as young parents, as young homeowners, etc. to fulfill their social 'duties' and make responsible choices. To endure all this and keep it together they 'use' religion, glamorized and self-directed. Their search for meaning is interactive: pick up whatever fits your life project. For this they appeal to the 'expertise' of the church.

Their cultural context is a *kairos*: not to steer them into church in view of the future and the vitality of the community of faith, but to bring them in touch with the flow of grace that streams from the religious tradition of Christianity as a possible answer to their longing for a final orientation, or at least as a clarification of their questions concerning this. This answer is not a mere blind to take away the pain of daily contingency management, but a critical eye-opener to review their own life project and make it tolerable. Gérard Defois, bishop of Lille in France, calls this 'wide angle ministry'. Michael Ebertz speaks of 'communication ministry' (1998, 144-145). The large group of interested, who seem to be looking to approach the church, are not left out at the gate. They are invited to move into the space between the inside and the outside of the church, in the passage between culture and faith.

This openness is not a form of church expansionism, but a contemporary understanding of how Christians can be present in the world. Their presence in society is no longer monolithic, their message not to be taken or left. They can be inspiring on the road to the truth, a truth that in accordance with human life consists of many facets. The times of the massive 'opposite' of Christianity have passed; the temptation exists of withdrawing with like-minded in a 'snuggle strategy'. I wonder if that suffices – evangelically speaking. Can Christians take the liberty of losing their flexibility and of being put off to the side? For the time being quite a few people are still in and out of the church. Often they come into contact with it through traditional pastoral activities: a funeral, a marriage, a baptism, the first communion and confirmation of their children. All of these activities, however, are diminishing (especially marriage) or are experienced as being without a meaningful future (especially confirmation). The traditional forms of social presence of faith are dampened down further. How will the story of faith become visible in the future: authentically, sensibly and evangelically flexibly?

In line of the above I make a plea for religious education of young adults. Instead of continuing to invest the available energy in the catechesis of children (first communion and confirmation at an early age), the church could ask itself f how it can serve the longing for religious orientation of young adult contemporaries. Partly this is done already in connection with the sacraments of marriage and of the baptism/first communion of children. At parents' evenings one can notice that young parents like to pass on something of value in the moral and religious upbringing of their children, but that they usually lack the words. Their anthropological experience of birth and parenthood does not get enough response and religious interpretation from the highly sacramental message of church baptism. And when young children grow up and start asking questions about life, young parents are often at a loss for answers or an attitude of answering (Schweitzer 2000). In the meantime – i.e. now that it is still not clear what to do with the catechesis of sacraments – it seems very important to me to involve the parents as much as possible in the religious education that is part of the sacrament (of their children).

There are other ways, however, to address young adults from the side lines. I think of encounter groups (for instance in higher vocational education and universities), of intervision groups of young people in the same profession (for instance new nurses, teachers, etc.) and other intensive meetings (like summer camps) and forms of cultural service of churches to young adult meaning seekers (through websites, publications, information evenings), etc. This calls for a different kind of engagement of the church: it offers its own house and its own expertise as a forum, as a space in which the process of searching of young adults can grow and be enriched.

It is not about actualizing or adapting the Christian message, but about rereading of the particular context of young adults from the perspective of the gospel. Often the 'process of revelation' starts with opening the senses, with learning to read one's own life again, with reconnecting with one's own sources of imagination and creativity. Because it is shocking to see how much goodwill, how much desire to live a truly good life (in relationships, at work, during time off, etc.) is undone by the media, hard work and hyped up relationships at the age of young adults. Many of the small stories are trampled by the big story of the market. The gospel can refute this ruthlessness and show images of truly good life. Fact is that young people cannot be talked into anything. If they are unable to see for themselves how an old story is capable of uprooting the self-evidences and/or brokenness of their story, nothing happens. If the flow of grace does not come from the inside, can be rediscovered and worded from their own experience of longing for grace, nothing happens. The social river bed is present, it should be broadened and deepened by encounters with contemporaries and wise insights from the past. However, the question is: will there be enough people left in churches who are willing and able to inhabit this meeting place in an inspired and sensible way?

**Conclusion**

These reflections fit in the broader perspective of renewed attention for adult religious education. In the Dutch and Flemish dioceses many initiatives have arisen during the past five years, see respectively the documents 'De glans van Gods woord' (2004) en 'Volwassen worden in geloof' (2006). It is realized that no longer all salvation is to be expected of religious education of children. In addition to that, religious communication takes on a different hue in a society of choices, especially that of personal engagement. I conclude here that these initiatives take many forms corresponding to concrete local needs and requests. It was my intention mainly to make clear that the new generation young adults, just like the currents one, has the right to a personally appropriated experience of faith. However, the complexity of this experience in the given circumstances is much greater for future adults. That is the reason why this kind of work is even more exciting than it already is with 'normal' adults, but paradoxically also relaxing, since nothing has to be proven.

# Chapter 4

# The Vulnerability of the Post-Modern Educator Raising Children as *Locus Theologicus*

Some fifty years ago, the coming generations were almost automatically socialized in the Christian narrative. In such a mono-cultural setting there was no doubt about the sustainability of religious and moral convictions that were handed over to children. This 'filiative' concept of faith transformation is now fading out, slowly but surely. A new faith experience and related educational approach have emerged since Vatican II. The 'meta-noetical' model of faith formation germi-nated: the 'new believer' is expected to re-imagine critically (noetical) the Christian narrative on the basis of his personal biography (meta) (Englert 1992). A person should reflect on the tradition in his own way of analyzing, articulating and reconstructing his moral and religious environment. Nowadays, this process of 'bearing' witness to a personally appropriated faith is a central issue in faith formation. It all boils down to a new form of faith formation conceived as adult 'religious literacy', the discernment that empowers and enables adults to make religious sense out of their daily lives (Dumestre 1997; Regan 2002) and helps communities as a whole to determine what is vital to the future of faith within their own context (O'Brien 1997). In this chapter, I want to show how such a biographical and communal approach can be adopted in the accompaniment of young adults who are raising children. By helping them to tell the story of the boundaries and opportunities of their educational efforts, they can learn to re-imagine the basic insights of the Christian tradition, as a valuable source of information, discernment and spirituality for their daily dealing with children in education. What is needed for the future of faith formation within families and congregations is a renewed correlation between faith and life, precisely within the experience of the non-evidence of this link (Boschki 1998). This is only possible if the contemporary generation of young parents re-appropriate the religious story from within (thus meta-noetically), on the basis of their own struggle with the religions and world views in which they were raised themselves as children (thus filiatively).

## 1. Beyond blind faith in educational progress

Education is learning to live with separation and finitude; it is an exercise in modesty. No one can appropriate for oneself a child's life. The life of every child is unique and therefore holy. Especially at a time when the demise of the grand narratives has accelerated this experience of contingency, parents and educators have found it difficult to educate, to offer meaning in the tension between bringing up and letting go. The ongoing temptation to construct the perfect child in a ruthless world and the deeper yearning of every educator to provide the child with grace and holy ground to grow up and to flourish uniquely within, constitutes the ambiguous act of educating. Many young parents are yearning for a language game that goes beyond the language of education.

This can already be perceived when they ask for adequate pedagogical support. They want to make their child resistant to violence, calling for solid values and norms that should be offered by schools, churches and institutions. In the cases of problematic educational situations, parents examine extensively the approaches of educational therapists. 'Pedagogical voluntarism' is enjoying its heyday where much, if not everything, seemingly can be solved by education (read: well-adapted pedagogical and didactical methods). If you but believe in the education of your children, you will be fine. Theological voluntarism (read: don't trust your own experience, only put your trust in God) has given way for an exercise in pedagogical willpower. This leads to a paradox. Never before was the faith in education so great, never before were people so concerned about their children, never before was the family held in such high regard, but also never before was the confidence in its beneficial results so shaken. Can parents today live and educate with such a shattered faith in education? Are they sufficiently grounded in order to remain firm in times of doubt and hopeful in times of failure? Does pedagogical voluntarism offer this solid ground? Could it be that many parents and educators relegate their educational task to professional pedagogical assistants because they have lost the nerve to face this situation of fallibility, vulnerability and temporariness personally? Could it be that the obstinacy of everyday education is unbearable because traditional sources of meaning have disappeared and in the meantime people with pent-up frustrations have to work out a new spiritual base by themselves?

In this chapter, the pedagogical efforts of people are not denied or ignored but taken up in a theological reflection. How can a transcendent perspective on education free us from 'pedagogical stubbornness' and empower us for a more honest and sound experience of our dealings with growing children and fellow educators? I wish to point out a number of pedagogical-experiential hints and articulate them from a theological perspective. As argued in the introduction, the personal quest for religious meaning is strongly present in a modern context where old confessional solutions no longer satisfy in order to cope with complexities. People have to discover in their own right 'the relational ties between, in themselves, disparate goals in life' (Ziebertz 1995, 60). A solid faith tradition can offer a rich stock of images in order to articulate the trans-ethical moment of educational efforts. It aims to surprise, not to alienate. It forms a dramatic moment that challenges people to review the usual state of affairs in a different, in a new light. Opened up is the space for 'passage' and encounter (Grözinger 1998), undefined and yet full of potentialities, radically different from dogmatic and collective answers in former days. A renewed awareness of transcendence can but unfold on the basis of the religious traditions taken up in an autobiographical way. The uprooting of grand religious narratives can only be meaningful when concrete people give them shape in their own lives and speak about them to others meaningfully (Moore 1993). In the following section I will develop five structural experiences that concern many in education today. These experiences are also five educational goals or competences to be achieved by children. In the third section, I will recast these experiences in a theological way from a Christian faith perspective. Education then can become a solid 'locus theologicus'.

## 2. Education as an exercise in modesty

The five experiences described below can be recognized by every concerned educator. They are about five competencies that he can consider to be characteristic for a well-educated person and thus wants to impart to a child. What he expects from the child should be learned, formulated and demonstrated in all modesty by the educator himself during the educational process. He never fully knows *a priori* how to behave in a concrete situation. One learns to educate in the process, standing amidst the concrete questions and musings of children. And, one can only educate but once: childhood never returns, you can no longer make radical changes once the dye is cast. This temporariness of every pedagogical project makes the educator modest. In the third section, this experience will serve as material for a theological re-interpretation. These five competencies, belonging to the five basic pedagogical experiences, are: the rational, social, moral, existential and eschatological competence.

### *To reflect on life, not evade it*

Education is essentially linked to *rationality*. Parents, schools and pedagogical supervisors expect that children will learn to articulate and account for their personal lives reasonably, that at least they will avoid the misfortune of deceiving themselves or living an illusion, that they would be prepared for the dynamism of their own story. Education is directed towards justification: knowing what awaits you and shaping goals. Ancient philosophy expressed this direction as a person's connection to two different worlds, that of one's birth and that of humanity (Nussbaum 1993). One learns to be at home in the community of humanity by gradually cultivating it, by being interested in it and by discovering it because it is usually hidden beneath as well as by our prejudices highlighting the transparent immediacy of differences. An education worthy of its name leads people from one community to the other, from learning the good life at home to gradually discovering the relativity of this learning, aiming at an independent life project imbued with one's personal commitment. The English philosopher of education, Richard Stanley Peters (1980, 113) gives a good example of what this could imply: "An unreflective businessman, for instance, might visit an undeveloped country with a view to setting up a factory. But, on going into all the details of what this would involve, he might become more and more aware of the disruption of a way of life that is entailed. He might 'not want to know' or he might begin to question the whole enterprise. And if he began to question this particular feature of business life he might begin to query the way of life more generally."

When education's central goal is this competent life or the acquisition of rational competence, it is then obvious that educators can only reach this goal by living it out themselves, with all their trials and errors. Education is initiation, an introduction into a world of insights, attitudes and behaviors, replete with value and meaning. But this initiation is never static. Out of its very nature, it is always dynamic and personally involved. People educate each other through communication and the conscientious involvement with each other (see Chapter 1). Fundamentally, this involvement is ethical in nature: I hold myself responsible for the countenance of the other, more concretely for the child, the partner(s) in education, the society, etc. The 'rational' life to which children are educated and for which educators are responsible is therefore inextricably linked with the 'good' life. One only learns morality by being taken up in a meaningful (or rationally loaded) and therefore personally involved (or ethically loaded) network of insights, attitudes and behaviors. Young people have a right to this rational-ethical counteraction in order to move forward and lead a personally competent life.

## *To deal with one's fear for the otherness of the other*

A second competence that occupies an important place beside the rational one is *social* competence: people are deemed to learn to live together in diversity. To have respect for the otherness of fellow humans (in terms of customs, lifestyles, convictions, etc.) has its repercussions today in all sorts of initiatives in global, intercultural and inter-religious education. There is something strange, however, with this dimension of education. Young children have no problems with this at all. They talk to each other with the language of play and immediate involvement. How they relate to each other from different cultures and backgrounds with a disarming and groundbreaking ease criticizes the pedagogical serious-ness with which educators enforce so-called higher initiatives among older children and young people. It seems pertinent to me that adults should ask themselves whom they actually want to convince of the values of respect and tolerance: their children or themselves? Isn't their own fear for the stranger – a fear that can be rationalized away in education – often a factor? Don't educators or adults particularly aim at tempering the violence that can ensue from a confrontation with the stranger, a violence that lies both in the other and in themselves? Intercultural education remains very much a pragmatic matter. Many cultures live together within a small area, and are thus obliged to negotiate minimal procedures for a peaceful co-existence. This is a formal concept of tolerance that stands in sharp contrast with what intercultural education is actually all about, namely the highly esteemed 'mutual enrichment of cultures' or a perspective change that offers me the opportunity to discover myself anew (van der Ven 1998: 257-282; see also Chapter 7).

## *To appreciate one's own possibilities for growth*

For the educator, the raising up of children also means coming to terms with his own educational past. What I deem valuable for the future of my children as an adult is also colored by experiences from my own childhood. One's injuries also count: people sometimes take revenge for the humiliations they bore as children by repeating them on their children. Adults often swear that this will not happen to their children. Those who grew up with a strong authoritarian figure can be very authoritarian or, otherwise, be very permissive towards their children. Those who grew up with less opportunities either impede their children's unfolding or hope to find atonement *post factum* for their achievements ('Study well, then later you will be better off than us'). In both cases, however, people think and act in terms of an injury and they repeat the past. These injuries cannot entirely be effaced; they cannot and need not. It is a mark of self-knowledge, however, that people are aware of them and bear them in mind in the educational relationship.

A complete identification with the child (think of the father who strives for a passionately desired but never realized football career for his son) leads to the instrumentalization of the educational relationship and to the disappearance of the individuality of the child. The adult then is no longer free with respect to the child because he is no longer free in himself. He then wants to heal his injuries in and through the education. Children and childhood, however, should never be instrumentalized for the well-being of adults. The sexual abuse of children is the most extreme form of this disdain or instrumentalization of children's lives of hope. This is precisely what we mean by *moral* competence. Adults should give an account of the moral integrity and freedom of conscience of their children. Never to be used as means, children are ends in themselves. Children are subjects in themselves and deserve respect on the basis of their inalienable moral autonomy (Eid, Elsässer & Hunold 1995; Roebben 1995a).

## *To be challenged by 'the risk of living one's own life'*

Education also wants to contribute to the acquisition of *existential* competence: a child should take his life in his own hands, he has to learn to recognize his uniqueness and act on it in a fitting way. In this sense, education is encouraging children and young people to learn to see themselves within their own existence. Nevertheless this task is paradoxical: ultimately the educator can never take the place of the child, and yet in a surrogate way he must pluck up the courage to stir the child to freedom and responsibility. Education is an empathetic challenge to the child 'to take up the risk of his own life' (Bonnett 1986, 131-132), to leave the beaten track and trace one's own life-dynamism. Obviously, this must be engaged time and again in concrete situations (as in choosing a course of study, a partner, a leisure activity, etc.). It is therefore a lifelong task.

The educator who takes this task seriously is up for a challenge. It requires much critical-creative capacity for making distinctions to guarantee the well-being of the child both out of one's own certainties as an educator as well as out of the unpredictable yet necessary path the child must take. While the dynamism of initiating and sending off, of surrogate action and independence, is logical in an ideal model, it is often irrational in life itself. How will parents react, for instance, when their child reveals them that he is homosexual? Will they learn to accept this as a situation radically different from what they perhaps hoped for their child, or will they oppose this severely preventing the child from accepting himself?

Educators require their children to become signifiers, to 'become narrators of their own story' (Ricoeur 1986), to cope meaningfully and consciously with the reality that surrounds them and color their 'narrative identity'. In this claim, however, they are also confronted with their own existential quest, with their own trials and errors, their own moments of lucidity and involvement, of aridity and 'living in passivity'.

## *To bid a lifelong farewell*

The most paradoxical task linked to education is learning to bid farewell. An abiding summons to 'dégagement' is present precisely in the most direct 'engagement' people enter into with each other, namely giving birth to children and raising them. The French-Jewish philosopher Emmanuel Levinas calls this 'ethical motherhood': the human person gives birth to the life of the other by committing himself wholeheartedly to the service of the other and by exploiting all his capacities for this service (Roebben & Burggraeve 1992, 206-214). But when years go by and the child grows older, the educator becomes gradually an outsider in the identity development of the child. Then, separation is at stake: you entrust your child to others and to his ability to manage on his own. You hope that he will find his way, but at the same time you know it will not be easy, for the world can be a harsh place for children and vulnerable people. In this experience, you are confronted with the uniqueness of this life project that you wanted and to which you are committed, yet it can never be your private possession. 'Your children are not your own', says the prophet Kahlil Gibran. In the life-giving event of education, death and the awareness of separation is constantly present like a throbbing pain. Many forms of 'over-education' can be explained precisely out of a lacking *eschatological* perspective: people fear to let go of their children and dare not acknowledge them as self-reliant participants in the society of tomorrow.

An awareness of the transience of things of the world also lurks in the experience of separation. 'All things pass away, nothing ever returns'. This is unusually acute at the moment of a child's birth: you receive the child into your midst and call him by name. While this name is unique and significant (the child will bear it his whole life) the moment of name-giving is largely contingent. If given another name, the child could have been 'someone else'. Learning to speak, write, sing, ride a bicycle, etc. are colored by the same experience of contingency. At the moment an educator demonstrates a process and the child spontaneously and responsively learns and reacts, he already gains insight (partially or fully), stored up forever in his mind and no longer appropriated for a 'new' first moment of giving meaning. It all boils down to paying close attention, to watching and enjoying the growth of children. It presupposes a factual presence, to be around during important moments, to be approachable and touchable. Some fathers never forgive themselves for having missed their little boy's first goal in an official football match.

## 3. Education as a trace of transcendence

In this third section, I attempt to re-interprete the experiences of a post-modern educator described above from a theological perspective. This is a thought experiment that presupposes a religious openness, a readiness to recast the perspective of finality named above in concepts that transcend the person and society and point to the Holy. For believers this is a good thought experiment: they are required to concretize their faith option over and against the horizon of inquiry of post-modern education. For non-believers, this can also be a fruitful path: they can give different and new meanings to their educational experiences with images derived from traditional meaning-givers such as religions.

I undertake this reflection from a Christian background. I cannot think about education apart from tradition. But I can attempt to clarify, account for and critically evaluate, insofar as possible, the internal argumentative force and persuasiveness of my tradition. The considerations below have a tentative character: they are intended to be exploratory, to find traces in the landscape of meaning today. This quest was not easy for the path is bumpy and not well arranged. The scholarly, practical-theological explorations are not always helpful for they remain empirical and descriptive on the one hand, or merely normative and doctrinal on the other hand. A sound existential and hermeneutical-theological re-imagination of educational experiences is the sort of groundwork that needs to be done in concrete processes of adult faith formation (Roebben 2009), as I argued in the introduction of this chapter.

## *To respond with circumspection to 'a voice from elsewhere'*

A human being is called to give a rational account, to learn gradually to understand oneself as unity of speech and action, as a person who can face reality in an independent and sensible way. This responsibility comes from elsewhere. Humans experience unique answers they give to their lives as a counter-reply to a question from outside. The competent life does not appear out of the blue. It is a wrestling with the strangeness of reality, encountered in the path of one's life. In the Christian tradition, this strangeness is linked to God. He reveals himself, lets himself be known in the obstinacy of personal and social life as someone challenging the person to change the history of contingencies into a history of salvation (Schillebeeckx 1977). This thought is central in the covenant with the people of Israel: God has liberated his people from the slavery of Egypt (indicative) so that in and through this experience they can be radically committed to bring about justice (imperative).

What is exciting about education is that adults must demonstrate, on the one hand, how personal accounting as a principle works and, on the other, must step back to give the child practically the floor and grant him the opportunity to formulate an answer with regard to the strangeness of reality. This tension can be experienced in concrete educational moments as grace. An educator does not have to be the origin and horizon of responsibility for a child, but has instead to encourage him to learn to understand himself as 'called', as someone who gives an answer to a voice from elsewhere. The paradox lies in the temporariness of the adult voice so that the child will be encouraged to understand his own voice.

This tension is strongly present especially in religious education where the 'voice from elsewhere' is articulated in a characteristic way, namely as coming from God or a transcendent being. Here, the educator initially avails of the dangerous possibility of steering and influencing the child towards 'a voice', of presenting the divine being as a radical opponent of human longing for self-understanding and self-reliance, and so make oneself indispensable as an educator. On the other hand, the experience that the child himself – initiated into the actual religious tradition to which the educator belongs – can learn an attentive attitude in order to understand the voice about his own life, reveals a strong potential for liberation. The avenue for a personal commitment in faith, is paved.

## *To dare deep encounters*

While real social competence goes further than neat agreements about formal tolerance ('we shall do no harm to each other') and procedural communication ('we shall come to an agreement about how we speak to each other'), it ties in with the surprising character of the encounter with the other. The fact that reality's claim can resound only by means of dialogue makes people modest. No one holds a lease on the truth; together we grow and become one. Together we are engaged in a quest for truth (Alexander 1995).

This perspective is particularly enriching but likewise quite vulnerable in a religious context. Believers in every religion lay claim to a definitive articulation on the presence of salvation in the world (e.g. 'Jesus is the only savior', or 'No salvation outside the church'), but the full weight of that articulation is learned in dialogue and consultation with others. Despite the fact that religions should be understood from an original and constitutive experience of transcendence and otherness, they often lack the courage to learn from each other. They do not dare encounter the other out of fear of blemishing their most trusted and 'holy' presuppositions (Duffy 1995-96; Geffré 2000). Many religious forms are therefore absolutely powerless and, as social systems, empty and useless, thus Cardinal J.H. Newman. They have nothing to contribute in the social debate for a culture of encounter:

"Perhaps the reason why the standard of holiness among us is so low, why our attainments are so poor, our view of the truth so dim, our belief so unreal, our general notions so artificial and external, is this, that we dare not trust each other with the secret of our hearts. We have each the same secret, and we keep it to ourselves, and we fear that as a cause of estrangement, which really would be a bond of union. We do not probe the wounds of our nature thoroughly; we do not lay the foundation of our religious profession in the ground of our inner man [sic]; we make clean the outside of things; we are amiable and friendly to each other in word and deeds, but our love is not enlarged, our bowels of affection are straitened, and we fear to let the intercourse begin at the root; and, in consequence, our religion, viewed as a social system, is hollow" (From the *Sermon on Christian Sympathy*, quoted by Moore 1993, 90).

## *To believe in the sustaining ground of existence*

Children belong to themselves. They do not exist so that their parents can show them off or use them to erase their wounded past. Children possess a potential moral autonomy, their own radius of action that indeed initially requires material and mental support during education. Meaning, one must demonstrate to a child what meaningful autonomy can be, is always radically linked to the humanity of human beings and thus to this unique child. No one can arrogate another for oneself. It is easy to say that adults should be aware of their own injuries in the education of their children. While being confronted with the truth about themselves can be playful and liberating in education, it can also be extremely sobering when violence and destructive forces surface. Here again, the religious experience can bring clarification – the experience wherein is mediated that people ultimately do not have to bear everything themselves. In the end, they come to realize they themselves are borne, in their attempts to educate, inclusive of the injuries that are thereby laid bare. Even here it all depends on how you are able to reconcile your own responsibility (and its accompanying injuries) with the fundamental experience of 'I am not surrendered to myself'.

The psalmist in Scripture also describes this experience of incomprehension, hurt and the incapacity to accept otherness in one's own life. Amidst the defiance and discontent he formulates a prayer of surrender to God. It is so authentic because it is anchored in the reality of the injured human being and offers the prospect of healing at the same time. This prayer of trust is a passage from Psalm 73. The ultimate ground of meaning for reality is here expressed in images that point to the biblical God, experienced in history as the Liberator. Initially, it is an encounter for an entire people (the deliverance from Egypt), and later radically and universally for each individual who addresses him:

'When my soul was embittered, when I was pricked in heart, I was stupid and ignorant; I was like a brute beast toward you. Nevertheless I am continually toward you; you hold my right hand. You guide me with your counsel, and afterward you will receive me with honor. Whom have I in heaven but you? And there is nothing on earth that I desire other than you. My flesh and my heart may fail, but God is the strength of my heart and my portion forever' (Psalm 73, 21-26).

### *To turn from post-modern greed*

Children should become the signifiers of their own existence. Again, this is easier said than done. Adults indeed experience an irresistible drive to control everything, to leave nothing to chance – at least this is how it is constantly suggested to them by employers, the media, public opinion, their acquaintances, etc. When the life project of children turns out to be radically different from what parents had intended, it often leads to tension and frustration. To trust that a child will turn out right – whatever the so-called wrong paths and sidetracks may be – is a learning process that requires much time and reflection.

My contention is that our century is characterized by 'post-modern greed', a concept that seems to have cross-cultural grounds – at least in the rich part of the world. People are literally full of themselves, there is no room left anymore for the other, for the stranger in oneself. People do get obsessed with the stranger outside of themselves, but always from a recuperating disposition: 'How can I draw this new thing into my *own* life project?' This is likewise so in dealings with children. Children often act as signboards for parental post-modern well-being. Parents go through much trouble to show how good they have this complicated stage of life under control, how they are able to manage perfectly the 'children-market' and how they can give 'everything and everything immediately' to their children (Mercer 2005).

So that children would feel more at home with adults, we should not let them simply be 'open minded', but we should give them the chance to warm-up by the hearth of our commitment. This raises the question on the 'inhabitability' of our homes, the quality of relationships between people therein, the cordiality in our dealings with each other, and the honesty that surrounds our traditions and customs. To live and deal with others in graciousness imparts a different face to an often merciless and grace-less world.

## *To learn the art of dying*

As already mentioned, education is one of the most paradoxical undertakings of humankind. The human being engages fully for the well-being of the child. At the same time this turns out to be the most disengaged event thinkable: separation is ingrained in the work of education. This human experience is both vulnerable and lofty. To promise the child that he will be 'a sign of hope for the future' is to efface the self in engagement towards the child in order to realize this. It is to admit being but a modest part of a much greater whole, that one can but provide a one-time contribution to the greatest life project of this concrete future adult.

Death is the final and most radical experience that thwarts my project as a self-conscious and self-actualizing educator. Willingly or otherwise, this radical break makes me overcome my anxiety, however good and noble, in order to care for my child and hope for his the best. The ultimate consequence of the education-separation paradox is perhaps that one cannot and should not take a child along to one's own grave. This is the ultimate letting-go, to relinquish the right and the duty to mean something for the other, let go of the child.

Since time immemorial, religions and philosophies of life have formulated answers to the human question on an ultimate healing of brokenness, separation and death. As I indicated in the beginning of this chapter, these answers function today in new contexts. In the dismal story of the wrecked lives of young children, victims of ruthless violence and greed, glimmers of hope shine through as a 'happy ending'. A God who does not take away human responsibility but takes human freedom seriously can still move people today towards a life of trust, even in the face of death – precisely because death does not have the final word.

**Conclusion**

This chapter has become a pure investigative endeavor, an attempt to do theology 'from within and towards life'. If, after a critical evaluation, this attempt turns out to be meaningful, it requires a theological recasting in the framework of an adult faith formation. In my assessment, the challenge lies in addressing people in what inspires and engages them. Adult faith formation will have to understand itself as an aid in narrating the narrative, the fragile searching and groping for a meaningful life, a narrative that will perhaps often refer to a sensible transcendent perspective, but will also often be dominated by people's fear of becoming meaningless. Telling the story (over and over) again is then the only thing that is left, because human beings live to tell and they tell to live.

# Part 2

# Education, Religion and School

# Chapter 5

# Narthical Religious Learning
# Redefining Religious Education
# in Terms of Pilgrimage

## 1. Religious perplexity in the classroom

The modern multi-cultural and multi-religious environment has a pervasive influence upon the moral and spiritual mindset of young people today. Pursuing an emancipatory concept of education my position is that young people have the right to gain insight into the diversity and complexity of the religious phenomenon: what religion does with people and what people do with religion. The school is the place par excellence to learn, to observe and to interpret this impact of religion on moral and spiritual convictions, decisions and practices in contemporary society and culture. 'Religious literacy' in combination with the formation of a 'religious self', a sort of pivotal point of reflection, evaluation and communication within the learner, seems to be the generally accepted goal of religious education in recent theory development. One could argue that this hermeneutic-communicative concept, based on observation/interpretation and communication *about and from* religion, is also the leading concept on which teacher education programs in Western Europe are built (to mention only a few: Hermans 2003, Jackson 1997, Lombaerts & Pollefeyt 2004, Mette 2000, Roebben 2001c, Schweitzer 2006, Ziebertz 2003).

However, there are indications that this approach is reaching an impasse. In observing and discussing religion in the classroom it could be the case that the underlying religious experience is not accessible to learners, because of their deep-rooted ignorance of the topic. This is not only so in secondary education, but even in teacher training programs in higher education. In modern secularized societies not only the grammar but also the 'lived' or experiential language of religion is increasingly lacking. De-traditionalization, combined with individualization and pluralization of religion, often causes perplexity in the classroom. 'What in heaven's name are they talking about?' is then a frequent question. 'What do you personally think?' is then a sort of final appeal to the teacher's wisdom when the atmosphere becomes too emotional. The teacher often turns out to be as dumbstruck as the pupils.

Three different observations are underpinning this view. They emerge from recent developments in religious educational theory, accelerated and challenged by the very spiritual experiences of children and young people today. First of all it seems more and more the case that a detached religious studies approach in the classroom cannot but lead to issues of personal meaning giving (Bowman 2006, Simmons 2006). The passion of religious people can after all be spread to the novice and can encourage expectations such as: 'Can I also get a taste of that experience?' A second development is appearing in the field of inter-religious dialogue and inter-religious learning: in order to become fully involved in this dialogue the learner needs to be able to speak from some personal stance, however minimal. Without an initial 'thick' description of one's own position or without an insight in the lived theology of the particular tradition to which one belongs (Hussain 2004), the learner is not motivated enough to engage in a tolerant exchange of ideas and practices (Schweitzer 2007). What is needed is 'a re-defining and a re-dignifying' of one's own spiritual home (Halsall & Roebben 2006, 448), a 're-cognition' of one's own religious experience in a provisional framework, not as a undeniable certainty but as something to put to the test during the encounter. And thirdly, the whole field of 'children's spirituality' (in German: *Kindertheologie*) is raising new thoughts about the radical (some even argue the 'infinite') openness of children to the world of the sacred

(Bucher 2002, see also Chapter 6). Their un-inhibitedness towards other spiritual beings, their 'relational consciousness' of the world and their spontaneous childish attitude of living a life of dedication and expectation, provide a critique of the 'culturally constructed forgetfulness' of spirituality in modern forms of education, even of religious education, which cannot be ignored (Hay and Nye 1998).

These three observations, critically reframed by the latest developments in theory, make us aware of the challenge to religious education. My point of departure is not the deficiency of the modern hermeneutic-communicative concept of religious education, but its potentiality. Or, the perplexity can be a surprising starting point for the communication on religious experience on a deeper level. Young people are open to this quest, because they do not carry any burden of proof for the old system. They want to get involved and are waiting for someone who leads them into unexplored land. In the following paragraphs I invite the professional reader to rediscover the dynamic of the hermeneutic-communicative model of religious education and to go beyond it, in order to uncover the original religious experience that lies underneath it. I invite the reader to participate critically in the way of the pilgrim and to explore the metaphorical language of this essay. What counts for children in the classroom, could also count for the professional and the teacher: "Through the challenge of 'unpacking' another worldview one can, in a sense, become a new person" (Jackson 1997, 130-131).

## 2. The pilgrim's way of learning

You can travel like a tourist: consuming, greedy and always demanding. You can also travel like a pilgrim: contemplative, open to surprises and taking time to digest the experience quietly. In post-modern culture, traveling is often thought of and perceived as a tourist event: you 'book' a trip (and not a journey), 'do' some sight-seeing, 'arrange' an insurance etc. Maybe it cannot be otherwise, considering the hastiness of our time (Bauman 1996). Traveling is affected by our consumer culture: traveling people often fall victim to a competitive spirit and supermarket behavior. To illustrate this with an example: recently I learned that sherpa's collected four tons of tourist garbage on Mount Everest.

The true challenge of traveling, however, is to be open and receptive to what you encounter on the way and what rearranges your course of life. True travelers notice differences, and become conscious of significant things that were missing in their frame of reference and of which they were previously not aware. Journeying people are open to others and to circumstances that are different. Traveling like a pilgrim supposes the willingness and the skills to change one's perspective on the road. True travelers are at home on the road. Like pilgrims they feel like a fish in the water when they have to experience the elements of nature and culture and rearrange them in view of their own path of life. The challenges of their journey, being so close to the elements, help them to be continuously aware of this transformation process. Anyone who has never had blisters on their feet from walking, or strained calves from cycling, who, in other words, has not experienced the elements, has never really traveled at all. Experience (comes from the Latin *experire* which means: to go outside) is breaking out of yourself and being moved by other things that inspire you, mentally as well as physically, and to stand still and listen to them.

Is this traveling also possible in a purely mental form? Is it conceivable to travel between four walls, such as in a classroom? Can an intentional learning process evoke the same experiences as those of a pilgrim? These are difficult questions. Some will say that the learning experience of the pilgrimage cannot be attained at school. Children would no longer be sensitive to casual observations, they would rather be inclined to react to immediate and radical sensations they experience. Schools should therefore be suppliers of 'travel kicks', which use every means to let children experience new matters. In this way children learn about the latest material equipment, have exciting adventures and visit exotic destinations, but they do not learn what it means to enrich themselves and to be absorbed on the road. Learning in this way is artificial; it is too smooth and too soft, it lacks the challenging predicament of a continual search and discovery, such as is shown by a pilgrim.

Young people long for life perspectives that are consistent and meaningful and which truly deal with something. They want to travel, but they also want to reach a home. Restlessness is of all ages: each generation wants to rearrange reality in accord with its own visions. The question of young persons today however is whether or not they should take the effort to bother at all. The essentialism of meta-narratives is over. It is not present any more in the mindset of young people. They have not experienced these narratives and they are unaware of the accompanying emancipating process. Their key question today is: how to cope with plurality and profusion without becoming violent or depressed? Is there a horizon of meaningfulness that fills our search with sense and sensitivity? Are there images of successful lives that can inspire us? Or do we have to find out every-thing ourselves? Traveling and being on the road seem to be the current keywords for a vital and resilient attitude towards life, but do young persons truly possess sufficient guarantees to be 'at home on the road'?

## 3. Post-modern religious education and the *discovery* of meaning

Religious education encompasses *meaning giving*. This is a modern and active term: it supposes a high degree of thoughtfulness and stems from the idea of creating your own life journey and destination. It sometimes happens that from this perspective religious education unintentionally receives the status of a tourist event: teachers go on a journey with their students and show them the different ways in which people give meaning to their lives. At home again, they invite the students to make a choice. The danger of this approach lurks around the corner: young people do not feel involved and will in the long run show a tendency to escape – looking for distraction and non-commitment.

*Receiving meaning* is a good term to describe the pre-modern process: the meaning of life was imposed upon people; it was described and defined by church and state. In the past, 'traveling' was not an option during religious education. There you learned that the world outside was in agreement with the world inside. You learned that a world of difference did not exist, unless someone deviated from the right doctrine – an expression of behavior that was not permitted in those times and that could result in radical exclusion.

What can be considered as the post-modern alternative, in correspondence with the longing of young people today? I propose the term *discovery of meaning*. During religious education classes, young people learn the skill of re-reading reality from a philosophical and religious point of view. That perspective is handed over to them through the life stories of others who themselves dealt creatively with reality. They discover the concept of their lives by making a detour through these stories. Nobody has been given the ability to directly observe the meaning of life (the pre-modern perspective). A merely descriptive analysis of possible perspectives of meaning (the modern perspective) is considered to be insufficient. A literary 'detour' (a term of Paul Ricoeur, quoted by Streib 1998) could be an alternative and is like a thought experiment: it challenges young people to reconsider their own stories from a different angle, from the possibility of 'it could as well be otherwise'. That confrontation is always surprising ('I have never seen it that way before'), but never alienating.

This type of 'discovering' learning does not provide ultimate answers but opens the hermeneutic space in which seeking can be transformed into a meaningful and fulfilling practice. By means of stories of good and deepened life young people learn to discover that these stories could make a difference in their lives as well. The fundamental question is not whether schools should translate and customize religious traditions into a perfectly fitting lifestyle for the young or that they should leave their traditions as they are. The question is whether schools are able to apply the communication of religious tradition in such a way that it inspires and *moves* young people to deepen their lives and to discover the very meaning of them.

## 4. A hermeneutic-communicative approach to religious education

'Most trains ride along the back of life', thus sings the Dutch theatre performer Herman van Veen. This is a striking image of religious education. Students are taken along on a journey, gathered in a train (communicative) where they can learn from each other and from the stories from outside, how to understand and to cope with reality in view of the reconstruction of a sense of meaning for their own lives (hermeneutic). This approach assumes that it is possible to invite young people in a communal quest in which a profusion of alternative life views and clear-cut communication contribute to an elucidation (if not enlightenment) of one's own position and opinion. In this respect religious education wants to give young people the opportunity to formulate and justify their religious origins and future. The objective is not to initiate them into one particular world view, but to make them aware of the diversity that surrounds them and to hand them skills to deal with this abundance. The point of departure is that there is a correlative effect on a pedagogical level between the themes of life that tend to puzzle young people and the (many and possible) answers that have been generated through religious traditions in time, and which today are presented by the teacher, the fellow learners, the curriculum, the handbook etc. Meaningful words and gestures that could contribute to their own meaning giving process are *revealed* to young people. Or put differently, young people *discover* new meaning in old stories and traditions and learn precisely through this religious appropriation how to define themselves.

Stories form the access road to this learning experience: small stories which show the back of life and which have not yet been flattened out by the big overruling scripts of market and media. Children and young people will not be left to their fate. They will be taken on a detour and safely brought to meaningful contexts and perspectives, where meaningful words are spoken and meaningful actions are undertaken. The teacher is willing to uphold their learning environment with new impulses, unsuspected views and sometimes even raw and uncensored reality. Thus, there will be discussions about what is and what could be. This concrete utopia is what stimulates and compels religious educators to be at home on the road. In this 'pilgrimage' they are leading their students.

## 5. A mystagogical-communicative approach to religious education

This correlation between what actually is and what proactively could be is of a *pedagogical* nature. Young people are enabled to make the mental detour, to broaden their perspective and to ask critical questions of the material at stake. They develop their interpretive competence in the dynamic tension between available knowledge and newly presented interpretation schemes (Roebben 2001c, 263-265; Schweitzer 1999, 205-207). This correlation however initially is not of a *theological* nature, which refers to the interaction between experience and revelation. The model of the correlation didactics, grounded in a correlation theology, was successful in Roman Catholic religious education in Belgium, Germany and the Netherlands until the late eighties. On the basis of a relatively solid religious socialization at home, the teacher used to disclose theological contents by referring to the related religious practice in everyday life. Moreover, there was the conviction that divine intervention was effected in this process as a solid answer to the needs of the searching religious individual. This particular religious background can no longer be assumed. Children enter the classroom without language, tradition and community (hence without the possibility of theological correlation) but their questions of life remain, often unspoken and sky high.

I am strongly convinced that something 'strange' happens to these children when they are brought into the hermeneutic-communicative process of religious self-enlightenment and are invited to 'co-express' themselves with the meaning-exploring stories of the other side. The *pedagogical* correlation (which they request for: 'listen carefully to our needs so that you can guide us on our journey and can support us with your insights') can erupt into a new *theological* correlation ('where do I find new life for my soul?') Those who introduce young people to an environment impregnated with strong and meaningful didactical impulses, those who escort them into the powerful space between human ambivalence and the longing for wholeness that evolves out of this ambivalence, cannot but admit that questions will emerge like water from a fountain. Those who for example come up during the class conversation on 'loyalty towards your parents' with the story of Isaac's relation with Abraham are assured of a weighty discussion. And this will be likewise in the case of Job's story considering 'suffering' and Moses' story regarding the question of 'vocation'.

These questions are near and related to the turbidity within learners themselves who abide between longing and perspective. These questions are powerful because they refer to the ultimate questions to which religious traditions and people time after time have formulated meaningful answers by ways of contents (dogmatics) and lifestyle (ethics). Those teachers who during these important learning moments restrict themselves to offering information and encouraging communication cause, in my opinion, serious damage to the religious learning process of modern young people. Indeed, they offer an overview of the digestive system, but they tend to forget (or are afraid to admit or cannot bear the thought) that young people crave for *soul food*. In this process of dealing with perplexity one does not have to be afraid to catechize or to encourage the young to formulate a confession of faith. Catechesis after all presupposes pre-catechesis which in its turn presumes religious socialization. And this is no longer available. Young people often appear empty handed in the classroom. Are schools courageous enough to critique their overemphasis on didactical organization 'in religiosis'? Are they brave enough to participate in the religious 'emptyhandedness' of young people, trusting therein that new spiritual experiences originate when young people experientially learn to re-define and re-dignify themselves through religious traditions?

I plead for a willingness to leave behind a religious education in which young people are just ferreting tourists who – however well intended it may be – learn to functionally deliberate every possibility in consideration of their identity formation. Religious traditions do not solely function as 'identity providers' (Joas 2004, 12-31). Rather, they are sources of wisdom that quench the thirst of the soul. Of course this supposes a critical reading of those sources and a condemnation of a fundamentalist use of sources, an application that defiles the soul and fills it with hatred. A virtuous religious education justifies the genuine language game of religion. And this language game is referring to what is unsystematic, ironic, subversive, in-definite – and in that sense open for the indefinite, the undefined, the a-functional (see Chapter 8). I plead for a religious education that is explorative and informative, which learns to discern congealed traditions in 'key stories' (*pedagogical*: hermeneutic-communicative) and which also and foremost learns to 'de-congeal' or 'to liquefy' these traditions (Roebben 2007, 121-140 and 169-173), so that the original 'key experience' and underlying 'key question' (Schweitzer 1999, 205-207) can come to the surface, key elements that enrapture the soul (*theological*: mystagogical-communicative).

This mystagogical approach (in combination with the label 'communicative' because of the need for exchange between pupils, teachers and classroom materials) is grounded in the positive anthropology that the human being is radically open for the mystery (from the Greek: *musterion*) of existence. The soul after all is susceptible to the mystery of reality as it unfolds itself in the life of the human person. In the learning process the soul can be encouraged to reveal itself to the learning person. In this perspective the teacher is acting (from the Greek: *agogein*) as a midwife who time and again helps the learner to give birth to new insights (pedagogical), to new life (theological). After the deductive model of 'kerugma', after the silent death of the inductive model of theological correlation in the late eighties (Englert 1993) and new pedagogical forms of correlation theories in the late nineties within the context of religious modernization (such as the abductive correlation theory, see Prokopf & Ziebertz 2000), there is a new interest in religious experience in the realm of religious education praxis and theory (Grümme 2007a, Klie 2003, Schambeck 2006, van den Berk 1999). This approach makes us aware of the paradox of education in general and of religious education in particular.

## 6. Narthical religious learning

The pedagogical space between longing and perspective, the passage between the searching of the learner and the proposal of the teacher to undertake a mental 'detour', can bring about a dynamic which exceeds the learning process. To describe this unforeseen 'teachable moment' within the intentionally organized learning zone, I use the metaphor of the narthex. Its original meaning refers to the entrance hall of the church, the buffer zone between the outside world and the inner sacred space. The narthex, in its metaphoric sense, is both a pedagogical and a theological place of confrontation. In the learning process a space can be offered for what cannot be learned but only can be 'received'. In the narthex we can come to understand that we cannot ground our own existence, that we are not the source of our thoughts, that in our search we have already been found and that we never revert to definitive senselessness when we might get lost or lose sight of the track. The German theologian and educationalist Helmut Peukert calls this 'transformative learning' (in contrast to most of the learning forms which he calls 'cumulative learning') and considers this the educational method of the future: losing oneself in the encounter with the Other (or the other), to experience oneself in a completely different way as 'being found' (Peukert 2002). According to the author churches and moral communities especially have to fulfill a unique role in this 'new learning', since they represent traditions of openness that teach people to deal faithfully with situations of radical transformation (like healing after breakage, forgiveness after sin, life after death etc.).

Religious education then can become a pilgrimage. The learning span could then be compared to the situation of pilgrims who find themselves craving for water and coolness on their journey and who are confronted with something completely different from what they had expected and hoped for in the narthex of the church building. An almost perfect example of this learning span is the narthex of the Madeleine church in Vézelay in France. On their journey through the hills of Burgundy, along one of the four central axes of the French route to Santiago de Compostella, pilgrims turn into two-legged shambling creatures craving refreshment. Is there anybody who can quench their thirst and offer them a cooling breeze? Something extraordinary happens when entering the narthex: their entreaty for refreshment is answered with beautiful sculptures of the Christian salvation history. The triumphing Christ wants to offer them 'inspired water', something completely different for what they expected and hoped for. But at the same time a sigh of recognition resounds in their souls. They let go of their overarching search for salvation and let themselves be found (in this case by Christ). The quest receives new meaning, the longing is rearranged, questions that have been asked along the way are not solved but rephrased. Life receives new meaning: a new sense (pedagogically) and a new direction (theologically).

## 7. Implications for religious education

The metaphor of the narthex is vulnerable. It could be misinterpreted and to some extent it invites misinterpretation. The narthex as universal symbol is (literally) connected to a singular church building which represents a particular faith tradition. The danger therefore exists that the narthex will be considered an anthropological steppingstone for the 'real deal' in the sacred space of one particular faith tradition. The metaphor however by no means intends to uphold the narrowness of such a stringent view. I use the image to explain that the existential question will only be recognized in the feeding of the tension of longing and perspective. Religious experience will only appeal to the imagination (as a possible answer to that existential question) when this tension is conceptualized, in other words when the human longing comes across words and images that intrinsically elucidate and renew. This encounter between longing and perspective is, as has been said, doubly layered: the pedagogical handing over of new insights for the developing narrative identity of the pupil ('Who can I become?') can give rise to another more radical longing to tackle the mystery of who one really is ('Where do I belong?'). What are the implications of this metaphor?

1. As a religious educator one does not need to be worried about a 'hidden curriculum' of catechesis or confession of faith. Catechesis after all supposes pre-catechesis, based on the explicit request to become a member or participant of a faith community. Within the narthical learning model I assume that many no longer adhere to that idea – they may have been baptized but in practice that means very little. I assume that a lot of children and young people today have not experienced a religious socialization at home and that a pre-catechetic 'longing' therefore is out of the question. The longing that I am talking about in this narthical learning paradigm is of a totally different nature. It resonates in the question that children ask their teacher: 'Do you truly believe yourself what you are telling us? What does having

faith mean to you? How does it *work* for you?' The longing is therefore open and unbiased, a typical situation that in a post-secular living environment is increasingly gaining ground. The question therefore is whether or not contemporary religious education has the courage to cultivate this space and to show how concrete religious people and groups engage in the clarification of that space of existential longing. The narthex for that reason must not be misunderstood, in the literal sense of the word, as a pre-catechetic portal of which the outside door is closed like a barrier once people have set foot in the 'keel' of the church, in the intimate (read: liturgical-sacramental-catechetical) part of the church.

2. This model bridges the 'classic' division of sacred church versus secular world as prescribed in 'modern' secularization theories. The profane after all can manifest itself in the inner space of the church, the sacred can be disclosed outside of the church. In the thoroughfare of the narthex both worlds meet thereby mutually affecting each other. That this approach requires new demands of Christian theology scarcely needs saying. An exciting task for future theological reflection is to ask whether and how the sacramental experience of wholeness, characteristic of a good liturgy, rises in the 'ordinariness' of human existence.

3. Within the narthex it is necessary to awaken and nurture the already present 'transcendental openness' of the tension between immanence and transcendence, so that learners think of themselves as open questions and hope to find fertile and steady ground to answer this existential question. This implies that narthical teachers must carefully listen to what the longings of (young) contemporaries are and that they must be able to voice the often unarticulated issues in their lives. Moreover, they need to encourage them in their effort to articulate their own experiences. For that reason they must constantly enter the market place of life to observe conscientiously the longing of contemporaries for life fulfillment and to (help them) conceptualize this.

4. Another aspect in the bipolarity of narthical leadership is, besides the observation of longing, the cultivation of perspective – or in other words, the maintenance of the 'religious backpack'. What should it contain? What kind of provision do teachers take with them for along the way? The answer to this question requires a lot of hermeneutic sensibility. Which biblical key stories are able to illuminate and illustrate the existential questions of today's contemporaries? What is of eminent importance? Which 'hierarchy of truths' prevails? Which central ideas of salvation deserve to be conceptualized today? And what can we leave behind as lumber? I strongly believe that this line of thought implies a renewed engagement of academic theology with the religious-educational discourses of today. There is a desperate need for biblical, ritual-liturgical, political-ethical and cultural-religious focal points to help understand and stimulate the quest of our young contemporary fellow sense-seekers.

5. The narthical space is also a place of encounter where one has the freedom to theologize. Many kinds of questions and experiences after all can come up within the continuum of immanence-transcendence. Some will talk about the radical 'alteriority' in their lives, while others will tell about a life in human solidarity. New traditional patterns, interpretations and even contents will originate in this creative encounter. It is obvious that (religious) traditions within the narthical space will be reanimated and reactivated, if young people are given the chance to acquire them, however irreverent this may seem to the 'traditionalist' who hides in every teacher!

6. 'Learning by doing' is an important principle within the narthex. I believe that a merely educational and didactical approach to religious education has put the cognitive competencies to the forefront. Modern religious education needs to stimulate 'thoughtfulness' and aims to teach children how to phrase effectively and view their own religious identity. But religious literacy in my opinion surpasses the reason of this rational approach. It is also a matter of taste and inner (and inter-

nal) familiarity. In the fear of indoctrinating young people, we no longer dare to initiate them into the religious experiences of actually lived faith through symbolism, rituals, church social welfare work and tangible encounters with believers and faith communities.

7. The narthical perspective ultimately confronts us with the inevitable question of energetic communities. Do they still exist? And if they do, are they correlative and narthical enough? Isn't it true that we often have to conclude that religious communities fail to address the need of today's sense-seekers, the 'believing without belonging', because they themselves are so soulless and their members so 'belonging without believing'? Is there anybody home in the inn? Is there life in the inn? Is anything 'cooking' in there? Or has the last person already turned off the light and closed the door behind them?

**Conclusion**

In the context of the increasing mobility of young people and the growing number of *diaspora* communities, of syncretism and religious tourism (Cohen 2006, 148-150) the narthical approach is more than worth examination (Engedal 2006). In the meantime the great religious traditions leave their traces. A pilgrim's image that illustrates this impact marvelously is from the Dutch novelist and journalist Herman Vuijsje, who walked the Camino, the pilgrim's road, in the opposite way, from Santiago de Compostella to Amsterdam. He writes: "All those kilocalories that fell down from the pilgrims through the ages, where have they gone? On the Camino! After the Middle Ages they remained there unused, nobody noticed them: a layer of pure energy, compressed and crystallized under the feet of thousands of new pilgrims. Now the pilgrimage is moving up again, after all these centuries, and old routes are rediscovered, they are woken up out of their slumber and they offer the pilgrim in our days unsuspected power" (Vuijsje 2003, 159 – translation BR).

# Chapter 6

## Children's Theology
## Concepts and Contexts, Problems and Horizons

The academic discourse within practical theology and religious education (RE) is widening its scope and becoming more and more globalized. Local practices are communicated all over the world and global trends are shaping local contexts. Through the Internet the world has become an open learning space. The approach of 'Kindertheologie' ('children's theology', abbreviated as KT) in the German speaking world is reaching the international discourse and encountering with the (mostly Anglo-Saxon) movement of 'children's spirituality'. In this chapter I focus on the following questions: what is the original idea behind KT in Germany and how does it enrich the theory and praxis of RE globally? I start with referring to the need of contextualizing the phenomenon of KT and describing its conceptual outlook. Then I integrate KT in the global themes and questions of contemporary RE research. Thirdly, I discuss some basic problems in the research, study and praxis of KT and finally I point to some promising horizons of KT for the development of global RE in the near future.

### 1. Local concepts and contexts of RE and KT

In discussing the role and impact of KT for global RE, there are several issues to be solved. The point however is that these difficulties cannot easily be overcome because of language barriers. Efforts have been made to compare internationally the developments in the field of RE (Schweitzer 2004a), but the local concepts (or words) are always related to the social, cultural and political contexts (or practices) through which religions and religiosity are articulated in different educational settings – in school, family, church and public life (Osmer & Schweitzer 2003). This makes it extremely difficult to learn from each other and to evaluate what one has learned and/or 'mislearned'. My experience in international circles has taught me that steady and self-critical 'live' encounters with others – 'learning in the presence of the other' – offer the best results (see Chapter 7).

The encounter of RE professionals therefore is and should always be an inter-cultural and inter-religious learning process in itself. Most of their time they need to spend in finding common ground about the words they use and the contexts in which these words were born. To give only a few examples: the Dutch word for RE, namely 'godsdienstonderricht', can easily be misinterpreted by a German as a systematic introduction in the celebration of the eucharist (in German: 'Gottesdienst'). And the Polish school subject 'katechese' can be misunderstood as catechetical instruction in the full life of the church. The German school topic 'Religionsunterricht' is legally and politically constructed for denominationally separated classrooms in public schools, in which Roman-Catholic, Protestant and in some cases Islam classes in RE are provided. But the term is also used for the project 'Religionsunterricht für alle' (RE for all) in the city of Hamburg, as a multi-faith concept that crosses the confessional borders. Another issue is related to this: how are institutional religion and personalized religiosity present in education, both in public and private schools, beyond the mere RE classes, for instance in pre-school settings (Dommel 2007), in the spirituality of the whole school (Roebben 2003), in the broader 'ritual repertoire' of the school (De Wildt 2012) and through its ethos and presence in public life (Jäggle et al. 2009; see also the European REMC-project on the possible tensions between religious socialization at home and in the primary school, cfr. Roebben & Dommel 2013)? And how do these complex constructs of 'religion' in schools can be "a contribution to dialogue or a factor of conflict in transforming societies of European countries" (see the European REDCo-project: Jackson et al. 2007)? Such questions arise out of interesting international encounters.

The same can be said about the German term 'Kindertheologie', literally translated into English as 'children's theology'. How does this term and the underlying movement relate and respond to the Anglo-Saxon developments in children's spirituality? Is it a more academic reflection (therefore theology) on a more educational praxis (therefore spirituality) in the life of children? Are the German RE specialists building on the 'lived theology' that comes out of the Anglo-Saxon empirical and hermeneutical research of children's spirituality? Is this theology a solid block of new theological information or rather 'a way of doing things'? Is it theological theory or theological praxis? And how does this 'theologizing' with children can be compared with the 'P4C' (or 'philosophy for children') movement of Matthew Lipman and many others? What is the difference between philosophizing and theologizing with children?

In an interesting set of English essays on KT (Yde Iversen et al. 2009), that originated out of two international consultations in the Danish Løgum-Kloster in 2006 and 2007, the participants in the discussion came roughly to the following interesting positions in this discussion. KT can be divided in two streams: it is about philosophizing (or wondering philosophically and reflecting systematically) with children on religious subjects or it is about philosophizing with children in the form of religion. Hans-Bernhard Petermann and Andrew Wright adhere to the first stream. Petermann wants to invite children in RE "to make faith (also in the sense of its communication) reflective as an elementary dimension of human experience" (Petermann 2009, 144) and does this through a Socratic dialogue that is well prepared and structured by adults. For Andrew Wright this kind of learning process implies clear insights in the appropriate terms and conditions of the learning and in the variety of answers that is plausible for the typical sort of questions raised in RE. Especially when children are dealing with ultimate reality, there should be a clear definition about what we perceive as daily reality, this is the form in which people practice their daily relationship with ultimate reality, according to Wright (2009).

Ekkehard Martens and Jørgen Huggler go one step further. The basic human questions of Immanuel Kant cannot be solved by mere reason ('reine Vernunft'), argues Martens (2009), but need another language game, namely that of morality ('praktische Vernunft') and/or religion. In the Christian tradition the "responsible imagination" (according to Sharon Daloz Parks, see Chapter 2) plays an important role in the thinking and acting of the agent, even if he/she doesn't know where this new information comes from. But it stimulates, criticizes and organises one's daily life. For Jørgen Huggler this knowledge through faith, this orientation in thinking ('Orientierung im Denken', according to Ingo Dalferth) needs to be reflected itself. Theology is always 'fides quaerens intellectum' – faith in search of reason. "One of the best things the teacher can aim at (…) is to give the pupil entry to the company of other people in history who have dealt with religious issues (…). However, it is an important part of teaching to let the learner have an opportunity to experience the contingent nature and limited usefulness of these structures through material that is able to resist these attempts" (Huggler 2009, 125). Huggler continues: "We have to learn to decode and to talk about these expressions and their significance. In some way, this is not only to learn about or from religion. It is indeed to learn to live with religions and to live without losing the capacity for thinking and enjoying freedom of mind" (Huggler 2009, 127). And Gerhard Büttner correctly adds: "Anselm's insight that belief requires rationality also means that theological and Christian patterns of argumentation are worthy to be discussed, regardless of whether one can identify or not" (Büttner 2009, 35).

The relationship of the concept of 'spirituality of the child' with the way it is described and pedagogically used as 'KT' remains a complex issue. The international discussion will need further clarification to find out how these two terms fit together and how they do open up two different ways of looking at and working with the same phenomenon.

## 2. Global themes and questions of RE and KT

Working theologically with children and adolescents in RE differs from country to country (for an interesting overview of RE in Europe, see Kuyk et al. 2007, and the comprehensive REL-EDU project at the University of Vienna). There are however some striking tendencies that can be found on a larger international scale, in Europe and worldwide. At least three global developments influence nowadays this discourse. They are reflected in KT in Germany and give birth to new RE concepts all over the world.

The first element encompasses the awareness of the dignity of every child. KT is first of all an acknowledgement of the radical dignity of every child as a unique human being. Children need to be protected in their vulnerable situation as growing human beings. Children's theology is therefore in the first place a theological reflection on and approval of the status of childhood ('child' as *genitivus objectivus* in KT). Every human being has the indefeasible right to be small, vulnerable and in development – to be 'at home on the road' – looking out for his/her inalienable destiny in life (Mercer 2005). Theologically, this right refers to the basic condition of every human being in faith: living with open hands and an open mind, not afraid but confident, living in dedication (see Introduction and Chapter 2 § 3.2), expecting everything from others and from God. One of the most exciting theological reflections on this dimension of humanity can be found in the work of Karl Rahner (1966). "Theologising with children brings theology back to its own foundation in the experience of faith" (Petermann 2009, 142), namely faith understood in its double meaning as belief and confidence. Children can teach us what we as adults have lost or misconstrued: our "culturally constructed forgetfulness" about spirituality (Hay & Nye 1998, vi), our confidence and rootedness in the Mystery of Life. Out of this follows generically the place of children within theology itself ('child' as subject of theology, as *genitivus subjectivus* in KT). Children not only have the right, but they actually do theology as 'theo-logy' or literally 'god-talk'. They show us ways of dealing with transcendence in their own right. If we listen carefully to them, we will discover some of the deficiencies in our mostly academic and highly cognitive theologies. "Children have not experienced the reformation, they have not experienced the enlightenment, and this sometimes allows them to uncover blind spots which 'expert' theologians may have developed" (Roose & Butt 2009, 49). The theology of children can stimulate academic theology to understand its original position as a theology of childhood a-new…

This element relates to a second observation: KT can be seen as a postmodern modus of doing theology. Faith is only plausible when it is personally appropriated. KT cannot flourish in a context of dogmatism, fundamentalism or even cultural pessimism. KT brings "more joy, more tolerance, less anxiety – or briefly: more fun!" (Anton Bucher). This kind of theology is anchored in a positive anthropology. The human being (including the child) has the necessary resources and tools to think critically (to philosophize) and to articulate a personal relationship with the transcendence (to theologize). This disposition is already there, it only needs to be dis-covered, revealed or un-vealed by a companion in faith, by a parent, a teacher or (metaphorically) a midwife. Such a postmodern approach to RE and KT is rooted in a 'modern' approach to theology. Karl Rahner calls this the transcendental openness of every human being for the Mystery of life. In his opinion every human being can and should theologize, because he or she has the capability to reflect systematically on the complexity of his or her own existence in the tension between immanence and transcendence. The difference between children and adults, between the "ordinary" theologian (this is the believer who reflects on his/her belief) (Astley 2002) and the academic professional theologian is not substantial, but gradual. The difference between a child and an adult doing theology also is gradual and not substantial (Bucher 2002, 11). Every human person has a unique destination in life and has the right and the duty to discover this gradually. Theology should therefore be a democratic enterprise. It cannot only be the privilege of religious educators, ministers, theologians or bishops.

And finally, the discussions in RE on content versus competence, on handing over versus discovering, on content-centered versus child-centered, etc. are reflected and overcome in a dialectical way in KT. Children's theology (understood as the theology or god-talk of children that reminds us of the original position of theology as a theology of childhood) is practically divided in three moments (Schweitzer 2003b) of doing theology:

- Theology *of* children (listening carefully and empathetically to their religious language, the way they understand revelation and Gods presence in our world);
- Theology *with* children (helping them in finding good questions and solid appropriate answers, or when the answers cannot be found, to leave these good questions open);
- Theology *for* children (showing the courage of one's own convictions as an adult and telling them about the solid answers one has found as an adult).

This triadic approach to RE as doing theology seems to be extremely interesting to understand basically what needs to be done in concrete RE globally. A well trained teacher of RE should be in a position to give answers to these three questions: where do these children come from personally and socially (context), how can they be appropriately accompanied by adults in their search for meaning (communication) and what is a good elementary selection of key knowledge that helps them in their search (content)? Children should not be left alone in their search for meaning. Within the complexity of late modern (detraditionalized and multi-religious) societies, educators are not allowed to leave kids alone with their moral and religious identity formation. It all boils down to bringing children into exciting *narthical playgrounds* (see Chapter 5), into enriching 'green pastures' of thought and action, where their own theological imagination is stirred up by Bible stories, classical texts, meaningful others, sacred spaces and practices, such as old and new ways of praying (Kammeyer 2009), to mention only a few.

## 3. Problem areas in KT

KT is a promising, but relatively young branch in (practical) theology. Many aspects still need to be further defined and researched. The central concern of many researchers is to remain respectful for children and not to functionalize or romanticize their voices for the sake of a new vitality in theology as a whole. As far as I can see the awareness of the position of children in theology is part of the ongoing (and never-ending?) hermeneutical turn in theology (Dillen 2007). We are still struggling with the actual presence of living human beings in our theological fabric. Giving young people, let alone children and infants, the floor and listening carefully to their longings and concerns seem to be a difficult and often embarrassing matter, not only for church leaders, teachers and ministers, but also for academic theologians. Children and youngsters often tell us the truth: the success stories but also the painful failures in the adult world. The central question therefore is: how to do sincerely justice to children's voices? In what follows I describe four problem areas in which I mainly raise questions about KT. The impact of these questions on churches, societies and academic-theological and -educational circles needs to be discussed urgently.

## 3.1. Methodological problems

How can we be sure that we are doing KT, that our research can be validated? Do we really perceive the children's voices? Or do we rather hear our biased adult interpretation of their voices, something that we long for, something that we hope to achieve or something that is at least helpful to connect with? As argued before, there is a great deal of agreement on the role of philosophy in KT. As Martens argues: "Altogether, the characteristically philosophical aspect of children's philosophy can thus be said to be methodical, gradually more skilful thinking on issues drawn from a practical engagement with the world and the self, undertaken in a spirit of radical openness towards new ideas and insights" (Martens 2009, 109). But then the question is: whose world, which thinking? We want children to grow and to discover their own thoughtful identity in growing, but for whose world and based on which kind of thinking? For instance, do we really understand the emotional dimension of their "relational consciousness" (Hay & Nye 1998, passim) or do we go too fast with our cognitive evaluation of this reality, because we are in hurry and we are lacking research time and instruments to see what this really means to them? Do we respect their first 'naivité' or do want them to achieve as quickly as possible the second 'naivité', the ideal stage of post-conventional and personal faith? And moreover, do we expect them to participate in the intercultural and interreligious debate as well? How much differences can a child bear in its fragile learning process? What remains important is this: in KT children are encouraged to question what seems to be undisputed and they are encouraged to keep difficult questions open (Schwarz 2003). They are allowed to think for themselves. Do we – as teachers – give them the chance? And do we – as theologians – take their thinking in their own world seriously?

## 3.2. Didactical problems

More didactical clarity is needed in KT. Three questions can be raised here: what is the goal of KT, what is the road to be used, and – even more important – where do children actually come from? Learning outcomes, learning methods and learning contexts need to be explored. What happens when children do not have any religious socialization as background? How can they be involved in storytelling when there are no stories told at all, or even worse, when nobody introduced them in the importance of "telling stories in order to survive" (Chapter 8 § 2)? How can we invite also these kids to speak for themselves? What kind of methodology do we need? And what is the relationship with other didactical models such as elementarization (Schweitzer 2003a, Valstar & Kuindersma 2008), hermeneutic-communicative RE and interreligious learning? Most important seem to be the apt didactical conditions for learning in KT – conditions that are necessary for every learning process: "They [= moments of pure reflection] will be all the more successful the more they are a) elementarised, b) interesting, which also and especially means rooted in the concrete experience of the children, c) intuitive and immediately accessible, d) challenging and didactically designed to be open to a deeper and a wider exploration of the initial problem, and e) condensed and to the point" (Petermann 2009, 143). And finally, what are the goals for a successful learning process in KT? Is it just a process thing or can we also appropriately wrap up the process and consolidate new and commonly found results for later – for new KT moments, for identity development, for life, for the good life for all?

### 3.3. Theological problems

What is the normative role of Christian theology? Should it only clarify the relationship between Christ and culture, or should it also critique culture? In other words, does theology also fulfill a liberating function in KT, in pointing not only to what is reasonable, but also to what is the best option with a view on full human flourishing for children and their fellow human beings? What is the relationship between folk religion and market religion, between the small narrative of the local stories and the new grand narrative of market and media that shamefully annex these small stories? Can children still develop their own vulnerable story? Who defines what is accepted in contemporary culture and not? Who has the power to determine the spiritual or religious meaning of stories? What could be the critical and helpful role of the master narrative of the Gospel as a liberation story in this respect? And what could possibly be the role of the churches in this debate?

### 3.4. Academic problems

Will academic theology get more and more distanced from 'ordinary' or 'folk' theologies such as KT (Grümme 2009)? Will it disqualify these lived theologies as 'humbug'? Will the practical sensibility of every sub-discipline in theology finally disappear in favor of a cool systematic theology? Will practical theology continue to struggle now through KT to be a real academic discipline and not just a translation or making 'fluid' of so called 'solid' dogmatic ready-made answers? Will the waterfall system from systematic theology into practical theology into RE (and KT) continue to be the default position of RE? Will every form of non-academically approved theology, to be found in RE and KT, finally water down to a sort of 'lite' theology (Freudenberger-Lötz 2009, 92)? How close is our theology to daily life? How close is it allowed to come?

## 4. Promising horizons for RE provided by KT

Raising too much questions can be paralyzing. KT is under construction and the answers to these questions will slowly but surely be formulated. The least one can say is that KT definitely has its momentum in late modernity. It makes us aware of bold theological discourses that have lost their youthfulness and vulnerability, or to put it more succinctly, their innocence. It helps us to delve deeper into the real meaning of theo-logical language. In the final part of this chapter I refer to some of the promising horizons of KT for RE, for practical theology and theology as a whole.

## 4.1. Rethinking RE teacher education and theology curricula

In line with the three functions of KT (theology *of, with* and *for* children, see above) new approaches to RE teacher education in theological faculties and schools of education are urgently needed. Or, a lot of hermeneutical work needs to be done, this means helping children and young people to find meaning within conversations. A lot of 'clouds of unknowing' need to be addressed, so that future teachers become aware of their own possibilities and boundaries (Ward 2012). Old and static mono-religious standpoints need to be overcome and teachers should first learn for themselves to raise and to tackle the difficult and open questions that are raised by their children, e.g. "What if God does not exist?" This means that (future) RE teachers need "sound expert knowledge in structuring school orientated education (…)". Their role should be threefold, related to the 'of-with-for' perspective of KT: "the role of the attentive observer (perceiving how the children understand the theme), the role of the thought-provoking member of the discussion (encouraging the children to advance their understanding), as well as the role of the supporting expert (bringing expert knowledge into the discussion)" (Freudenberger-Lötz 2009, 90).

## 4.2. Doing local theology

The enlightenment paradigm which forms the basis for the concept of KT (everybody can think for him/herself) should be more than just a formal framework, in order that local stories can be told and can be heard. Every regional or local context has its own dignity (Sedmak 2002): the grandmothers in the North-Eastern part of Poland are doing local theology with children in family catechesis (Osewska 2011) and they do it differently from the teachers in Norwegian schools, who invite children to tell their small stories in workbooks and logbooks (Haakedal 2011). In this respect KT-educators are aware of the need for 'slowification' in learning processes (see also Chapter 10 § 3). Children and youngsters have the right to define for themselves the places where they live and belong to, the particular places that are ordinary and at the same time extra-ordinary and holy to them. Reconstructing narratively one's life as a journey implies also the acknowledgement of time and space in which people are journeying. In order to come to terms with our contemporary complex and multifaceted societies, children need time to discover who they are and where they are. This seems to be extremely important when KT comes to life in inter-religious learning processes. Then the central issue should be: how can we help children and youngsters to "re-define and re-dignify" themselves within their own traditions in communication with others (see Chapter 7 § 7). Interesting reflections on the relationship between inter-religious learning, dialogical learning, children's spirituality and KT can be found e.g. in the work of Julia Ipgrave (2009a and 2009b).

## 4.3. Developing a new religious language

The above mentioned REDCo and REMC research projects (both sponsored by the European Commission, respectively in the FP6 and FP7 frameworks) are univocal: children are interested in each other's beliefs. They perceive differences spontaneously on a daily basis: in the classroom, on the playground, on the street, in the local football club, etc. Unfortunately these experiences remain open without further interpretation and communication. Nobody is using the great educational resource they offer. Children are often left alone. On the basis of the interviews from the REMC group it became extremely clear that children expect adults to be able to handle a religious language, but that these adults feel uncomfortable to do so, because of the complexity of today and their totally different backgrounds in the past. Links with religious communities have often disappeared, families are culturally and religiously mixed, religious mother tongues are absent and the general grammar of religion to perceive and interpret religious diversity is not even thought of. Schools and parents are indeed deeply connected in this situation. In the framework of this book one can of course raise the question if schools are able to offer a linguistic shelter to this general religious homelessness at all.

## 4.4. Telling stories in order to 'keep the faith'

Storytelling is an extremely powerful educational tool. In many conversations on the road, during my trips to the post-Communist countries in Eastern Europe, I recognized the longing for a 'time out' of people living there – for their children, for themselves and their educational systems. Literally they only wanted to tell their stories in order to 'keep the faith', in order not to collapse in the difficult social and political processes of transition in their home countries. Their voices sounded like: "Give us the time to reorganize our fragmented 'histories and her-stories', the small narratives that helped us to survive communist ideology – give us time to learn democracy and to change our school systems, time for de-marxization and de-ideologization – give us time to deal with the identity vacuum in which young people find themselves and time to overcome traditional RE and address this new situation appropriately – and stay in touch with us!" If we really take the vulnerable voices of children in KT seriously, then I interpret this call of our colleagues in Eastern Europe as a reminder that storytelling – *of, with and for* (young) human beings – is indispensable for the development of good RE. It is my contention that we are not yet aware of the full impact of the biographical and narrative shifts in contemporary RE work.

## Conclusion

KT is an exciting new way of looking at the world, of reflecting and acting in it, of doing local theology with a radical focus on the young storytellers and learners at stake. Many are the challenges of KT to those who get involved:

- KT challenges parents to become better – or 'good enough' – parents.
- KT challenges the whole of theology to become better theology
- KT challenges other disciplines in child studies to become better child studies (and not to forget that spirituality is important and that children have a 'right to religion')
- KT challenges the society and its educational system to become a more just society that provides better schools.
- KT challenges churches to become better churches that are prepared to give up their power and help people to find new and surprising ways to God and to other people.

# Chapter 7

# Learning in Difference
# Inter-religious Learning in the Secondary School

Cultural and religious diversity shape our living and learning environments. In recent years they have become the subject of considerable debate. Indeed in many parts of Europe the explosive ingredients of multicultural conflicts and multi-religious tensions have been given significant media coverage. Nonetheless it is interesting to note that in schools and other places of social empowerment, the steady work of mutual exchange and enrichment between culturally and religiously diverse groups seems to enjoy far less media attention. Since 9/11 societies are acutely sensitive to the destructive power of religious fanaticism and inevitably this sensitivity has permeated European classrooms. Indeed some scholars claim that religious education (RE) can no longer be omitted from the curriculum of modern state schools and should be provided as an examination subject for *all* students (Miedema 2000 for the Netherlands and 2007 for Europe as a whole). This chapter concurs with this argument and adopts a pragmatic approach to RE. It argues that since religion is a worldwide phenomenon young people in school are entitled to be educated in the dynamics of religion. They must also be educated about how to handle the possible 'dynamite' that might ignite when people play dangerously with 'religious fire'. Information and interpretation are key words in this regard. It is vital that young people are given information and interpretative skills to enable them to learn how to recognize, understand and respect their own and other people's religious backgrounds. In such an environment successful education contributes to mutual understanding in the midst of differences.

Learning about religious difference is a multi-layered task. Those who engage in the encounter with the other will not only be confronted with diversity and with the other's 'difference' *(la différence)*, but also with the other's radical strangeness or otherness *(l'altérité)*. In class, students meet each other in a direct way, as a classmate, as a person and as a human being with their own origin and future. The students are not first and foremost representatives of ideological and religious groups. They are human beings, blossoming in pursuit of happiness, starting to develop as moral people. I am convinced that young people not only learn to recognize and respect the *origins* of the other, they also learn how to become open to the inalienable authenticity and life project or *future* of the other. This future will resound most strongly in the other's (non-)religious convictions. In these convictions, a glimpse of the mystery of the other will be revealed. When this glimpse occurs in class it often occurs as an invisible and unintentional pedagogical outcome. It happens when a student in the encounter with the other, begins to address the fundamental question 'Who do I want to become as a human being, and what is *my* future?' In the wake of 9/11, the authoritative Dutch rabbi, Raphael Evers, phrased it as follows: "We have here a culture in which we think highly of tolerance. (…) And that is what you should teach young people. To learn in school (how) to live together with one another is of even greater importance than to learn how to read and write, or to know where Paris lies. We all make a huge mistake if we look at each other and think: there sits a Muslim. And: there sits a Jew. We forget that the other is a human being in the first place, who happens to be raised in a Muslim or Jewish culture. In our religious zeal we often forget the human being" (Sjah 2002).

This deep layer of inter-religious learning involves learning to recognize, know and appreciate differences. It implies an encounter, at a profound level, with the otherness of the other. Mary C. Boys refers to this as *learning in the presence of the other* (Boys 2008). This encounter usually happens after preliminary acquaintances have taken place, and after one has done one's best to acquire information about the other and to talk with the other about differences and similarities. Those who then dig deeper come across differences in interpretation that require clarification. Through this encounter students not only learn to perceive these differences and to communicate with others so that they can have a better understanding of their positions, they are also invited to open up their own religious experience to one another. The encounter involves posing the question 'Who are you, I want to become captivated by you?' and the response 'Come and see, let yourself be captivated!' The encounter presupposes difference and enables the perception, communication and holding of different positions represented by fellow human beings. In this regard inter-religious learning is, without doubt, a stimulating invitation to learn how to articulate and take responsibility for one's own (non-)religious point of view.

## 1. A contemporary profile of RE as a school subject

In a plural society, RE can no longer be considered exclusively from a catechetical orientation. After all, explicit initiation into one (for instance Catholic) religion requires a community of believers, yet many modern state schools are not composed of a community of faith. A model of pure application or adaptation to the secularized culture also falls short. As a subject RE is not identical to social or moral education and it necessitates that religion as a complex reality should be studied from a critical perspective. RE helps young people to listen more carefully to 'slowly fermenting questions' within their own multifaceted lives. In a classroom context it enables them to vocalize their own questions in a reasonable manner. In a plural and often religiously indifferent culture, young people are not only entitled to receive solid information and guidance concerning life-questions, but also to learn to ask their own critical religious questions. In 'children's theology' [the German *Kindertheologie*], a recent development of 'children's spirituality', the skill of asking critical questions is deliberately stimulated in childhood (see Chapter 6).

Generating religious questions embraces two competences focusing on a hermeneutical nature which concentrates on identity clarification and a communicative nature which looks at the communication of worldviews (Roebben 2001c; Lombaerts & Pollefeyt 2004). It is important to spend some time exploring these two areas. Contemporary young people grow up in a European society where many intersecting and competing ideas exist. The co-existence of multiple ideas does not only occur within groups of youngsters, but also within the lives of individuals themselves. Today, identity is formed in radical plurality. The master narratives that once imparted meaning are no longer plausible and people are now entrusted to one another and to their own inner compass in order to obtain clarity in their quest for meaning (Crawford & Rossiter 2006). As a school subject RE offers students advice relating to their own lives, along with a safe place where they can learn to deal with confusing and compelling experiences and questions (Mette 2007, 235-255; Schweitzer 2006, 81-96). After all, the environment in which they grow up is often threatening, confusing and overwhelming.

Young people must also learn to express and account for themselves in their relationships to others. They must be challenged to examine critically the world of hazy opinions and to position themselves within a solidly grounded and well-documented vision of their interaction with others. The class group plays an important role in the process of religious communication, as it is the locus for a learning process where opinions are clarified, explained and substantiated. Class group interaction provides insights into pivotal questions such as: 'What are religious people really talking about? What motivates believers into seeing their lives from a perspective of radical commitment? How do I formulate the questions of life which concern *me* unconditionally?' In this sense the dialogue never takes place exclusively in the class group, but ties in with the ongoing dialogue of humankind which poses the great life-questions as well as the answers that religions and secular world-views offer.

## 2. RE and the educational dynamics of the modern school

RE is part of the intercultural dynamics of the contemporary school, which in turn responds to great social and cultural questions. Just as schools never stand alone neither do school subjects. Since 9/11 religion cannot be considered a private issue, but is placed at the core of education, and must be considered as a part of intercultural dialogue. In Europe, RE has become a matter of public awareness, even within the realm of religiously affiliated schools (for Protestants, see the work of Karl Ernst Nipkow in Miedema 2008; for Catholics, see the work of Mette 2007). This awareness extends nowadays explicitly to the mind of European politicians and legislative bodies (Jackson et al. 2007). It should offer students the opportunity to identify, describe and clarify concerns about their living environment while operating as a valuable building block for a new world. It invites students to transform the chaotic field of talked-about opinions and threatening information, into a powerful living environment of insights and skills, which have both a liberating and invigorating effect, and which make a positive future possible. In order to understand RE's role in the public space of the school, the traditional paradigm of handing over (religious) information and life patterns to the next generation should be radically transformed into a paradigm of (religious) awareness of the social context of this and other (more secular) forms of 'handing over'. Traditionally, RE was about initiation into one particular religious tradition. Today, RE implies the recognition of the unique resilience of education in society; an awareness of the attractive and frightening presence of religion in society; and the unavoidable need for religious communication in society, at the heart of modernity.

Learning to deal constructively with differences is a primary objective of the present-day school, all the more because dialogue with other beliefs takes place, not only in the depth of time (intergenerational), but also in the breath of space (intercultural) and in the perspective of hope for the world (global). The factual presence of people from other cultures (via migration and asylum), the large mobility of people and services, the supply of the media (TV, film and internet etc.), ensure that our living environment remains in an ongoing atmosphere of cross-fertilization. This process shapes our outlook and ways of life, and creates both challenges and tensions. Values Education, Education for Citizenship, Personal, Social, Moral and Spiritual education are partial answers to this intercultural and plural situation. In schools, one strives to create a safe space to address this situation so that differences are not evaded but examined in their directness and power while being tested for their ability to promote humanity. This means that threatening and closed concepts of the 'good life' can also be critiqued and freed from fanatical and fundamentalist biases. Religion is not immune from the process of critique (Lombaerts 1997). As the whole social and cultural horizon of meanings shifts, religion also changes. Nevertheless, this process of awakening runs its course slowly and laboriously, and religions tend rather to neglect the existing state of affairs and mask the contingency of existence (Van der Ven 1994).

Christianity faces the historical challenge of confronting this situation directly. The temptation to escape into religious or ecclesial 'platonism' (by arguing: 'this situation does not affect us, so let us just carry on as if nothing ever happened') is great (Valadier 1990). After all, for centuries Christianity has determined the agenda of Europe's social and cultural systems, and as a consequence it now finds it difficult to disentangle its internal truth-claims from their institutional interpretations. The role of women in the Church and society is one example of this. Despite forceful statements from the Church about emancipation and equal rights for all human beings in society, women do not enjoy equality of opportunity when it comes to ordination to the priesthood in the Catholic tradition. The great challenge for the Christian tradition is to re-contextualize itself in an environment of moral and existential plurality and indifference. This view of tradition as a 're-sourcing process' implies that Christians are prepared to review and re-experience the internal reflective, affective and dynamic strength of their tradition against the background of social and cultural developments. They will fulfill this task especially with a strategy of encounter that goes further than doomed self-preservation on the one hand, and half-hearted adaptive behavior on the other. Therefore the primary task of the contemporary Christian school is to put its learning resources at the service of its student's quest for meaning (Roebben 2003).

## 3. The post-modern multi-vocal identity of young people

Contemporary children grow up in a world of difference. As a result, their personal identity frequently comes under pressure. They must perform the vulnerable developmental task of self-clarification in the context of a society and a culture that is unclear about its own perspectives on development. We may question if this situation is qualitatively different from situations in previous times. In response we can say 'perhaps not'. In previous times children's identity conformed to the self-image that they received from others ('generalized other'). Contemporary children also draw the other-pole into the self-pole: they weave the stories told and attributed to them by others, into a web of intertextuality. When someone asks young people what they are like, they turn the text material of significant others in their environment into a personal texture and conclude: 'This is just the way I am'.

However, a plurally structured environment is more confusing to grow up in than a background that is neatly and clearly singular. Some children lose themselves in fragmentation (the other-pole outstrips them), others cling obstinately to one perspective (the self-pole takes in all the differences). For a contemporary, well-considered outlook on education and the life cycle, one therefore speaks of a 'balanced identity' or 'multi-vocal identity' (Meijer 1995; Streib 1994). One can describe it as follows: I try to keep myself in sight by acquiring insight into the attitude and background of the many significant others who shape my self. I try to be aware of where I come from and what my life story is thus far (*diachronic* multi-vocal) and I try to obtain clarity in and to live with the many and often conflicting voices that operate in me at this moment (*synchronic* multi-vocal). Diachronic and synchronic are terms that refer to two logics or ways of ordering things. Diachronic involves looking at sequences, origins, history and change whereas synchronic refers to connections and patterns at a particular moment. The school's hermeneutical task in general, and of RE in particular, is therefore accelerated and strengthened by the circumstances in which contemporary education takes place. Cultures and religions have never existed in a chemically pure condition, but today the weight of plurality breaks right through the safe initiation boundaries and impels young people and their educators into intensified reflexivity. Those who want to know where they stand must consciously go into the many voices that resound in their narrative identity.

According to this perspective inter-religious learning is a form of intensive RE. It does not replace RE, but substantially deepens its dynamics of interpretation. It takes place in the first instance, not between representatives of ideological and religious groups, from a kind of outsiders' perspective but rather, in the dynamics of the worldview of the individual person. This involves intra-religious learning. Explicit religious socialization involves setting up an interpretative search process in communication with others, where one searches in order to acquire clarity in one's diachronic and synchronic aspects of identity. Young people experience a superabundance of ideological ingredients. There is no shortage of religion and worldviews. Indeed one could posit that, if anything, there is an over-supply. Indigestion lurks round the corner unless the learning process helps young people to digest this multitude and to gradually but surely connect themselves to their own life-project, no longer in a noncommittal and freely experimental manner, but intrinsically tied up with the truth-claim of that project. Pastiche, sampling and syncretism are some of the indications of the way in which youngsters try to maintain this plurality in themselves.

This search for identity in difference characterizes the educational environment in which religious educators carry out their work. An often-heard lament among religious educators is that they themselves partake in this pluralism and no longer stand for uniformity in their own tradition. One cannot and should not want to resolve the crisis of tradition, the Church and of the Christian belief by assuming that the Christian heritage is one and undivided and can therefore be passed unproblematically onto young seekers. Discourse about whether children first of all need their own religious feeding ground before they can deal with inter-religious dialogue and learning, is often ideologically tinted (Mokrosch 1999; Schweitzer, 1999; Dommel 2007). One must ask 'What is the underlying idea of religious responsibility and commitment to tradition?' 'Is it true that children must firstly "know" everything about their own tradition before they can be truly responsive to others?' 'Does the crisis of Christian belief instead not render us sensitive to the fact that trouble-free initiation zones no longer exist and that even the most closed religious congregation is intruded upon by the "world" of religious pluralism and secular worldviews?'

## 4. Three learning models dealing with religious diversity in school

RE should contribute to an understanding and appreciation of religious differences between people. Two key objectives in RE involve learning about all that religion implies and learning how religion influences the lives of people. In this way RE can deal with ignorance and indifference, two negative developments that hamper the peaceful coexistence of people. In the broad sense of the word inter-religious learning refers to the religious insights that youngsters gain when encountering others. In a narrow sense it refers to the element 'interpretation through communication' (*learning from religion*), that is followed by the second element 'information through documentation' (*learning about religion*) (see first and second column in schema at the end of this chapter). Inter-religious learning attempts to make the pupils sensitive to the unique nature of a religious position and, in (dis-)agreement with others, invites them to situate themselves within this field (Pollefeyt 2007). In general there are three models which outline the learning tension between particularity and plurality in RE. These are 1) the mono-, 2) the multi- and 3) the inter-religious models (for the two latter ones, see Grimmitt 1987). In addition three key questions help to critically assess these models. These are: 'In which way do they do justice to the particularity of one's own tradition?' 'How do they deal with the phenomenon of religious plurality?' Finally 'How do they situate themselves in the tension between these two?' (Sterkens, Hermans & van der Ven 1999, 163-165).

1. The mono-religious model ('learning in religion') consciously aims to immerse young people in the dynamics of a particular tradition and render them full-fledged participants of that tradition. A possible exclusive variant of this model radically ignores other life views, while an inclusive variant is salvifically optimistic and claims that salvation - perhaps in fragments, never *in extenso* - is to be found also in other traditions. In evaluating the mono-religious model critics argue that its underlying concept of tradition is extremely static. For even in the most closed community crises occur in the manner in which people understand themselves. Further in this model the uniqueness of others is not recognized, and there is a strong correlation of this attitude with forms of ethnocentrism. Moreover, people are blind to the possible tension between what is familiar and what is strange.

2. The second significant model is termed the multi-religious model

('learning about religion'). Here one assumes that young people can be introduced simultaneously or successively to various religious traditions and world views, since they have no specific affinity with one or other tradition and can thus decide for themselves purely on the basis of information given. A variety of approaches have developed from this model in the last decades including 'Religionskunde' in Germany and 'Geestelijke stromingen' in primary education in the Netherlands. Critics of this model suggest that it leads to indifference. Further no conscientious commitment is stimulated between the child and the tradition. If all viewpoints are the same, if nothing makes any difference, then there is absolutely no reason to consciously engage with and interest oneself in any one particular perspective. Finally, this model does not take seriously the pluriformity of religious experiences. Students adopt as it were a religiously clinical attitude and study the religious phenomenon from a spectator's perspective. It is akin to learning about the digestive system by devouring information, without ever being tempted at any single moment in the process to really taste and savor the flavor of food, let alone to alleviate hunger. An emergency exit is substituted for a search for truth. This model runs the risk of being ideologically misused. In a non-committed presentation of various religions and views of life, the idea that it does not matter whether one is engaged or not threatens to resonate throughout. This kind of education is counterproductive as it does not inform, but deforms. It renders young people into a species of religious tourists who put themselves through the anecdotic, exotic, adventurous and 'kick-generating' facades of religions. Differences between traditions become leveled and depoliticized, and their potential as moments of learning on the road to a more conscious humanity, is lost (Giroux 1996).

3. The inter-religious model ('learning from religion') thematically explores the deep questions of life, to which religious traditions and worldviews answer in parallel and/or differently. The outlook of a religion or worldview can be analyzed and communicated in four

forms through a) story, b) community, c) moral outlook and d) ritual. At these four levels, the internal-argumentative strength of interpellation of religions and world views can be investigated and tested in one's own life and brought before conversation partners for investigation and testing in an ongoing dynamic of perspective exchange. Real pluralism assumes a multitude of beliefs that are deeply significant to real people. These beliefs cannot be swept into one pile and labeled as being 'all the same', but must be acknowledged as being able to deepen and broaden the vision of various conversation partners in conflict and convergence. Critics of the inter-religious model state that an intrinsic commitment to one's own tradition, however minimal, is expected from the students, so that people are prepared to study and present this to the group for perspective exchange. There is much openness to other beliefs, but the question remains whether a real rapprochement in the religious realm is possible, and if the post-modern multi-vocal self is capable of withstanding this diversity. Will the multi-vocal self be sufficiently socially agile to resist collapse into indifference or fundamentalism? In evaluating this model it is important to keep in mind what could be termed the 'shady' side of inter-religious learning based on a realistic view of pluriformity, which analyses the negative aspects of inter-religious contact such as non-communication and oppression (van der Ven 1998, 273). While these negative aspects exist it is important to recognize the positive developments evident in the spontaneous multicultural sensitivity of young people who express themselves in world music festivals, international exchanges, root- and folk-music and folk-culture etc. Furthermore many young people seem to recognize polyphony in their own life, and integrate and celebrate it as spontaneous energy.

## 5. From multi-religious learning to inter-religious learning

Since RE no longer takes place in a trouble-free zone and interactions with the outside world criss-cross the life patterns of young adults, in my opinion, the inter-religious model has the best chance of success. This model supposes a thorough knowledge of the religious backgrounds of fellow-classmates and when this happens prejudice is inhibited and respect for the opinions of others flourishes. This inter-religious model does not exclude but rather includes the multi-religious model. Observing religion as a societal phenomenon ('What does religion do to people and what do people do with religion?') *(learning about religion)* offers students the opportunity to gauge the life questions to which religious people, over the course of time and in the depth of society, have given answers *(learning from religion)*. This contributes to a better understanding of one's own worldview and can help to clarify one's multi-layered identity. Therefore one can say that multi-religious learning and inter-religious learning presuppose and complement each other.

In this dialectic, two forms of inter-religious learning regularly occur in the classroom. Some students are strongly convinced that their religious beliefs and behavior emphasizes the necessity of providing others with information. Other students are more timid and insecure when it concerns their own religious position and they require more help with the interpretative aspect of the learning process. Both of these forms of inter-religious learning occur in the classroom and pulsate the teaching and learning environment. The German RE expert Karl Ernst Nipkow (1994) called these forms respectively the (a) hard and (b) soft form of learning in plurality.

(a) The hard form of learning in plurality invites young adults, through conversation, to rename, document, and clarify their religious origin in conversation. For instance they are asked to think about the implications of their baptism for themselves by consulting their parents and/or grandparents. The presupposition is that those who have a traceable religious history and origin must also be able to relate to it, and respond to questions such as: 'Does this mean something to you or does it leave you indifferent? Do you know what you are talking about when you say that you are non-religious, when in fact you have been baptized?' In this process of documentation young adults bring their religious backgrounds into focus. Through the search for similarities and differences they learn to understand and express the richness of their religious backgrounds to each other. While for many their religious origin may not be relevant to their own life-quest, neither can it be denied. For those who are religiously convinced, it is often a closed chapter. It is up to them to open the book up again and learn to communicate its story.

(b) The soft form of inter-religious learning connects more with the polyphonic identity of young adults. After all, a lot of young people know so little about their own religious background that they may not know which religious 'nest' they may have been hatched from. Therefore it is pointless to enter into conversations about (supposed) elements of explicit religious initiation. This form opts for a broad perspective on worldviews, and from there it searches for connections and invites young adults to identify where they fit into these worldviews. It presupposes that religious ties, which are often not expressed in words and images, interconnect people. This form of clarification is essentially a communicative issue. It is about teaching young adults to ask pertinent questions about their own existence and to put their own perspective between parentheses and through conversation with others to learn to accept its relative status (Rickers 1998, 135-137; van der Ven 1998, 266-282). According to the British RE expert Robert Jackson, this leads to the *edification* of the person: 'Through the challenge of 'unpacking' another worldview one can, in a sense, become a new person' (Jackson 1997, 130-131).

## 6. Problems and possibilities of inter-religious learning

Religion is vulnerable, because it involves questions as old as the hills. Young adults who discuss religion will increase this vulnerability. The school subject can manage this field of experiences but it cannot prevent the rise of hermeneutical conflicts which could bring the planned learning process to a standstill. At these moments RE cannot suffice with a didactical 'procedure' of such bottlenecks or differences in interpretation by documenting students well and by letting them communicate with each other in a 'house-trained' manner. It is my opinion that the learning process must be deepened during these moments. In many instances this will also 'actually' happen. When the themes of life are touched, none can remain indifferent. The convinced will demonstrate their strong belief, the doubters will hesitate, and the indifferent will withdraw under the demand of others. Some youngsters have received a strong opinion about their religious perspective towards certain themes from home (hard form). Others need to rely on themselves and are exposed to chaotic and unclear dispositions (soft form). Needless to say this requires quality leadership. The educator should not keep clear of contradictions. He does not harmonize the learning process, but is competent to explain the complexity and return the situation to the students. He moreover raises the question of truth by helping to describe and assess conflicting claims of truth: 'On grounds of what assumptions do people or institutions give this particular religious answer to a question of life? What does it do with them? And what do they in turn do with the answer? Can one understand the fervor and zeal of religious persons, and does one understand why they exactly give these particular answers? Does the answer really come from them or has it been installed in them through an institution? Does it contribute to being a better human being or does it instead dehumanize people?'

*Three barriers* exemplify that inter-religious learning in any given circumstance may be problematic. The *first* difficulty relates to classrooms that students perceived to be unsafe for the disclosure and discussion of diversity. In such instances students might feel themselves and their religious position threatened, disrespected, and even ignored in the classroom. If trust is absent, especially when it comes to the vulnerable domain of exchanging experiences and ideas in religion, then inter-religious learning will not occur. On a more profound level it is important to ask how students and teachers cope with competing truth claims in the classroom. In the name of tolerance and for the sake of continuing a respectful conversation, one must ask how far a teacher or student should go before criticizing and challenging an intolerant position. A *second* problem which may arise in inter-religious learning relates to the individual development of the student. In some sense inter-religious communication in class supposes an advanced degree of personal development. Only those who are able and willing to represent their own position can fully participate in the dialogue. This does not imply that all students need to be pocket-theologians. Moreover it does not mean that they should be able to present a neat and fully worked out map of their lives. However, it does imply that students should be willing to reflect on their worldview and their own religious story, both in a synchronic and diachronic perspective. Or to put it in Kohlbergian terms, they should be able and willing to grow from a conventional viewpoint – through clarification – to a post-conventional viewpoint. From sixteen years onwards this approach has significant advantages. That is not to say that children and pre-adolescents cannot be sensitized to the plurality that surrounds them. In inter-religious learning to date a crucial question that has not been satisfactorily addressed is the question of whether there is a definite moment in the person's transition from monophony to polyphony. In other words, how many different voices can a child withstand before it hears a deafening cacophony? A *third* problem is that young adults may feel insecure and 'socially disabled' from engaging in inter-religious conversation with others. Hans-Günter Heimbrock asks 'How far can one walk in the shoes of the other?' (quoted in Streib 2001, 140). Certain aspects of the conversation might remain inaccessible and radically different because they stem from completely different religious traditions or because they cannot be expressed. Moreover when one listens to other religious stories one can become confronted with the internal fallibility of one's own religious conviction. Certain elements of one's own conviction might in principal be incompatible with those from other traditions (for example resurrection versus reincarnation). One could also fall into the hands of *holy envy,* a sort of religious jealousy, 'experiencing something so profound one wishes that his or her own faith community also had or practiced it' (Boys 2000, 276; Lubarsky 1996). In summary one can become quite entangled, not only within the conversation, but also within oneself. It is precisely in and through reshaping these hermeneutical conflicts into a successful learning process, that the teacher could address the question of the narrative identity of the young adult.

*Three possible reactions* could be outlined within the practice of the classroom regarding this rather 'profound' form of inter-religious learning: a realistic, an optimistic and a fatalistic. As for the *first* reaction: research in the Netherlands makes evident that most of the young adults between the age of sixteen and eighteen years have a preference for multi-religious and not for inter-religious learning (Roebben and Van der Tuin 2004). They valorize diversity as a great good, they want to learn about other opinions for their own personal enrichment but at the same time, however, they are not really willing to revise their own point of view. There is a matter of tolerance, as long as this implies that people remain unharmed (through for example arbitrary and useless violence). Each has its own truth; one doesn't have to doubt that, neither in a negative nor positive sense, thus the commentaries of Dutch youngsters. Hans-Georg Ziebertz has come to a similar conclusion in Germany (2005; see also Riegel and Ziebertz 2007); but at the same time he complains that religion should be more than just a transfer of information: "One should not only be acquainted with the different religions, but also allow oneself to be affected by their messages. This is inherent in religion as religion" (Ziebertz 2005, 219). In Flanders the reactions are not so downright (yet): pupils have some reserve to the contribution of encounters with believers from other traditions (Pollefeyt and others 2004). This brings me to the *second* reaction: young adults should not only interest themselves in the reasons that can be found in the diversity of religious opinions, they are in fact already doing so. This is the optimistic view. The fact that young adults are raised in a sphere of polyphony does not have to be a problem. This might probably and predominantly be the problem for educators who themselves have been brought up in a time of a linear-chronological education and who therefore assume that one first need to feel at 'home' somewhere before one can engage oneself in a conversation 'outdoors'. Most of the young adults however seem to recognize, integrate and celebrate polyphony as a kind of spontaneous zest in their lives. Some authors for that matter point out that a detached presentation of religious positions in a subject such as 'religious studies' at the university naturally eventuates in matters that involve individual meaning giving (Bowman 2006; Simmons 2006). Today, young adults are easily appealed by religious traditions precisely because there is nothing to lose or to win. Their personal growth is not at all mortgaged by confusion about religious diversity: they enjoy spiritual practices themselves in a sphere of abundance. Moreover, the outsider perspective in 'religious studies' (or the multi-religious model in secondary education) is outdated in the eyes of young adults. It perhaps only exists in the perception of educators who through this subject want to rebel against or discern themselves from an insider perspective of traditional theology. A *third* reaction finally consists of what I would call fatalism: a cry for help to find a way out of a hermeneutical, in this instance an inter-religious, intersection. Young adults will than cry out: 'It is all fine by me. I can see how religious people respond to the profound questions of life. But what does it mean to you, sir/madam? How did you come to terms with this question, how did you struggle with your tradition in this matter?' They want to learn what a human being made out of flesh and blood, someone who moreover speaks with authority, has to say about some or other matter. At that moment they lift the hermeneutical learning process to another level, namely that of authoritative and reasonable testimony. Then they ask (almost as if in an act of despair, because education sometimes can really leave them ravenous) for the difference of a dissident point of view, for the otherness within the perspective of the other, for a human person who in his peculiarity lives by the choices he has made. The other turns out to be completely irrecoverable, his point of view remains strange, but it gives food for thought, it can jolt people awake from their religious complacency. I think that this fatalism on the one hand, coupled to the new susceptibility for spiritual forms of life on the other hand, creates opportunities for RE (especially in a multicultural and multi-religious setting). It expects teachers who are willing to pedagogically and theologically open up the learning space for the variety of religious traditions and communities in the lives of young adults, and who are willing to invite them to gauge and explore their religious experiences. Through model learning and social learning, they will invite students to participate in and create an ambience in which the actual differences and strangeness can be broken open into utopian otherness and newness. The Dutch religious educationalist Cok Bakker is on the basis of his research findings rather optimistic. He is convinced of the practical knowledge of the teacher as a reflective practitioner. They solve problems of religious diversity in the same way as they deal pragmatically with other diversity issues in the classroom (2007).

## 7. Learning in difference and inter-spiritual dialogue

'What can I learn from you if we cannot be different from each other? Why would I learn at all when it does not make a difference where you come from, who you are, and what you stand for?' Educational meeting places originate where differences in interpretation occur. 'You are different from me, your way of acting is strange to me, but I want to know you, you intrigue me. This is where I stand, where do you stand?' These questions can open up the learning process of religious 'diversity' in class (this involves multi-religious and inter-religious learning) and form it into 'learning in difference'. Here the sole objective is not a transfer of information that enables interpretation to occur through communication. One also has to challenge the authenticity of the human being and enliven the soul. When this happens people are ushered into the unfathomable mystery of the uniqueness, immanence and transcendence of the human being as a member of humankind. In this exchange of dialogue each person is initiated into religious experiences and the mystery these experiences relate to. It is obvious that this 'learning in difference' is diametrically opposed to 'learning in indifference'. Learning in indifference does not only happen when differences do not stand a chance, it also happens when diversity is wiped away. Students will then drop out of the process because there is nothing for them to learn. They are not stimulated through a diversity of perspectives and neither are their soul's energized by the radical 'otherness' of the other.

This new type of learning can be called 'learning through encounter' or as the American practical theologian Mary C. Boys terms it 'learning in the presence of the other' (Boys 2008). Such 'inter-spiritual' – dialogue is not about having the last word on doctrinal or disciplinary matters, on the contrary it involves a sharing of spiritual experiences that lie beneath the different positions. I am convinced that, considering the eagerness, ease, and interactivity of the spiritual search of contemporary young adults, this inter-spiritual model can be implemented and practiced in classrooms. The Indian theologian, Raimon Panikkar, suggests: 'It is about having an inner religious conversation with myself, an encounter in the depth of my own religiosity after I have met another person on the same intimate level' (Panikkar 1978, 40). One might wonder if 'inter-spiritual' dialogue is an unachievable aim in class. Perhaps it is a challenging and worthwhile aim for the future. For if one ushers young adults into the realm of the soul, the demands of class instruction are high, the desire for information great, and the longing for communication with peers limitless. Perhaps the most noticeable aspect of the process will be young adults' underlying questions of hope and the future: 'Is there a perspective possible that connects and unites people globally, that transcends humankind, and that at the same time helps human beings to respect and cultivate both their individuality and their difference from others?'

Such critical encounter with the other encourages me to look more thoroughly at myself. Inter-religious learning is not a youthful version of an adult and ripened inter-religious dialogue, but a religious learning process in which religious plurality (in class groups, but also in the individual person) is taken seriously. This critical encounter reinforces the ability to look deeper into one's own meaning-giving system and to explore further the existential resilience it offers. Through the intercultural and inter-religious encounter I am challenged to re-define myself, to know myself better, and respect myself more, as a human person with dignity, who makes a difference through encounter with others. Another person's view on a given (religious) question can only inspire me when I myself am committed to that question and begin to answer it. That is a point of departure. One has to start somewhere. Nobody can see and honor all perspectives at the same time. Without one's own spiritual view, it is even impossible for one to converse with another. It would not be worth the effort for nothing (new) would come out of it. So, in this approach the multi- and inter-dimensions are interrelated to the intra-dimension of religion. Encounter implies difference. Without difference there can be no encounter. So, one could argue that the intra-religious dimension is re-incorporated in this approach to inter-religious learning (Halsall & Roebben 2006; Roebben 2007, 156-160).

Inter-spiritual dialogue teaches people modesty and fortitude where the other is radically different and they can learn from them. For a truthful presence in this learning process, I need to be secure and honorable in encountering the other, in the hope and trust that the other will be secure as well. Learning through encounter is not easy. It requires time and energy to learn, recognize and respect other's views while not losing oneself in the euphoria of universal brotherhood (*'alle Menschen werden Brüder'*). On the other hand it implies a fundamental willingness to let the other be a unique and authentic self, and to respect their point of view, trusting that the other will be willing to express their own opinions. It requires a leap into the unknown, a hope for a willingness of communication with the other, a hope that can only be verified through an actual involvement conversation. In this conversation one does not wait for the other but has the courage to start it oneself. It is this mutual vulnerability that has urged Mary C. Boys to speak of a *hermeneutic of affections*, a willingness to lend one's ear, not so much to the opinions of the other, but to the inspiration (the 'spirit') that the other demonstrates by talking about their point of view (Boys 1997a, 353). It generates space for mutual acknowledgment, for admiration and respect for the unique way in which fellow human beings, each in their own manner, hear, experience, and fulfill the religious call without feeling obliged to take on or annul the authenticity of the other.

By way of summary we can say that this 'new' approach to the 'old' inter-religious learning can be schematized as follows. Inter-religious in the 'old' sense of the word relates to the middle column. Inter-religious learning in the broad 'new' sense of the word, as 'learning in the presence of the other' expands over the three columns.

| Learning *about* religion | Learning *from* religion | Learning *in/through* religion |
|---|---|---|
| *Multi*-religious learning | *Inter*-religious learning | *Intra*-religious learning |
| Knowing the other | Respecting the other | Re-*defining* and re-*dignifying* myself |
| Information through documentation | Interpretation through communication | Confrontation through encounter |
| Heuristic competence | Social competence | Existential competence |
| Teacher provides information as *expert* | Teacher manages the communication as *moderator* | Teacher confronts with lived religion as *witness* |

## Conclusion

Will education succeed in overstepping the contemporary accent on one's own ego? Will the other truly come into my life and touch it, no longer in function of my own ego and formation of my own narrative identity, but in the figure of the radical other, who gives me food for thought, who leads me away from old certainties and foreknowledge, and who refreshes me with new, 'bestowed' identity? In this chapter I have pleaded for an inter-spiritual learning process through 'learning by encounter' or 'learning in difference'. In this learning process there is room for impeding elements (conflict, disharmony, holy envy) as well as elements that are beyond didactical command. Is this learning of the 'practices of dispossession', this 'learning in dedication', possible and doable? (Geerinck 2004). Is there mental space for it in our high-tech educational systems? Is there enough creativity to implement a teaching of learning in difference? These are some key questions that RE must address.

# Chapter 8

# Modern Narrative Identities and the Bible
# A Subversive Concept of Religious Education

In this chapter I take the line that the term 'not anymore' (as for example in the sentence "Young people cannot be approached in a religious way anymore") is detrimental to education in general and religious education in particular. It is rooted in the melancholy of the educator and not in the resilience of the child. From an adult perspective it describes the deficiencies of today's children compared to those of the past, instead of creating latitude for a new way of dealing with the present and future culture. It resembles the idea of "Just wait until you're older", in the hands of adults who have given up all hope of a better world themselves. Young people are entitled to a better world: when the drive to contribute to this dies down, education becomes worthless and useless.

Not so long ago individual building-schemes in a person's life were drafted beforehand. Most of the lay-out had already been determined before someone started his adult life. Nowadays the plans are drawn up after the facts. Older people tend to feel insecure with such 'balancing identities'; but the young feel like fish in the water. Cell phones and chat-boxes on the Internet are their favorite media to undertake action, to develop patterns and ways of thinking on the move – in and through the interaction with peers, without building-schemes, purely for the pleasure of exchange. Action to them is inter-action, dynamics and involvement. Is this better than before or worse? In any case, it is different (see Chapter 3). It is obvious that learning in this context is completely different from what it used to be. Nowadays children determine to a large degree their own learning agenda. What is exciting is that the adults themselves wanted them in this context (by birth and education) and are therefore fully responsible (see Chapter 1 and 2).

This is also the case for religious education (RE). In this subject young people get a chance to become morally and religiously sensitive to themes that concern them unconditionally, personally and socially. The times of achieving this by means of school catechesis, as initiation in Christian faith, are long-gone. But what is the future of RE? We live in complex times and RE is not the solution to all problems. So far as (young) people are occupied with existential questions at all, it is at their own initiative. The *novum* of our times however is a first generation of young adults, who have not been religiously socialized in their home environment and still have to deal with important questions of life. Their religious knowledge and language is minimal or non-existent, so is their contact with religious communities. The tensions in school mount when one thinks of the people of foreign cultures who often know and dare to bring up their religious origins a lot more convinced than indigenous people. Low profile and high profile at the religious level often collide in the concrete classroom. For some this inarticulateness makes it impossible even to ask existential questions at all. And if it presents itself, sometimes in a harsh way at the decease of a classmate for example, many young people are speechless and frightened. In addition to this, traditional religious institutions are in a state of crisis: they are mostly unable to address people on their religious homelessness (Roebben 2001c, 247-250). They often show, however paradoxically, "an unwholesome disinterest in our souls", argues the Jewish philosopher of education Hanan Alexander (2001, 6). There is a social stratum to look for and find new answers, or better still, ask the questions anew. There are, however, few beacons to orient this process. Education as the 'holy ground' on which educators can stand for the guidance of children is no longer founded in solid answers, but it is crumbling and untrustworthy and continually in motion like a swamp (Roebben 2003). One can try to escape this situation in an attitude of fundamentalism or relativism. Both, however, are a source of cynicism and completely counterproductive to education. The alternative is complex. In this chapter, I advocate for listening more carefully to young people. Leading them implies learning from them. Whoever wants to speak with authority has to listen to the voices of those he is addressing. This paradox is pre-eminently present in our times. Young people want adults to take notice of them and not pass them by indifferently. This does not mean just sheepishly following their lead or wanting to blend into their world without a ripple. Nowadays education and schooling imply that adults account for what they do and say. And this presumes that they have heard the claims of young people, these 'modern narrative identities', with interest (of the Latin *inter-esse*, what is in-between).

The outline is as follows. I will start out with a description of modern RE in school as contribution to the religious self-clarification-in-communication of young people, a perspective that is common sense in contemporary RE curricula (par. 1). Subsequently, I point out the necessity of narratives for identity-building in a post-modern society and the position of Bible narratives in this process (par. 2). The crucial question, however, remains: why does one stick with Bible narratives in modern RE? Many other beautiful and inspiring texts are available, from profane and other religious traditions. What is the surplus of this curricular option and how can it be theologically thematized and founded? (par. 3). Finally, I develop some educational lines and make a plea for a subversive RE (par. 4). I will start out and I finish with a component of pedagogy of religion. The second part belongs to a general theory of education, the third to theology.

## 1. RE as religious self-clarification-in-communication

Most of the educationalists of religion agree about the objectives of RE in school. The general goal of main stream RE is the emergence of 'religious literacy': religious self-clarification-in-communication. In a plural society, RE can no longer be considered from a catechetic viewpoint. After all, explicit initiation in a particular religion requires a community of believers, a function which the modern school as a learning institution cannot fulfill. On the other hand, a model of pure adaptation to secularized culture falls short as well: after all, RE qualitatively differs from ethics or social competence training. The issue requires another approach. RE should lead to religious competence, to a critical and informed awareness of the moral and religious issues of life in the individual and collective realm. In a plural and often religiously indifferent or dogmatic culture, young people are entitled to receive sound information and guidance concerning these questions of life. Therefore a hermeneutic-communicative model is most fitting in this learning context (see Chapter 5 § 4).

Present-day RE has an important function in educating young people. It helps them to keep their attention alive for what transcends (socially, morally and religiously) that which is routinely taken for granted in (youth) cultures. It makes them also critically aware of certain destructive forms of social, moral and religious behavior and thought in the same (youth) cultures (Mette 1994a, 206-214). RE calls for attention for the in-depth dimension of life on the one hand, but warns against hasty transcendent conclusions attached to immanent perceptions on the other hand. In that sense RE is 'Sachwalterin des Allgemeinen' (Mette 1994b, 463) and radically fulfils a 'social-hygienic function' (Bitter 1998).

## 2. Telling stories in order to survive

No one can survive without an internal familiarity with a story that gives a sense of meaning to life. After the Enlightenment, modern human beings had the liberty to choose the story with which to write up their own life. Nowadays, people are in a state of narrative forgetfulness and embarrassment. The master stories have evaporated. If you are not able to become your own story, you are no longer noticed nowadays, you are trampled down by the latest 'master story' of the market place. It is a bitter necessity to have a story at all. Ontological despair arises when nothing has been named yet and people are at the mercy of the powerful language of the market place. Especially young people are heavily burdened in this respect (Roebben 1997; 2002b). Young people have a right to stories that testify to the human struggle with life's major questions and to the tentative and vulnerable nature of the answers. This is a central experience in education: young people ask for breathing-space, room to get a feel for the stories, always provisionally and in consultation with others, but fundamentally. They want to be included and not reduced to the perceptible bits and pieces. People want to be of one piece. Although present-day education is aware of the fact that the ancient master stories do not work anymore, it nevertheless still engages itself at the same time in a vulnerable reconstruction and enactment of master stories (Alexander 2001, 207-208).

While reconstructing one cannot draw on complete stories imprinted and passed on by religious socialization during childhood, since these are absent. The theory of the didactics of correlation of the 1970s and 1980s in its form of seamless connection between faith and life is definitely "am Ausgang ihrer Epoche" (Englert 1993). It is useless to educationally employ chunks of theological content in order to link faith and life. Young people prefer to personally assimilate the religious praxis and viewpoints that they encounter in their life's project. They surf the see of (cultural, social and religious) meaning and are continually designing their own "native language" as a permanent neo-logy. The direction has been reversed: the initiative now starts with the young, where the learning process as well as the religious consciousness is concerned. In that sense the time-honored theory of the didactics of correlation (as an educational theory, specifically to "learn to make correlations understood as to learn to as questions", Feifel 1995, 100) is revitalized and expanded by young people themselves. The relationship experience-revelation is a theoretical, theological-epistemological possibility. That this is no longer plausible in a post-modern climate, does not mean that the correlation principle in religious learning and learning in general has been overtaken, according to Friedrich Schweitzer (1999, 205-207): "Entwicklung von Deutungsfähigkeit is didaktisch nur denkbar in der dynamischen Spannung zwischen jeweils vorhandenen und neu angebotenen Deutungen" (206) (see also Roebben 2001c, 263-265). Young people absorb substantial elements of religions for the use of their own patchwork identity.

The Christian-religious heritage is subject to this semantic experiment as well (Prokopf and Ziebertz 2000). Young people do annex with irreverence (at least from a traditional point of view) religious meaning in order to construct their way of life. Therefore, the thesis of disconnection ("Entkoppelungsthese") between subjective religiosity and objective religious content is at least open to question (Bucher 1999). Young people weave a new text from ancient religious texts. This is a kind of pre-reflective experience. According to some scholars, RE takes than the role of "interpretive substitution" by fellow learners and by the teacher (Ziebertz, Heil and Prokopf 2001), since young people frequently do not know for which functional basic experience religion has the substantial answer. They often do not recognize the substantial religious elements that are employed in popular culture among others to interpret these basic experiences. They have the experience (that is the starting-point); but they lack the tools to determine on which ground rule (maior – substance) this experience is based and to which concrete question of experience (minor – function) it refers.

The modern school is guiding young people in the moral and religious dimensions of a modernizing society. It provides clarification of the loose moral and religious language games that young people design by introducing narrative elements of "Tradition, Konfession und Institution" (Englert 1998) in the learning process as semantic sub-stance. These elements function as a 'mental detour' (Paul Ricoeur) to achieve a reconfiguration, a re-imagination (Streib 1998) or reconstruction of the personal life story (van Knippenberg 2002). It is not given to anyone to view the meaning of life directly and this cannot be mediated either. A purely descriptive analysis of possible perspectives of meaning is experienced as insufficient. A mental detour, however, belongs to the category of thought-experiments: it challenges young people to review their own story from the dimension of the not-factually-present, from the possibility of "it might just as easily be different". This confrontation is always astonishing ("I have never looked at it that way"), but never alienating. In this model the advance knowledge of young people is not disposed of, but reconstructed from the perspective of the other or the stranger (Roebben 2001c, 265-267, see also Chapter 5).

The semantics of biblical tradition fit in well with this narrative concept, perhaps better than the confessional and institutional language games – because the latter are too formal and too less creative. The Bible is able to provide stories, images and metaphors to feed and/or strengthen the individual narrative identity. In the encounter and interaction between the listener, the "Hör- und Solidargemeinschaft" (Berg 1991, 146) and the text of the biblical tradition, educational meaning can emerge. The input of biblical tradition is not considered here in terms of the objectivity of the tradition (if this exists at all), but from the factual and personally appropriated interpretation of tradition by the listener in his interpretation community. At times the Bible confirms the personal story, at times it proposes a counter-world. Always, however, it offers a confrontation, the fundamental possibility of correlation, of being challenged. This identity building force of biblical learning is linked with the anthropological dimension of learning: it can be made recognizable to students because it is humanity-confirming (what I experience is taken seriously), because it is practically rational (what I learn can serve me in my concrete life project) and ideology-critical (I rewrite my own life story as a personal answer to the great hegemonic narratives of the market place).

There is much Bible-weariness amongst students and a confrontation is often avoided, in spite of the fact that it is a curricular requirement. At the same time, however, this situation of ignorance and distance can be a challenge to renew this exciting relationship, in the first place from a pedagogical, correlation-stimulating viewpoint (Schobert 2002). Biblical RE attempts to 'pioneer' ("anbahnen") this encounter (Ott 1995, 302-304; Feininger 2000-2001, 151). The German Bible educationalist Ingo Baldermann holds the view that well-considered biblical RE can contribute to moral and religious emancipation and strengthening of identity. The Bible offers an "Alphabetisierung der Hoffnung" (Baldermann 1996, 15-23): amongst humanly-recognizable experiences of contrast, the Bible expresses perspective of hope and promise to modern young people, a perspective that exceeds boundaries. This at least: 'What I have been thinking so far is not all that stupid after all. There have been predecessors – fellow human beings who have also entertained this type of 'healthy ruminations'. It's reasonable to believe, after all.'

## 3. Bible narratives: dangerous in the hands of young people?

Bible narratives and themes are eminently present in the newest curricula, as well in the Netherlands as in Flanders and Germany. Also in the concrete forms of the new textbooks the ancient exemplary Bible narratives are emerging again. What is their value in a renewed concept of RE? Which shift of meaning takes place when Bible narratives become associated with the formation of religious identity and literacy of young people, instead of with initiation in a particular religious tradition (such as the former catechetic-kerugmatic model of RE)? Granted, these stories possess a high degree of 'existential caressability', and they are a perfect illustration of the complex questions of young people today; in the sense of: "See? What you are going through now, people have gone through centuries ago in biblical times as well. Your experiences are illustrations of biblical experiences and vice versa". In that case, however, tradition and contemporary context merge, they overlap. Biblical semantics are domesticated and pacified with an eye to a 'smooth' process of RE. The final justification of the use of Bible narratives then boils down to the fact that the subject is offered in a Roman-Catholic or Protestant-Christian school and in a country with a (still predominantly) Christian heritage. Is this the final and only reason why it is appropriate that Bible narratives are told and explained in these schools every now and then? Is that a sufficient reason?

Criticism is passed onto the idea of functionalization of religion and biblical semantics – religion in view of the personal organization of the good life. The German systematic theologian Thomas Ruster holds the view that modern individualized religion and Christianity are so tightly interwoven that the latter has merged with the former (2000). The God of both systems has become interchangeable and therefore meaningless. The critical, prophetic shape of the biblical God, who leads people from (religiously) oppressive situations, has lost its impact. In times of 'God-forsaken religious entertainment' ('Gottvergessene Religionsfreudigkeit') (Grümme 2002), modern people worship modern idols, according to Ruster, and these only functionally contribute towards making life livable, towards contingency-control ('Kontingenzbewältigung'). Our modern, autonomous religious experience, according to Ruster, has become completely incompatible with the heteronymous language and religious reality of the Bible; therefore, we are not to trust our own experience anymore. The Bible has lost its subversive power and has been degraded to a purely cultural-historical contribution. The Bible is no longer a dangerous book (Pelletier 2002).

Assuming that religious socialization of the new generation is absent and that children are trying to give meaning to their lives in a subjective and syncretistic manner, resulting intentionally or otherwise in a functional approach towards religion ("religious awareness is something that you have to assemble yourself from loose fragments of meaning"), Bible narratives are employed in RE from a cognitive outside perspective. In addition to other examples of successful life the teacher shows how biblical characters from their particular religious background can be of assistance in the identity-building of young people today. Those are the goals of present-day RE in a Christian school (see paragraph 1).

The absence of an internal perspective that is structural and religiously socialized (by the home and the congregation) does not necessarily imply that children only extract external style-features for their own contingency-control from the cognitive learning process with Bible narratives (paragraph 2). Could it be that they get more from such a learning process? Not because the teacher or the official Church secretly hopes so in view of the continuation of the Christian tradition, but because young people themselves decide to do so, since it radically and subversively instills in them new layers of humanity? Could it be that through the functional nature of RE they manage to break into more substantial elements that we no longer think possible? In other words: if one invites young people from the inside of a particular (i.e. biblical) story to go through the religious experience behind the story, is this a purely catechetical pursuit – in the sense of 'invitation to a profession of faith'? Catechesis presumes pre-catechesis, and that is absent in this case. Moreover, young people will protest when they get the feeling that they are being indoctrinated against their own will. In other words, can contemporary RE, beyond objective-technical explanation and subjective-esthetical elucidation, open up the religious-hermeneutic meaning of a Bible text without fear of becoming catechetic (since this is beside the point, because catechesis presumes pre-catechesis)? This opening reveals the place where the question is posed about the 'eternally fertile breach' – between who I am and who I will be, between who I am and who the Creator intended me to be? (Ganzevoort 1998). Can RE open up this longing or not?

What is characteristic of this religious-hermeneutic experience of opening up? It can not be considered from a theological model in which revelation or tradition simply and heteronomously precede our humanity. In that sense Ruster's model falls short: after all, in his analysis nobody other than the radical insider is able to understand the radical, heteronomous interpellation force of the Bible. In this respect it would be of no use to communicate the Bible in any way to anyone, because a fundamental understanding has become impossible, since all autonomous human experience has been corrupted and is closed on principle to the complete Otherness of the Bible (Grümme 2002, 19-23). A new post-modern understanding of revelation and tradition is called for, that agrees with the Rahnerian transcendental openness of human experience, without relapsing into the old fault of trying to restore the plausibility of theology by means of correlative experiences.

A possible new avenue for interpretation is the following: the normativity of the Scripture lies in the future (Bieringer 1997). The Bible is not an objective observation-post from the past from which the religious experiences of today should be assessed. The Bible needs to 'be done' in the future. In agreement with the American Bible theologian Sandra Schneiders, Bieringer speaks of "a world projected by the biblical text" (Bieringer 1997, 65) and the desire "to allow ourselves to be transformed according to the coordinates of the world of the text" (66). The Bible has been revealed in the sense that a new content was revealed, but first and foremost in the sense that this content was revealed in a certain way, namely anchored in human experiences of salvation and calamity. "The Bible is revealing itself with respect to the world, to all of reality, including my existence and my history. Revelation is the feature of the biblical world." (66, after Ricoeur). Other descriptions of this view on revelation can be found, notably as 'orthopraxis' (Schillebeeckx 1977), 'submerging in reality to receive oneself from reality' (Borgman 2002), 'learning to learn' (Segundo, quoted in Borgman 1994, 29-39), permanent learning as 'Umlernen' (Koerrenz 1997, 237) – in short, living life from the possibility that everything can become permanently different. According to Koerrenz (1997), this is the central anthropological dynamic of biblical tradition: reading the Bible with an eye to one's own life story, is learning to learn. Nothing is immediately given, not even the biblical narrative. The human being is principally a learning being ('Lernwesen') and therefore must engage itself with reality and with its present interpretation schemes. This observation is especially valid in a modern society which is experienced in constant contingency and complexity. When biblical revelation is interpreted from this permanent "qualitative change of perception of reality and of interaction of people with each other" (Mette 1994a, 233, after Helmut Peukert) the theory of the didactics of correlation receives a new impulse. Biblical learning then stands in mutually-critical correlation to optimal human learning: it repeatedly breaks open the existing from the assumption that every 'already' refers to an eschatological 'not yet' (Grümme 2002, 26-29; Bitter 1996).

It is precisely from this perspective that new ways of dealing with the concept of identity-building are explored in RE. Norbert Mette argues that RE in school should go beyond a formal approach to world views ('Lebensgestaltung, Ethik und Religion'), beyond moral education ('Ethikunterricht') and comparative religious studies ('Religionskunde'). RE has to show that there is a God who liberates people from rigidity and isolation, so that they are able to follow new paths. RE is about this 'ability', according to Mette: an 'identity-from-gratuity', a possibility of being-human that is not separate from the present one (recognizable), but that exceeds it at the same time (anticipatory) (Mette 2002). Friedrich Schweitzer (1998, 207-209) holds the view that RE should offer the opportunity to young people to overcome a vague and enslaving deism and spiritism and achieve a liberating religious perspective. He advocates against a RE that allows young people to functionally fiddle with their identity themselves. RE should be about the perspective of God: how people in their vulnerability are perceived by God as coherence and continuity. Schweitzer quotes here Ingo Dalferth: "Nicht die Lebenserfahrung macht den Glauben eindeutig, sondern der Glaube lehrt, die Lebenserfahrung in ihrer Vieldeutigkeit zo durchschauen und unter den Bedingungen dieser Vieldeutigkeit dennoch eindeutig zo leben" (1998, 208). In connection with this, some people speak of the radical experience of alteriority, not as an objective compendium of truths that we can either take or leave, but as an experience of 'received humanity': my identity is dependent from how it is intended by others.

Could it be that this so fervently pursued personal appropriation (as 'Aneignung') of the religious in RE has not come about yet, because we are still organizing RE in terms of authoritative mediation from tradition towards students (as 'Vermittlung')? In modern RE the learning process has been handed over 'a little' to students already, but the experiences are still streamlined from a (often unspoken) Christian-religious viewpoint. We still do not dare to trust students with the subversive power of another perspective on life that is offered by faith; a perspective that young people are able to find themselves from their own experiences of salvation and calamity. Do we truly think them capable of being 'capacitas infiniti'? Or do we bore them with a school-like type of RE, because we view them as school-individuals who are only able to take in cognitive models for identity-building, and not as human beings with their own existential longing and resilience, with their own soul? Are they truly allowed to experience in their own particular story, and to raise the sort of ambivalent questions to which religious people and communities, including the Biblical ones, have been giving their answers – and this from an inside perspective (see the 'Biblos Project' of Terence Copley in Exeter)?

## 4. Implications for religious education

Let me give an example: telling the story of the vocation of Moses in the RE course, could this possibly open up the dialogical space for the work of interpretation on modern identity? Could this be helpful for imminent juvenile questions such as: 'What is the sort of life that I am looking for? How deep is my commitment? How far do I want to go? On what kind of holy ground do I stand?' For a Christian believer the narrative of the vocation of Moses (Exodus 3) ties in with the deepest layers of a person, with his or her soul (van Knippenberg 2002). In the announcement of his name ("I will be there for you") God gives the guarantee to Moses that he may become who he is ("liberator of his people"). Motion and emotion, involvement and support, go hand in hand. God and the human person go together: God saw the suffering of his people and the man Moses moved. A person feels a call and God guarantees that it is meaningful to respond. The conclusive force of biblical narrativity lies in the future. It is the type of knowledge that is achieved by beginning to move. Could RE be thought of in such a way, that it challenges young people to evaluate this perspective from within, without being forced of becoming a 'full' Christian believer or church member?

According to the German Bible educationalist Ingo Baldermann no mediation is needed in the appropriation process in RE. The Bible does not need a hermeneutic method of actualization ("Vergegenwärtigung"). The Bible is, as Luther argued, its own interpreter and focused on direct dialogue, since its inner-structure is nothing other than a continuous dialogical learning process (Feininger 2000-2001, 152). The pluriformity of voices and visions in the Bible spontaneously stimulate the learning subject to reorient. I seriously doubt that. In my opinion, the process of clearing the way ("Anbahnungsprozess") or of appropriating ("Aneignungsmodus") biblical narrativity for RE is of a much more complex nature. Instead of this subjective and direct commensurability, the Bible is more like a complex of mutually exclusive language games and fundamental convictions (in German: "zentrale Grundbescheide", "kerygmatische Aschen", "heilsgeschichtliche Abbreviaturen", see Berg 1991, 145 and Feininger 2000-2001, 152-153), that have to be explained and examined in the course of the learning process, and should be confronted with the equally great pluriformity of contemporary life questions. From this point of view the learning subject is expected to make decisions: 'Which basic line of the Bible do I want to follow? To which life question do I want to learn the answer?' After all, interaction with the Bible is interested in the future of the learning subject: What type of assistance is needed and what can be offered by the Bible in order to keep together and endure the diversity of life? (Ott 1995, 302). Therefore, the co-

construction of the answer to life questions and the better understanding of one's own quest for meaning are the two poles of the one dialectical learning process. Then occurs tradition, 'living' tradition: the ongoing process of *Resubjektivierung objektivierter Erfahrung* (the re-subjectivation of objectivated experiences) (Fend, quoted in Fraas 1989, 23), a constant process of re-plausibilisation of tradition's most fundamental visions and practices in new cultural and societal contexts.

Interacting with biblical narrativity is a "work of retrieval" (Alexander 2001, 12) and is never separate from an interpretation community, where the learning subject is challenged to take position through discussions with fellow human beings. In such a learning community identity-from-gratuity is never available in isolation, but assumes consultation and discussion. 'The experience of identity is never unconditionally true because it was announced in the Bible, but it is in the Bible because it is true' (Burggraeve 1991), this means that it can be recognized on anthropological grounds, that it can be discussed and that it can be realized in concrete individual and shared life experiences.

In this line of interpretation, biblical RE can contribute in the generation and/or clarification of *key experiences* (Schweitzer 1998): depth-experiences that are activated by the 'mental detour' of biblical *key stories*. In RE students have to actively carry out this correlation, it does not just happen to them. Through this process of clearing the way ("Anbahnungsprozess") initiated by the Bible narrative, fundamental insights emerge in which students have to choose on the basis of questions such as: 'To which crucial line in my biography do I want to find a religious-hermeneutic answer?' This interpretation process takes into account the stage of religious development of students and their ability to comprehend elementary contents ("Elementarisierung") (because not all biblical themes are suitable for all ages/groups) (Schweitzer 1998, 206-207). It checks moreover whether sufficient potential for change is present in a group to be set in motion.

This learning process has a subversive character: people change on account of the new transparency of their experiences. They decide to change perspectives and live according to the newly-found insight. The key experiences of biblical times, in the way they are founded and congealed in the key stories, are helpful to look alternatively to oneself and to discover new breathing space. For instance, the struggle of Job with his suffering and with God who is ultimately committed to him, is a key story to re-evaluate one's own experience of suffering and of powerlessness towards pain and calamity. The Psalms are helpful tools in re-enacting situations of distress, fear, hope and joy. As a listener of the narrative one can decide to believe it or not – but one is challenged to take a stance, anyhow. The key story provokes the reader to take the key experience seriously. Such experiences could be: exodus, time and eschaton, identity-in-gratuity, and/or discipleship (Schweitzer 1999, 209). I would add: creation, liberation, vocation, sin, new courage, and/or thirst for eternal life. Schweitzer is in favor of a more systematic reorganization of RE in line with such biblical key experiences/stories. Ingo Schobert (2002) argues that RE should always use this kind of educational approach: by using fragments of hope to re-imagine experimentally the personal quest for human flourishing. One has little to loose in RE by telling Bible narratives. These stories are no longer 'master stories'. RE teachers should not be scared to tell them at all, because other hegemonic stories have been taken their place. Surprising young people by telling them, is the biggest challenge for RE.

**Conclusion**

There are many questions remaining for further research and discussion. Which choices should be made in defining the key experiences/stories in curriculum development? Do we have a theological framework for this process? Where does the organizational energy come from: from theologians, educationalists, curriculum or handbook developers, teachers, and/or students themselves? Can we think of a new systematic theology that is able to 'de-congeal' or 'liquefy' (Roebben 2007, 121-140 and 169-171) the key experiences of biblical key stories as a platform for RE? Is there a systematic theology available that is able to rethink religious experience from the learning route of young people? Is the modern school a good environment for a subversive model of RE – or does it adopt its own rationality which excludes this kind of RE? Are young people still able to learn aesthetics and literature, in order to understand narrativity? And what about the spiritual resilience of teachers: will they be able to remain open for the ongoing process of tradition as 're-subjectivation'? And finally: are there any 'correlational communities' left in which a healthy connection between key stories and key experiences is alive and kicking?

# Chapter 9

# Between Professionalism and Spirituality
# The Education of Teachers in Religion

The preparation of future teachers in religion in general and in Roman-Catholic religion in particular is a complex and multifaceted issue. Or, the one and same person of the young adult preparing for a future position in religious education (RE) has to deal with the question of religious complexity and diversity in himself and in the educational setting of the school. Many streams of influence and expectations – input and output – are coming together. He is expected to become a good teacher with solid knowledge and teaching skills, an active participant in a school with its own culture and organization, a theological professional and a witness to the Roman-Catholic faith tradition. How does this complex cluster of competences and expectations relate to the personal religious identity of the future teacher? How does this situation affect theological education within a teacher education department at universities and institutions of higher education? And finally how can the official church support and empower its future teachers in their difficult job between professionalism and spirituality? These questions relate to the unsolved problem or, stated more positively, to the ongoing dialectic between the Christian faith tradition and the contemporary cultural debate. Young people may not become the victims of this lack of clarity. Hopefully they can become the future engineers of their own theological education and teacher education in religion. Are churches and theological institutions really prepared to listen to them?

In this chapter I will argument in four steps: firstly I will explore the canonical space in which the so called 'requisite suitability' of the lay teacher of Roman-Catholic RE is defined. Then I describe briefly the concrete religious-educational context in the last thirty years in Germany and Flanders and the interesting contextualized position of the bishops therein. The third paragraph refers to the contemporary situation of RE and the theological education of future teachers. I conclude with five statements in which the future of RE teacher education within the Roman-Catholic church is crystallized, both in a visionary and realistic way. What I mainly try to do is to 'think back' from the position of the RE teacher to RE teacher education and than again back to the undergraduate theological education of future RE teachers. The flow between these three is not going very smoothly. My argument is to clarify the need for more practical-theological sensibility, between church and school at the one hand and between theological education and the daily work of the RE teacher at school at the other hand.

## 1. Mandate and competences of the RE teacher

*"If the prescripts regarding the requisite suitability have been observed, they [= lay people, BR] are also qualified to receive from legitimate ecclesiastical authority a mandate to teach the sacred sciences" (Canon 229 § 3)*

In this canon of the 'Codex Iuris Canonici' of the Roman-Catholic church the rights and duties of lay people are defined, when they teach the sacred sciences. Some aspects need further clarification and this can be partly provided on the basis of information from other canons. Firstly, there is the concept of the 'mandate to teach': who is regarded suitable according to the prescripts of the church, can receive a teaching position within the wider proclamation task of the church (Riedel-Spangenberger, 2004). He is not acting in his own name, but in the name of the church. He should love the church, be devoted to her and be careful not to provoke or scandalize her. The one who teaches should opt for a loyal position which is critical and constructive at the same time.

What is meant by 'the requisite suitability' of the RE teacher? The canon remains unclear. Reading further in the Codex however, more specifically in Book III on the proclamation task of the church in the field of education, one comes across this regulation: "The local ordinary is to be concerned that those who are designated teachers of religious instruction in schools, even in non-Catholic ones, are outstanding in correct doctrine, the witness of a Christian life, and teaching skill" (Canon 804 §2). In Latin the wording is: "magistri recta doctrina, vitae christianae testimonio atque arte paedagogica." The combination of these three elements gives an idea of what is meant with requisite suitability. He who teaches future generations needs to be an authentic person who again is deeply devoted to the teaching and life of the church and who is able to transmit this knowledge to children and young people. The accumulated knowledge to be transferred relates to the so called 'sacred sciences'. What are these and is there a relationship between the teaching of these sciences in the academia and in regular RE at (the primary and secondary) school? The Codex remains silent about this relationship, but one could aptly presuppose that both teaching circles deal with the same content. The teacher at school has to organize his teaching formally according to the sacred sciences in theology and has to order his contents from this resource. In Canon 253 §2 the 'scientiae sacrae' are enumerated as follows: sacred scripture, dogmatic theology, moral theology, liturgy, philosophy, canon law and church history. Pastoral theology, practical theology and/or religious educational theory are not mentioned in this list! They could possibly be implied in the second part of the same paragraph: "(…) other disciplines which must be taught according to their proper methodology", but then their methodology would not be considered to be theological!

This is precisely my point. How a certain element of the tradition can be made transparent in a specific time and place, how a vivid connection can be installed between the lived faith in church and society at the one hand and the study in sacred science at the other hand, is more than just the application of a didactical tool. The practical-theological connection between theology and the life world of a specific generation is in the Codex apparently not a form of sacred science. However, 'reading the signs of the times in the light of the gospel' is an integral part of work of the church and her believers. It is strange that this practical-theological sensibility, one of the crucial elements of Vatican II (Sander 2005), is not mentioned in this list, and *mutatis mutandis*, not mentioned in the list of 'prescripts regarding the requisite suitability' of the RE teacher. With just some extra 'ars pedagogica' or teaching skills (cfr. Canon 804 § 2) the existing gap between tradition and contemporary experience, between theology and daily life, will not be bridged. With some extra help from the local bishop, who has to provide for initial (Canon 229 § 2) and post-initial education and for spiritual support and counseling, neither. It is my contention that the fruits of Vatican II have not been realized fully in this respect, that a lay theological reading of the signs of the times in the light of the gospel is still open for debate and interpretation, and that this is one of the reasons why RE is going through many trials nowadays. In paragraph three I will interpret this situation from a culture-theological perspective.

## 2. RE and the position of the teacher in Germany and Flanders

*"The Catholic religious instruction and education which are imparted in any schools whatsoever or are provided through the various instruments of social communication are subject to the authority of the Church. It is for the conference of bishops to issue general norms about this field of action and for the diocesan bishop to regulate and watch over it" (Canon 804 § 1)*

In order that the local bishop is able to regulate and control the work and the orthodoxy and orthopraxy of his teachers, general rules have to be issued on the level of the bishops conference, which define the aim, content and meaning of RE in the local context. More specifically the central question should be how the local RE can be included appropriately into the general educational mission of the school as a whole. In Flanders the subject of RE ('Rooms-katholieke godsdienst') is a compulsory course in the private Catholic schools (attended by 70% of the pupils) and is an elective course in public schools. In Germany RE is a confessional course, offered by the Roman-catholic or Protestant church, within the curriculum of public schools. Pupils can opt out and choose an ethics course. In Germany there are only a few religious affiliated schools, in which it is evident that RE (Roman-catholic or Protestant) is a compulsory course.

What are the goals for RE at school, to what extent do the bishops want children and young people become acquainted with Christian faith and what are the appropriate competences for teachers? As an example I will present the German and the Flemish situation. In 1974 the Würzburger Synod of the German bishops promulgated the text 'Der Religionsunterricht in der Schule' [RE at school, original text published in German in 1976], the starting point for the development of new curricula and handbooks in Germany. In 1996 the Flemish bishops presented their vision paper 'Het vak Rooms-Katholieke godsdienst in de scholen van Vlaanderen' [Roman-Catholic RE in Flemish schools (*Visietekst* 1996)], generating the same process in Flanders. With these two examples I hope to clarify the contextuality of aim, content and meaning of RE in two different locations and periods, and the fact that the bishops had/have to be flexible to respond to the real RE needs in the local community. It is evident that a specific sort of teacher is required to realize the expostulated model of RE.

## 2.1. Germany

In the seventies the aim, content and meaning of German RE are explicitly formulated in line with Vatican II. Children and young people should not be converted into Christians at school, but should have the opportunity to critically position them selves to a Christian-religious standpoint. The aim is no longer catechetical, as if young people should be prepared to confess their faith at the end of the day, but religious educational. RE enhances them to deepen and sharpen their own stance in faith. It could even the case that an atheist student will become a better atheist thanks to the RE course! Schematically the aims of RE in the German document can be framed as follows (Hilger, Leimgruber and Ziebertz 2001, 138, translation BR):

| General goal "RE should enable young people to think critically and to act responsibly in issues of religion and faith" | | | |
|---|---|---|---|
| Subgoals | | | |
| „RE stimulates and deepens the question of God, of the meaning of world and life, of values and norms, and it offers an answer to such questions based on the revelation and on the life of the church" | „RE familiarizes children and young people with the reality of faith and with the message of the gospel beyond it, and it helps to critically reflect this faith" | „RE enables people to express a personal standpoint in dialogue with other religions and belief systems, with world orientations and ideologies, and it fosters understanding and tolerance towards the position of others" | „RE motivates to a religious life style and to responsible action in church and society" |

This model is based on a set of important presuppositions concerning religious socialization. Children and young people learn to reflect on the faith that they received from home. They learn a specific language to make connections or correlations between that faith and daily life. Correlation theology is the pivotal point in this educational approach: there is a natural link between faith and reason, between revelation and experience. Correlation didactics is the 'school proof' form of this theology. People ask questions and Christian revelation and the life of the church provide the answers. Young people learn to position them selves in faith and can discuss this position in dialogue with others. This articulation or explication (with inclusion of the conscious position of an atheist) is important for responsible action and morality. Moreover, RE stimulates people to become tolerant and open for the positions of others.

It is evident that within this model of RE a specific claim is made to the 'requisite suitability' of the RE teacher (Englert 2007). Only the teacher who is able to move correlatively between question and answer or who can generate life issues and traditional answers and can connect them to each other, can be considered to be an apt teacher. Moreover he must be at home in the Christian tradition, live up to the ideal of it and show how to struggle with it. He must also be able to disclose the ideas of other traditions and convictions, although he is not a formal member of these. And finally, he must be able to facilitate communication between people and show in the mean time the courage of his own conviction. The 'requisite suitability' of the teacher, necessary for obtaining the mandate to teach at school, is now unfolded in a whole set of competences that give meaning to the elements "correct doctrine, the witness of a Christian life, and teaching skill" in Canon 804 §2. The suitable teacher is ready to bear witness to Christian faith, in word and behavior, he shows how to deal reasonably with this faith and how young people can be motivated to 'their' way of religious self-clarification, in confrontation with Christian faith. The teacher is so to say the living instrument of correlation theology. He is a living correlating model.

## 2.2. Flanders

The German model of the seventies, that by the way is still determining the Catholic-confessional RE in Germany, had a strong influence on religious education theory and curriculum development in Flanders. However, in 1996, twenty years after the German synod declaration, the situation has changed dramatically. Children no longer bring a religious background from home to the school. Just connecting with religious foreknowledge does not function anymore. Children not only lack the knowledge but also the experience in religious issues. There no longer is a living relationship with congregations. For the bishops this situation forms the starting point for a radical revision of curricula for RE.

In their vision text of 1996 the Flemish bishops recognize and valorize the new situation: the growing individualization, pluralization and detraditionalization of society have a strong impact on churches and congregations and therefore on RE. At school this field should be understood as a service to young people to critically evaluate their position to religion and faith in a plural society. Christian faith therefore is the criterion: in Roman-Catholic RE this option is presented to be the standard for personal faith development. Out of this a model for RE is developed for the typical context of the school, a model which is 'hermeneutic-communicative'. Young people are trained in the perception and interpretation of moral and religious phenomena in society, they learn to define their own stance (hermeneutic) and they learn to deepen, clarify and articulate their position with and in the presence of others (communicative) (Roebben 2001c, 257-261; Lombaerts & Pollefeyt 2004).

RE teachers are rendering this diaconal service in the name of the church. Therefore they received the mandate. The text of the bishops is clear: "RE teachers are Christians. They seek to be a teacher out of faith (…). This faith is lived up in connection with a congregation. Love for the church and critical loyalty include one another. Sometimes this faith will be like a search, faith against the background of doubt and unbelief. Especially then prayer, spiritual guidance and the support of the congregation are needed" (*Visietekst* 1996, translation

BR). RE teachers are not supposed to be super-Catholics, but should act as ordinary people who wrestle themselves with faith and therefore precisely are authentic leaders in faith communication.

In the curricula the Flemish Episcopal commission comes with the proposal to attribute a so called 'GSM' function to the teacher (referring to the common sense word for cell phone): in Flemish he is a 'getuige' (witness), a 'specialist' (expert) and a 'moderator' (facilitator). He is specialized in articulating live issues in culture and life world of young people, he is an outstanding communicator and knows how to involve young people into an enriching and tolerant debate. And finally he should be 'at home' in a religious tradition and bear witness to that tradition from inside. As already said, the Christian tradition is the preferential one in this dialogical learning process.

The "requisite suitability" of the RE teacher becomes more and more complex in the given circumstances. Several new RE competences are needed to cope with all the demands. The bishops have high expectancies of teachers: orthodoxy and orthopraxy, but more specifically high quality RE flexibility and professionalism to respond adequately to the new circumstances. The support from the bishops to the RE teacher has been augmented dramatically since the start of the new curricula: private consultancy and post-initial education have been provided by special advisers, teacher education departments implement the new curricula and the underlying concept to future teachers, the university is offering extra help and materials to relate to the moral and religious dimension of social and cultural issues in RE.

The crucial question however is what kind of spirituality is needed for this professionalism. When the future RE teacher cannot rely anymore on religious socialization in his audience and in his personal life experience, the question will be whether or not the religious language game and experience will be accessible as a tool for reflection in RE. How can children and young people be 'unblocked' for the deeper layer of reality in the way religious traditions do, when they do not have any clue of the key experience behind it? Which theology is needed for the complex religious educational 'handicraft' in a context of de-traditionalization of both pupils and teachers? With only a correct doctrine and witness of Christian life, drawn from an imaginary source of religious socialization, a source that is not present anymore, the task cannot be achieved. Neither will one arrive at the religious key experiences with only religious educational tips and tricks to apply pieces of the curriculum to the actual classroom. In the next paragraph I will present a short historical reconstruction – from the seventies till today – to better grasp the question at stake, namely how theological professionalism of RE teachers can be achieved in a context of religious 'believing without belonging'.

## 3. The preparation of RE teachers and theological education

In the eighties there is clearly a black hole in the succession of the correlation didactics. The correlation between experience and revelation through a lived praxis of faith, between question and answer in the life of the church, and the 'correlational' way this previously could be articulated in the classroom, is not evident anymore. In the eighties the educational principle of 'asking questions' (as the radical philosophical background of the correlation theology) is still standing in the classroom, but the undisputable and preferably exclusive relationship with the Christian tradition as the framework for answering these questions, is not present anymore. In the eighties children and young people are invited to reframe their questions from a multitude of possible answers. Cultural studies is entering the field of RE. No longer the world of human experiences is 'used' to illustrate the human dimension of Christian revelation ("you see, the world of the Bible is not far away!"), but children and young people have to deal with questions such as: what kind of answers of religious people can you perceive in society and culture, and what are the sort of questions to which these people are responding with their doctrine (belief), behavior (morality), rituals (liturgy) and praxis (diacony)? What does religion do with human beings and what are human beings doing with religion? 'Learning *about* religion' and 'learning *from* religion', perception and interpretation of the religious phenomenon in a communicative setting are the main goals of RE. Central to the learning process is the hermeneutical work of discovering meaning for one's own life: can religion or belief be helpful in my identity building, can it stimulate my critical asking, perceiving and thinking? And, how can I use religion for myself to become a more flourishing human being? Functionalization of religion is then not far away.

As far as I am concerned this functional approach to religion and RE is neglecting an important dimension of what could be and sometimes actually is articulated in the classroom. Children and young people ask questions such as: "Why be religious at all? What is the reason for adopting a religious life style? What happens to me when I enter consciously a religious or spiritual tradition? What is this famous religious experience and how can I become part of it? And you, as a teacher, a child could ask, how does faith in God affect you? What is your relationship with God at all? Do you believe yourself, or is it just a set of observations that you offer us?" This happens when young people are confronted with the otherness of the neighbor sitting next to them and being a member of a completely other religious community, when children philosophize and ask pertinent questions or when students go deeper into a religious studies approach and ask for the existential meaning of the facts presented to them (see Chapter 5). In my opinion, out of a good hermeneutic-communicative RE process questions emerge about the deeper existential convictions of the persons involved in the learning process. Or every human being has his story to tell and has 'to live to tell' that story, that secret, in order to find clarity for him or herself.

The following schema visualizes the different learning processes of modern RE. Horizontally one can discern the different religious educational competences of the modern teacher. Vertically one can read in a gradually intensive way the challenges for theology. He who wants to teach should be aware of the need for a theological 'backpack'. One does not only need pedagogical and communicative skills, one also needs to relate in a personal manner to the question of faith, of revelation, of God playing his/her part in daily life. And one needs stories and images out of the Christian tradition to present this relationship imaginatively and reasonably to future generations.

| Intergenerational learning  *Learning in the depth of time* | Theological-*heuristic* competence – teacher as expert (S) | Challenge of the knowledge society (training perception and ability to disclose knowledge) | Information  *Learning about religion/belief* |
|---|---|---|---|
| Intercultural learning  *Learning in the breadth of space* | Theological-*communicative* competence – teacher as moderator (M) | Challenge of plurality and diversity (learning to exchange knowledge with a view on personal identity building) | Communication  *Learning from religion/belief* |
| Learning in the mode of globalization  *Learning in the distance of the future* | Theological-*existential* competence – teacher as witness (G) | Challenge of globalization (learning to qualify knowledge in solidarity with fellow human beings in the world community) | Confrontation  *Learning in or through religion/belief* |

Sacred science, as was mentioned above, should include practical-theological reflection of (future) professionals in the school. In connecting educational skills with the contents of theology studied in the undergraduate program, new theology can emerge. Without this lay theology and lay spirituality within the framework of professionalism, the two will remain separated: the theory of theology (esoteric) and the praxis of RE (down to earth). A creational theology that helps future teachers to discover the holy in the daily public field of RE is much more creative and attractive than a sterile theology disconnected from an even sterile mandate of the bishop. This Roman-Catholic lay theology is still under construction (see Chapter 12) and reminds us of a deeper problem in theology: the lack of practical-theological sensibility, the lack of a "practical culture-theology" (Roebben & Zondervan 2008) within theology as a whole.

Pete Ward, a well known scholar in youth ministry, tells the story about his own undergraduate theological education at Durham University in the UK. There was a huge problem of "dislocation between practice and academic theology that I had been introduced to in my undergraduate studies" (Ward 2008, 25). He quotes Edward Farley by saying that "theological education 'atomizes' subject areas and fragments theological unity. So theological education tends to socialize practitioners into the view that there is a problem in relating experience and theology" (22). And remarkably "the pastoral circle tends to reinforce the dislocation between reflection and the everyday. This is perhaps ironic because the method is trying to do the opposite. The problem is that it separates both the analysis of a pastoral situation and theological reflection as particular stages in the method" (35) and distinct both "worlds that in someway must be reconciled" (36). For him this rupture was unsolvable at that time. It was only later that be became aware of a possible solution: when one is working in the field of the proclamation of the gospel (e.g. as a youth minister or teacher in RE), one is "already participating in the expression and circulation of theology" (48). Theology is a way of living, vision and discernment. It is about critical thinking within an epistemological perspective of faith.

Therefore I would suggest that every course in undergraduate theological education should include a component of practical-theological sensibility training. Every human being reflecting on important life issues is a theologian. People share with each other the ability to theologize about their personal and communal lives. The vocation of every lay person in general and of every RE teacher in particular should be 'fides quaerens intellectum', faith in search of understanding. The difference between professional theologians and ordinary people who reflect on their faith, is only gradual, not essential. Even children are able to theologize, because they can raise questions and reflect about the possible answers. The theological expert should therefore radically be trained in the work that he will do with non-experts, namely 'learning *in or through* religion/belief' (see schema above). Religious traditions, also the Christian tradition, are open to and stimulate this reflective process. Traditions are permanently developing, are being lived and lived through, are permanently being reconstructed. RE should be 'semper transformanda', the church should be an 'ecclesia semper reformanda'. Adult theological education therefore also needs to be 'semper reformanda'. The culture of young adults, rooted in the experience of real and virtual cities, open for renewal and new horizons, is a radical challenge to modern theology, to regauge its knowledge, wisdom about and engagement with the Holy in daily life. Future RE teachers and lay ministers have the right to reflect on these experiences and to see how these are organically interwoven with their ministry and their vocation. More research on and praxis within intentional learning communities is urgently needed. Reflection on already existing methods and approaches could be a first step in the right direction (for research on youth ministry, see Roebben & Zondervan 2008; on other ecclesial ministries, see O'Brien 2007). Here lies a splendid future for adult theological education.

## 4. Five statements as a way of conclusion

4.1. The canon law of the Roman-Catholic church offers a solid juridical structure and playground to creatively fill in the mandate of the

RE teacher with the requisite suitability or competences necessary in always changing circumstances.

4.2. Logically there should not be any friction between the official church and her RE teachers. On the contrary, new religious educational competences of RE teachers are needed and are solicited for by the bishops to face new religious and educational contexts.

4.3. The mandate or mission of the teacher from the bishop is based on mutual trust, in critical loyalty to one another. The teacher too should be able to give feed-back to the bishop and tell him how young people struggle with faith, how they play with it and get away from it – how they live "with, against, for and without God" (Kohler-Spiegel 2007). This feed-back is of the utmost importance for the development of the 'sensus fidelium' in the church.

4.4. Young teachers ask for more theological reflection and exercise in practical-theological sensibility and practical culture-theology – in other words, how they can read the signs of the times in the light of the gospel. This exercise to become sensible for the Holy in daily life, to articulate and to interpret this in front of the classroom, is for me a contemporary interpretation of what is meant with being "outstanding in correct doctrine and in the witness of a Christian life", according to the Codex. The local bishop needs to make sure that this professional spirituality is permanently cultivated and supported in the concrete life of young and 'not so young' RE teachers.

4.5. Theological faculties and institutions should encourage and empower their students more intensively in raising the vulnerable but necessary question "where God can be found in contemporary culture". They should take the 'lived faith' of their young adult students more as the actual starting point for their theologizing, for their teaching and research. They should articulate this question in a practical-theological sensible way ('theology as a way of living') in the whole package of 'sacred sciences' and not only in pastoral/practical theology or religious pedagogy. Only then, the RE teacher as a believer of his time can be sent aptly to the community and fulfill his theological mission with all the "requisite suitabilities" needed.

# Chapter 10

# Kenosis, Human Flourishing and Solidarity
# Re-Thinking the Goal of Education

What do we live for? What do we learn for? "Live to tell", would be the answer of the novelist (Gabriel Garcia Marquez) and the pop star (Madonna). "Learn to live to tell", would be the answer of the educator. Life as such does not exist. There is only narrated life, life in search of human beings with hearts and bones, who are able to articulate what they experience and believe through language, however vulnerable this may be. This ability implies a learning process: sharpening the perception of the surrounding world, learning to express oneself and learning to communicate with others. Both living and learning are aiming at participation in "the ongoing conversation of humankind" (Michael Oakeshott). In this chapter I present a concept of education in which the recognition of human imperfection, life as a growing process and learning as a practice of solidarity are central dimensions of narrative identity development. It is my contention that in the contemporary view on society and school these dimensions are neglected and need to be revitalized (Roebben 2011, 43-60 and 2012).

## 1. Living and learning together

It is striking to see how deeply the ideology of the market place has influenced the European educational space in the last decades. The concepts are *legio* (and mostly articulated in English, which is considered to be the top meritocratic language): "information highway", "knowledge economy", learning with "input and output", "managing" learning processes, focusing on educational "standards" and "competencies", etc. Pupils and students are closing a "contract" with the school, they deliver their "achievements" and they can expect achievements from their teachers. With the focus on a growing individualization of education, solidarity in the classroom is fading away. Every person is responsible for him/herself. Schools are doing their best to offer highly complex and individualized programs for their demanding "clients". And the latter are doing their best in turn "to adapt to the system". What should have been providing more freedom, namely education, becomes a strait-jacket. Not the human being with his/her inalienable dignity stands in the middle, but the issue, namely the augmentation of knowledge. The individual is expected to appropriate the received knowledge, to add his/her small contribution and then to hand this over to the next generation. People become solipsistic producers of knowledge. The strategies of privatization in the public realm of the school are giving birth to "strategies of immunization" (Simons and Masschelein 2009). The concern for the real other – the one who does not bring me necessarily financial or intellectual gain – is disappearing. Human beings are becoming rivals in money and knowledge production.

We need an urgent and conscious return to a personalist concept of education. Human beings have the right to grow as a human being, to develop as a human being. This generic goal may not be understood as a means for something else. Qualitative education contributes to the integrity of the human being, empowers him/her to become the narrator of his/her own story – coherent and fulfilled. Over and over again this ideal needs to be reformulated. The question today seems to me how this ideal of human dignity can be reconsidered from a solidarity-standpoint – from the standpoint of the person as companion or fellow of the other in his/her search for dignity.

No human being is complete, everybody is vulnerable. Moreover, human beings are not exchangeable. Everybody is unique and radically different from the other. These two experiences – vulnerability and uniqueness – culminate in the basic experience of the otherness of the other, conceptually crystallized in recent theories of the German RE discourse (in chronological order: Müller-Friese 1996, Greiner 2000, Boschki 2003 and Grümme 2007b), which in turn reflect on recent developments in intercultural and interreligious learning processes at school. These scholars confirm the idea that human beings are radically strange to one another and that precisely therefore they are delivered to each other in language and communication. There is no other way to become human, unless by education and dialogue. It is an interesting ascertainment to see how this development is taking place internationally, both on the academic and professional level. In this respect we urgently need more fundamental research in philosophical-educational (and theological-educational) anthropology: transatlantic comparisons e.g. between Martin Buber, Emmanuel Levinas, Hannah Arendt en John Dewey, or more recent work of e.g. Helmut Peukert, Hans Joas, Charles Taylor, and others.

One example of a new insight on human flourishing in and through dialogue comes from the Russian Federation. New forms of human communication are needed, thus the Russian RE scholar Fedor Kozyrev (2006), especially the spiritual one. Or even better, this communication already exists, in needs only to be unlocked in daily communication. How can this happen? Well, the human being is in his/her otherness always searching for self-clarity and self-understanding – and in this effort it collides with other human beings on the search as well. The dialogue as the encounter of these two becomes itself a "source of knowledge" (Kozyrev 2006, 217), sparkling from the depth of the encounter. Two souls are then meeting each other. On a deeper level every person remains different from the other in finding the meaning of life, but precisely in this difference they both can find *each other* as an answer to that search. The possibility of the answer is prevailing, not the perfection of the answer. By opening oneself to what Kozyrev calls, together with Mikhail Bakhtin, an "alternative coordinate system", another way of perceiving reality, shown by a fellow human being in living and learning, one receives a new insight in one's past and future, one becomes a new human being, closer to one's own presence – the latter literally understood as being there, being response-able here and now. Through *de-centration* of myself and *de-dication* to the other, I am becoming fully human. Real human flourishing is then taking place. The German philosopher Hans Joas confirms the spiritual dimension of this encounter and coins the term „self-transcendence", which is „ein Ergriffensein von etwas, das jenseits meiner selbst liegt, eine Lockerung oder Befreiung von der Fixierung auf mich selbst" (Joas 2004, 17).

## 2. Towards an educational theology of incarnation

This educational ideal of „growing in shared humanity" can have (but must of course not!) its foundation in Christian theology. The human being is made in the image of God and he/she is called (or pro-voked) to become perfect "as your heavenly Father is perfect" (Matthew 5, 48). This is not about spotlessness, but about focusing the human existence on true humanity or true human flourishing, on maturity, wholeness and completeness. The human person is called to become whole and holy in his/her quality as a human person, namely as a fellow or companion. The Jewish-Christian creation story offers a future vision, a permanent challenge to develop from fact to alternative, from 'is' to 'it could be otherwise', from self-development to living-in-dedication.

The event of the incarnation or becoming human of God in Jesus Christ is in the Christian theology both in substance as formally decisive of the commitment of human beings for and with one another. The Dutch philosopher Renée van Riessen (2007, 146-172) has in line with the work of Emmanuel Levinas convincingly demonstrated that the revelation of God always takes place in the form of 'kenosis', 'emptifying' or dedication. God compromises Him/Herself by delivering Him/Herself in the human condition to the world, not only in the (classical) ways of Scripture and Sacraments, but in ordinary daily encounters, out there on the street (Von Stosch 2012, 4). On the track of incarnation, this means that, when God withdraws from the absolute freedom to be God, He/She surrenders Him/Herself to the vulnerable image of a fellow human being who asks for our attention and hospitality. This is truly a creative act: deep human community and communication are then coming into existence.

Every human being can become in his/her otherness a guest but also a host for the other. We share *mutually*, as was mentioned before, the radical human experience of otherness, of vulnerability and difference. Moreover, human beings are gifted with reason, to define hermeneutically if and how they can become truly a fellow or companion to the other. De-centration of the self and de-dication to the other always imply a conscious decision that depends from many factors and circumstances. The revelation of God, understood as incarnation, must therefore always be spiritual-communicatively interpreted and tested. Therefore the Jewish and Christian traditions are "Bildungsreligionen" or educational religions. This is, according to the German religious educationalist Ralf Koerrenz (1997) the very central anthropological dynamic of the biblical tradition. Reading the bible to understand life means 'learn to learn' to understand life: everything could be different tomorrow, nothing can be extrapolated from today's experience. Nothing, not even the biblical language game, is a mere fact. Everything is perception and interpretation. The Bible fundamentally considers the human being as a 'learning existence', always dealing consciously with reality and with the interpretation schemata to understand that reality (see Chapter 8). Openness for living and learning conditions – what is the existential meaning of reality for me and for my fellow human beings, now and tomorrow? – are deeply engraved in an incarnational-theologically interpreted concept of education.

## 3. Five elements in the innovation of education

What now are the consequences of the educational concept of "growing in shared humanity", embedded in the Christian tradition of the incarnation, for education and school development in Europe? What could be the innovative dynamic in the midst of the great educational challenges that are facing our late modern schools and societies? About the normative character of this final part of the paper one could discuss. This is precisely my intention. While raising questions I open a discussion on what is really worthwhile for the future. This is a global exercise which can be done a local scale. As far as I can see five elements can be discerned as implications of the above elaborated concept of solidarity education: imperfection, non-planning, slowification, community and silence.

First of all, schools should be places, where people are allowed to be imperfect and can learn from their mistakes. The words of the Jewish philosopher of education Hanan Alexander are very clear in this respect: "Living up to an ideal was not the product of some external force, some hand other than my own; rather it was a result of a decision I made, a discipline I imposed upon myself, a behavior I learned to perform. There may have been other hands in the mix – parents, friends, teachers, lovers, even God. But all the help in the world could not force me to do good if I choose otherwise. In the final analysis, I was the one who measured up. What I do and think matters. I make a difference. I can make an impact on the world. When I stray from the path I believe to be right, even when the price is high and very little appears to be in my control, all is not lost. I can learn; I can return; I can repent; I can change (…). Not only do I matter; I matter just the way I am. This is the source of our deepest joy and greatest reason for celebration" (Alexander 2001, 155). The 'educated person' is not a finalized product, a perfect or complete individual, but a human being with a history and a future, "at home on the road" (see Chapter 5), who lives for an ideal and who is prepared to overcome the barriers that can be found in his/her way.

The second implication relates to the radical openness of learning processes – openness for what cannot and should not be planned, for surprising questions, viewpoints and multi-perspectivity. What children and young people actually learn in the classroom cannot be "seen, smelled or heard" by the teacher (Meyer 2009, 16). The most that he/she can do is orientate and adapt his teaching structure to the probable learning structure of pupils. Especially in the world of the new and social media this will lead us into radically new questions of educational research. We do not have the slightest clue what is awaiting us in this respect, which decisions should be made educationally and socially. One thing is clear: we will need to listen to the next generation, when we reconsider education, its goals and its relationship with tradition(s). Or, "a crisis of interpretation within any tradition eventually becomes a demand to interpret this very process of interpretation" (Tracy 1978, 8).

Furthermore there should be lots of interaction chances for children and young people to communicate philosophically and theologically with each other in the modus of (didactical) "slowification" (Roebben 2012, 1178). Fast food answers are not helpful in the digestion of slow questions! The materials of children's spirituality in the Anglo-Saxon world and "Kindertheologie" in the German speaking world are helpful tools for kids to address difficult questions and to learn to deal with tensions in interpretation of these questions (see Chapter 6). Children have the right to consider the complexity of life – of what surrounds them daily – in order to discover their own, fragile but worthwhile narration – coherent and fulfilling. In the Netherlands the school subject RE is called "levensbeschouwing", literally translated as "the consideration of life". Too often schools leave the difficult life questions "out of consideration" – and therefore do not fulfill their task of offering kids a qualitative RE!

The fourth challenge is community building. Like was argued before, the question "What do we learn from this or that event, experience, conflict, etc.?" is a question-in-plural. Deep learning communities offer space for *common* existential reflection and action. This goes hand in hand with slowification. Or, when we want to be sure that our classroom is safe for diversity, there needs to be a thorough and empathetic openness for those who remain silent, inarticulate, voiceless. De-centration and de-dication – giving the other a real voice – asks for awareness, attention, concentration (Greiner 2000, 286).

And finally the meaning and importance of silence should be mentioned here. "The core of everything is silent and endless", so the Flemish poet Felix Timmermans. He/she who is astonished by reality, becomes silent. The recognition of the grandeur of the world and of the emergence of respectful knowledge are filled with silence and awe. Silence relates to concentration and asceticism: to stand the restlessness, to wait till inner rumors disappear, to receive a new vision and a new heart to see the world differently. In silence the human person can become very wide and full of mercy for him/herself and others. Parker Palmer refers in this respect to one of the desert fathers: "Abba Felix leads his students into a wordless world. He wants to humble their language, to break down the illusions that we can create reality with our words. He knows where our words and our world come from – that true words and the true world are not mental constructs but a gift of grace, a gift we can receive only as we abandon the illusion that our knowledge manufactures the world. Abba Felix takes his students deep into desert silence, a desolate space where none of their mind-made structures can survive" (Palmer 1983, 42).

## Conclusion

It may be clear that this educational analysis, this theological concept and these pedagogical recommendations must become concrete in order to be efficient. However, we may not omit the foundational discussion. When we expect from young people that they will participate sustainably and critically at the society of the future and develop these talents already at school, we as adults will need to take "into consideration" the pedagogical and theological presuppositions behind this concept of solidarity learning. It is my contention that professionals in religious education can make a valuable contribution to this broader educational and social debate. They should not be shy to tell what they have learned. They should "tell to live to learn"…

# Part 3

# Education, Religion and the City

# Chapter 11

# Shaping a Playground for Transcendence
# Youth and Young Adult Ministry
# in the Global Era

In the turn of the year 2008-2009, we received a group of 120 young adults in our parish in Belgium. They came from Serbia, Montenegro, France, Germany and Poland to participate in the ecumenical 'Pilgrimage of Trust' in Brussels, organized by the Brothers of Taizé. More than 40,000 people were hosted in parishes around Brussels. In our family we had two Polish girls as guests. When we asked them what they were looking for, we were amazed to hear that they had come to Brussels, to the centre of Europe, to find inner peace and silence. Life had not been very friendly to one of them: her marriage stood under pressure. For the other young woman life was full of promises: 18 years old she was planning for the theatre education and had won this trip as a result of a successful poetry contest in her school in Warsaw. They are young adults on the road: looking for consolation or passion, seeking for sense in the city. In the middle of modernity, they hope to find reasons for living. The image is powerful: the train and subway system of the city of Brussels was overwhelmed by cohorts of young people, magically attracted to the centre of the pilgrimage. In the heart of bustling communication, media, business and market – in the eye of the storm – there was prayer, silence and faithful dedication. Together these young adults became brothers and sisters in worship and action, in the presence of each other and in the presence of God – gathered as human beings *coram Deo* and *coram homine* – in the midst of the global era. The social scientist and theologian Robert Schreiter has defined globalization as "the compression of time and space and the extension of modernity at large" (quoted by Mallon 2004, 140). The concern for a better world, for greater peace and human understanding, drove these people together on the crystallized holy space of Taizé-in-Brussels. Yet, at the same time this experience was radiated like sunbeams through the new media, via weblogs, cell phones, digitalized words and pictures 'all over the place' (Hess 2005; Roebben 1999c; Zondervan 2006). The good news was electronically extended to the whole world as well as conveyed over conversation to their guest families. These young people told their stories to anyone and everyone who would listen. Being there in Brussels meant for them being absorbent for the presence of God in fellow human beings, listening to the voice of the Sacred within daily experience, reading the signs of the times in the light of the Gospel – and spreading the good news to the world. Gathered by the same experience these young adults formed a 'liquid church' (Ward 2002); the universal and the particular interwoven, the globalized world compressed in Brussels and extended through new media as a radically new *locus theologicus*. Further research is urgently needed to describe the impact on lived faith and lived theology of young people, when they gather in big events like these or the 'World Youth Days' (Simon 2007). For now the questions are: where and how can adolescents and young adults learn to balance between the uniqueness of their own life project and the necessity of being 'wired' and 'linked' to a globalizing society and culture as a whole? Where and how can they find spiritual guidance in order to ponder the different options and horizons for a faithful live? Where and how can the local congregation be helpful in that quest?

The first part of this chapter focuses on the existential dimension of contemporary youth and young adult ministry, in relationship to present day youth culture. Adolescents and young adults are involved in permanent story-telling, in order to survive the harsh and overwhelming scripts of market and media. It is my conviction that school and (church related) youth work can help each other in encouraging young people to create playgrounds of transcendence and to foster their spiritual competences.

In the second paragraph I focus on young adults (between 16 and 25) and their 'developmental task' of becoming a true self in the age of globalization. The third part offers an outline of three different models of youth and young adult ministry in the congregation. I critically observe the possible links between young people, society and church within these models. I conclude with a short plea for more reflexivity in youth ministry.

**1. Narrative identity and spiritual competence**

Let me start with a provocative statement: our 'human resources management' of young people does not work, because we lack the courage to listen to the voices and 'sources' of young people themselves. Young people amplify the longing of our culture, but we are not able to capture their non-common-sense analysis. They are looking for adults and ask them for attention for what is truly worth while: honesty, a good life, a clear balance between work and leisure time, between professional and personal life, peaceful living together in diversity, teachers with a heart, safe streets. They have always been asking these vital things from adults. But I have the impression nowadays that their voice is not heard, despite all the communication tools we have today. Although they often seem to be very loud with their cell phones, chat boxes and facebooks, they abide in an atmosphere of deep silence – even worse, in radical dumbness and "systematic inarticulateness", thus Michael Warren. "There ain't no point in talking when there's nobody listening" (1998, 25-42).

In the previous chapters of this book I have been stressing the need for personal identity development within an explicitly religious framework. For that purpose young people acquire skills through education and schooling, in order to situate themselves in time and space, to locate themselves hermeneutically in their own story and to communicate with fellow human beings on their developing narrative identity. With the mystagogical-communicative or narthical approach to religious education in Chapter 5, I pleaded in favor of a non-instrumental way of dealing with the religious dimensions of life. True religion is always dialectically interwoven with human experiences – in line, but also in tension with them. True religion is about transcendence (clearly always in a human horizon of immanence), it is about de-centering the human story (clearly always in reflection on this story). True religion opens the living and learning space for the surprising coming of God, for His or Her radical alterity within diversity, immanence and self-reliance.

The Dutch pastoral theologian Tjeu van Knippenberg calls this the 'spiritual competence' of the human person, a third competence beside the hermeutical and communicative competence (van Knippenberg 1998, 199-245). I have argued before explicitly that a comprehensive religious education necessarily needs to encompass these three and that, also at a regular school, the spiritual competence should be and can be trained. This competence makes young people and their teachers aware of what cannot be 'taught' but should be 'caught' within the one and same learning process. In these moments of didactically empty hands the soul can be moved. This can be happening in the school; this should be happening in ministry with youth and young adults. It would be an interesting research question to investigate how these two fields of education can intensify and enrich each other.

## 2. Young adulthood as a developmental task

Most of the young people do survive these hectic times rather well. They experiment with the splendid artefacts and ideas of the consumption society. They enjoy all the good things it has to offer, especially for coming generations. In the complexity they survive: they give meaning and clarity to what they find on the darks streets of the global and/or virtual city. Being young was always difficult, but nowadays it has become a real challenge. Young people are asked to be socially flexible, to live with ambivalences, to engage with the games of society without losing themselves in these games. Identity building today is a multi-vocal construct (see Chapter 7 § 3): it means to re-consider oneself as wholesome within fragmentation. To be oneself means to become of 'one piece'. Young adulthood was previously an indication for a specific age group, namely the 'post-adolescents', between 16 and 25 years old. Since the beginning of the 1980s this term has become more and more the reference term for a societal phenomenon: abiding in the grey zone between childhood and adulthood, an elongated zone, no longer defined by sharp demarcations, but a hazy zone in which doubt is reigning about what has to be thought, said and done. In youth studies literature one can read about the 'individualized youth biography' (Fuchs-Heinritz 1990; Roebben 1996c, 197-205; Schweitzer 1996 and 2004). The adolescent period is prolonged because young people delay decisions, first because they lack the financial means and secure relational ties for a livelong adult commitment, later because they just like this kind of comfortable, provisional life style. They flirt with the ambivalences of life. They are at the same time autonomous and heteronymous, they should take decisions but postpone them, they dispose of new sources of knowledge, but they loose depth, they are mobile people with their own car or driving license, but they are longing for the homeland.

Since the 1990s young adulthood is reconsidered in the context of the hectic stream of post-modern life in a global era. Young adults are considered to be the 'unwilling pioneers of a multi-optional society' (Greiner 2005). The seductions are permanent, the options innumerable, the actual power of realization minimal. Flexibility means in fact fragility. In the midst of this ambivalence young people 'live to tell' (Gabriel Garcia Marquez). Some of them learn to master the tensions critically and personally. Others get stuck in a sort of lifelong post-adolescent crisis and are confronted with school fatigue, youth unemployment, dysfunctional working infrastructures, deficient relationships, addiction problems, etc. Young people need more biographical advise. But adults do send out contradictory messages: "Adults love youthful energies that remind us of what we have left behind". But also: "Youth must ignore their hearts and become what the market needs (…): to be compliant, productive, and consumptive" (White 2005, 19 passim). It is not an easy job to be young: 'I am expected to become myself, but how can I realize that developmental task when I am permanently obliged to comply with the rules of market and media? Do I have a spiritual playground at all?'

Without being exhaustive, in my opinion the following elements play an important role in this process. People nowadays are shaped by the illusion of visibility and accessibility. Whoever has not been seen by the new media, for instance, is ruled out and cannot participate in public life. The 'big brother' mania, the illusion of ultimate accessibility by cell phone, the hidden norms in using electronic devices between home and the working place, illustrate this development. Through the new media and our permanent connectedness to them, we life a drunken live of the illusion of immortality. 'I can be reached anytime and anywhere, so I must be irreplaceable and immortal'. For postmodern people death has no grip on the feast of living permanently on the edge.

The master narratives are long-gone. The new ones of media and market have replaced the former and absorb the lives of promising young people. In the meantime they are craving for guidance to survive the daily rat race with which they are confronted. They organize their life patterns according to the market anthropology, because this is often the only format they know about in their young lives. Their crucial question however is related to the possibility of building a narrative identity at all: 'Am I allowed telling my own story, or do I need to comply exclusively with the given prescripts? Is there anybody willing to listen to my story? Has anybody noticed me in my fragility and vulnerability, when I am trying to find words and gestures for my way in and out of the moral and spiritual swamp? Has anybody noticed my loneliness? There is so much communication in the air, but where can

I find a true community? Is there anybody who carefully listens to my longing to have life and to have life abundantly? (John 10:10) – the ultimate longing of every human being. Is that so strange?' (Roebben 1997, 337-340).

## 3. Paradigms of youth ministry as answers to this situation

After the analysis presented in the first two paragraphs, a critical question remains: can we simply continue our traditional efforts and methods of approaching young people in their search for personally reflected meaning and authentic commitment to the community of the future? Can our pastoral strategies remain the same against the background of the radical change that young people's environment, and society as a whole, has gone through? Is it justifiable to rely on traditional homogenous forms of religious socialization while the whole universe of youth experience has scattered in a plurality of traditions and meaningful others, and the claim for a new spiritual playground can be heard in different tones? My point here is how religious congregations can interrelate with this complex set of questions, how they can contribute to the clarification of these questions, based on the assumption that religious traditions always have been and are struggling with fragments of answers to this and other questions, questions that are in fact, as old as humankind: birth and death, relationships and emotional commitment, eternal life, why to be moral at all, etc. It is not so much the answers that count, but the sound thematization of the questions. In and through mediating their narrative answers to these basic questions, religious congregations can contribute to the pastoral task of assisting young people in the telling of their own stories and in the organization of their own biographies. In the following three subsections, different paradigms for youth ministry are presented, each with its own focus on the relation between youth-society-church.

The description and critique of, and the terminology for, the first and the third paradigm are existing in literature and reflective church work with youth (for example, Bopp 1995; Warren 1987, 13-20 and 21-29). The underlying assumptions and a key concept to connect these two, however, need to be reconsidered over and over again. This socio-cultural and political dimension of pastoral ministry may not be omitted. The permanent integration of the broader societal dynamics of youth cultures into the discussion on youth ministry, in order to clarify the possible role of vital churches for a new and global era, is inevitable. The second paradigm therefore plays a crucial role, because it articulates the longing of young people and their critique to a modern (adult) society and church alike. In the United States this cultural and political analysis was instigated among others by the stimulating reflections of Michael Warren on the 'politicization' of youth ministry (Warren 1982, 89-102). The question however will be how this intuition of the 1980s can really become a strategy to re-imagine the vulnerable life of young people in the horizon of globalization today. I described these paradigms for the first time some twelve years ago (Roebben 1997). This is a still a good framework in my opinion. The work of recontextualization, fleshing out the framework, however did not stop at that time.

### 3.1. The secularization paradigm

Let me now turn to my own church, the Roman-Catholic church in Western Europe. An observation that is crucial in this respect is the radical dissociation between the life of the official church and the cultures of young people. The church seems to give answers to irrelevant questions and, at the same time, remains silent on what people find to be authentic personal and societal issues. She is a "tranquil church in a volcanic society" (Nadeau 1994, 92-93), she seems not to allow herself to be moved by society's ongoing debate on contemporary human flourishing. She holds her old and honorable traditions in a definitive way and is not prepared to dialogue on the weight of these decisions and visions with others, fearing that she will become only part of the societal debate, and so allow herself to be criticized and lose final authority.

Well-meaning youth ministers are seduced into making this traditional bulwark more attractive to young people. They make different attempts to reach them by adapting liturgy to their language and customs, by decorating the place of celebration, by re-conceiving the array of Christian ideas in new rituals, ways to offer spiritual assistance, community formation, etc., in short, by adapting to the situation of secularization, by welcoming young people in an old building with new decorations. Another strategy is getting involved into the real world of young people and to encounter them where they actually live: in youth movements, on playgrounds, youth clubs, action and discussion groups, etc. Peer ministers share the life of these young people, listen to their questions, undertake different endeavors with them, etc. The gospel is their basic inspiration, which they are witnessing during some well chosen occasions. Sometimes their criticism of the official church is uttered, but most of the time they remain silent. Thus, opportunism and pragmatism come to the fore: they minister to and with youth, but they likewise minister to and with their superiors.

Both approaches can be found in every local church, and the pastoral choice between them often generates discussion and conflicts on the pros and cons of both positions. However, they are in a way identical, while remaining tributary to the secularization paradigm. They are both based on the assumption that the relationship between church and youth can be expressed in terms of inside and outside and that the efficiency of the strategy depends upon how one is willing to bridge the gap: by welcoming them into the church or by going out to encounter them in the real world (ministry *ad intra* or *ad extra*). The idea of the church as eternal counter-story is continued by this strategy. The church seems to be prepared to allow some 'cosmetic' changes in order to look better, but will not enter into a radical process of 'indigenization' (Warren 1987, 17-20) into the environment of people today. Yet, young people will ultimately not be attracted because they feel it is not about them. In the end, the church is too opposed to their questions and experiences to truly meet them. This observation does not mean, however, that we should stop our church work with young people. What is important is that we must be honest in our approaches, realistic in our expectations, and not feel guilty when our best attempts fail to 'work'. We cannot and should not attempt to convert whole groups of postmodern young people by merely adaptive strategies of the church. Young people are very sensitive to, and critical of, hidden proselytism. This experience in youth ministry serves as a sort of warning: we must go deeper and become more authentic; we must focus on the real aspirations of young people in the global era.

## 3.2. The reflection paradigm

How is this closer relation between church and youth possible without thinking and working in terms of adaptation? Will there not always be a gap between them? Can this gap be bridged in postmodern times? Is this bridge needed at all? Some youth ministry and religious education researchers have recently opted for a more modest attitude toward the problem, in which listening, sharing, and empathy are central categories (Drehsen 1994; van der Ven 1995). For these researchers, young people are the seismographs of the lack of a spiritual playground of our society, and in their different reactions to this problem they express their desire for a new world, as I have argued above. Young people reflect this experience to the world of adults and force them into new ways of thinking and responding to the crucial existential questions of our times. Reflection has a double meaning here: it is used in the sense of reflecting as in a mirror (these ideas are mirrored to adults), but also in the sense of interpretation (they interpret the ambiguity of our culture).

The central idea in this paradigm is that the church is no longer opposed to the world in general, but is an exponent of the world. The church is part of the same competitive ethos as can be found in society. Young people do not feel at home in the church for the same reasons they do not feel so in society. They feel that, wherever they go, they are assessed by adult values and norms and, consequently, are not taken seriously enough in their own personal, moral, and existential development. Ultimately, they find that in the church, as in society, they lack the experience of communication with others, a hermeneutics for their ambiguous life and integration into a vital community (Drehsen 1994, 74-75). In the eyes of young people, the whole complex of not being heard and accepted is as applicable to church as to the world. It is this very attitude that is criticized by young people. In so doing, they make the church aware of her inability to communicate at all and to create a world of interpretation that makes any sense to them. In the end, the church seems to have no other message for them in their search for meaning than a religious justification or reduplication of what is happening in the world ethos. In fact, one could argue that young people's existential distress is an appeal or an 'exhortation' to the church (not coming this time from the official teaching office, but from the basic teachings of the 'sensus fidelium') to revitalize her tradition of interpretation and liberation as an alternative to a fatigued postmodern environment. Young people are challenging the church to become authentic and radical again. They are longing for a church that is ready to go back to her roots (radices), namely, those of the liberating gospel that criticizes oppressive moral and religious institutions and is open to a new solidarity. Only then can the restructuring of the spiritual playground begin (Lechner 1993). This "awareness of the institutional structures that shape and sometimes oppress young people [can and] must create a new range of options in the way we actually minister to and with young people" (Warren 1982, 95).

One critical remark, however, needs to be made about this paradigm. Church leaders and youth ministers can be seduced by referring to this paradigm to instrumentalize young people's environment in an even more hidden and refined way. Young people's criticism would then be experienced and used as an historical catalyst for a fatigued adult church in order to procure new ideas and refreshment for the future. Youth ministry would then only be a reflective mirror (and not an interpretative one) in which the adult church can decode her own incompetence to read the signs of the times. Such a scenario would be an extreme form of religious retro-socialization.

## 3.3. The evangelization paradigm

The previous considerations lead to a challenging paradox: young people express a provocation (from the Latin 'pro-vocare': call to the fore) to the congregation to become itself again. In the same way they are asking adult culture to open 'interaction situations' (Norbert Mette, quoted in Roebben 1997, 334), they summon the church to bear witness to her story of liberation again. The tragedy, however, is that the church is hesitant to do so. The church observes the contemporary spiritual distress, but does not seem to be aware of the necessity to create a new language in order to ease this problem, a language that neither condemns people nor polarizes communities, but one that respects the multifaceted search of people to come to terms with the existential paradoxes of our times. The church's message, her tradition of mediating salvation, is fading away and is badly received, owing to the lack of communication with the actual life of people in and outside the congregations. In other words, the official church is standing in the way of her own story. She is too busy reclaiming and restoring her identity in a pluralistic world, and is neglecting dialogue with people on the crucial problems and paradoxes of personal, social, and global life that need the clarification of religion. It is in the historical search of young people for a spiritual playground that the official church needs to be re-anchored in tradition and to drink from its own wells once again. This historical process is the form in which the traditional adage "Ecclesia semper reformanda et purificanda" needs to be accomplished today.

Youth ministry therefore has to fulfill the difficult but challenging task of 'evangelizing' again in the life of young people. It should rid itself of old instrumentalizing strategies for reaching young people 'somewhere outside there in the dark', outside the church – it should engage in the ongoing dialogue of a new spiritual playground for young and old. Its aim is not to bring young people to the church or to bring the church to young people (secularization paradigm), nor to make the older generations in the congregation more vital and capable of facing the future while reflecting on the situation and the questions of the younger generation (reflection paradigm), but to shed the light of discernment upon the ambiguous answers that are now being given to young people to the age-old questions of life. The evangelization approach to youth ministry is aiming at a materially qualified and communicative salvific commitment to young people, one in which humankind's love of God can be experienced and become transparent for individuals and congregations (Bopp 1995, 403-404). This salvific moment can help to clarify questions concerning the past and the future of human engagement, questions about the underlying principles of what we do or don't do, about the basic trust in the meaningfulness of reality and the perspective of forgiveness and reconciliation. This eschatological commitment to the life of young people today should be at the center of our concerns, not as a warning to convert them from a dark presence into the light of an eternal future, but as a new mode of being human, liberated and challenged to rebuild a new world of solidarity, inter-subjectivity and to undertake a communal search for reliable and life-giving truth.

The word 'evangelization' then has the meaning of a preparedness to bear witness to this process of discernment, this struggle with reality (Roebben 1995c). Only when young people are confronted with adults who show the courage of their conviction, who live from the gospel in which they find 'enlightenment', can religion be experienced as a valid option, as an "inspiration auprès de la manière intelligente" (Thévenot 1993, 31). Only then it is reasonable to say that it is reasonable to be religious. Thus, no longer can the question of youth ministry be: "How shall we adapt the gospel to the situation of youth in order to bring them into the congregation?" It will be: "How should the (Christian) praxis in the congregation look, so that it can bear witness in a reliable and open way to the salvific coming of God to humankind, to which only a free and personal commitment can correspond?" (Roebben 1995a, 306-311).

Youth ministry will therefore be founded in a permanent movement of adult authentification and communicabilization of its roots which is the gospel. What is really important for a healthy youth ministry is not a good looking and attractively 'decorated body', but an 'inspired body' that is ready to face the question whether it is authentic and communicative, whether it can open itself to be a playground for transcendence. Only then it will become truly attractive.

**Conclusion**

A huge challenge is to be faced in the world of young adults. These people are listening to the voices of passion and responsibility, they are searching for good reasons to ground their hope for a better world, and therefore they are desperately looking for 'soul food'. Churches cannot and should not leave them behind. Religious traditions and communities should be aware of their quest. Fast answers are not helpful to their slow questions. The German humanist philosopher Jürgen Habermas 1992; more explicitly in 2001) argues that, without the reasonability of faith – the reflected images, stories and practices of the good life provided by religious communities – the good life itself will dry up. "Without the stories the people will be running wild", says Dorothee Sölle (according to Proverbs 29:18). In a complex and globalizing world this intelligibility of the story of faith is to be re-discovered. Every generation will need to tell the story again and think about how it illuminates 'the signs of the times'. The old lesson of Anselmus of Canterbury – *fides quaerens intellectum* (faith seeking understanding) – needs to be actualized in every new generation (Roebben 2009, 9-23). Young people deserve therefore good ministers who encourage them to see, to reflect and to act with the eyes of faith – especially in times in which many people decide to close their eyes for the Mystery of Life.

# Chapter 12

# Reading the Signs of the Times
# Prolegomena for a Theology of Youth Ministry

Learning to be faithful to the signs of the times on their way in daily life: that seems to be the central task of Christian believers in line with the teachings of Vatican II. But what vision do they need to remain spiritually 'at home on that road'? How can the gospel illuminate the journey of the faithful, especially of young adults, in a scattered world? How can they (learn to) make sustainable decisions in contexts of politics, economy, society, culture and religion? Christians are convinced that every era has to formulate and to live out its own interpretation of the gospel. But the question remains: how can they be sure that the right spirit, the spirit of discernment, is guiding them in this effort? In order to clarify this issue and based on a 'narthical' approach to the church as a learning community (see Chapter 5), I first contextualize my own story as a theologian. I will then focus on the importance of religious experience ('living with open and empty hands'), in order to create an educationally relevant theology of youth ministry in paragraphs 3, 4 and 5 ('theology of embrace'). I will conclude with some thoughts on lived theology as a reminder for every form of academic theology.

## 1. Forty five years of living in and reflecting on faith

I was born in 1962, the opening year of the Second Vatican Council. About twenty years later, I became a student in theology. Today, some twenty five years later again, I am teaching and researching in a department of Catholic theology in a large *high tech* university in Germany. A lot has changed since. During my university studies in the 1980s my heart began to beat faster, every time when we read the theological concepts of Karl Rahner, Edward Schillebeeckx, Gustavo Gutierrez and Jürgen Moltmann. They offered us insight in the motion and movements of a vital Christian faith that was anchored in everyday life. I still remember how Moltmann's theology of hope in those days radically influenced my spiritual and ethical behavior. How liberation theology inspired me to closely examine social injustice within my own living environment and how the interdependency of grace and free will (the classic theological tussle) appealed to my imagination when I read Schillebeeckx' oeuvre. And how deeply moved I was by the idea of a God who touches and calls upon each and every soul, as explained in Rahner's theological anthropology. These theological concepts emanated from a recovered Christian faith, embedded in living communities which passionately went in search of God's providence in the world and which strove to find some powerful (read: mystical and political) answers.

At the present it has been claimed that this kind of coherence, this correlation between living and faith has been broken. Correlation-theories seem to be of the past. Correlative religious learning is outdated and correlational communities no longer exist. After all, faith has no longer been passed on to coming generations, families no longer commit themselves to religious socialization, sacramental catechesis has become empty, and schools limit themselves to a strictly cognitive encounter with religious traditions in a multi-cultural society. To put it more boldly: the *fides ex auditu* (faith through hearing the word) has dissipated. Or as our children as regular as clockwork on a Sunday used to ask: "Where are my friends in church? Didn't they also celebrate their first holy communion and confirmation?" For long churches have thought: "Well, make the church visible again, bring it to the attention, make it more accessible and easier to digest." But apparently that didn't work out. The malaise is more deep-seated. Beneath the *Tradierungskrise*, the crisis that makes it difficult for churches to connect the Christian faith with everyday life, lies an *experiential crisis* (Roebben & Zondervan 2008, 258-262). People say:

"There doesn't have to be a relation between living and faith. I can easily do without a faith in God. I will manage just fine." A religious attitude or openness seems no longer to be optional. Why should one 'live in dedication' and trust in God when you know you have to stand up for yourself: at school, at work, in your relations, in your spare time, and in your church community?

What about Divine Providence in the meanwhile? If God is not been searched for by his people, does that imply that he no longer exists? Or has he withdrawn himself from this world and sought shelter in the safety of heaven? Does God no longer want to hear from us? Those thoughts are far from meaningless. They are present in Scripture, both in collective and personal faith stories, just think about the exile literature. If we no longer matter for him, how could we then function as a symbol of salvation for the world? Or does he want us to be a symbol of contradiction, like a holy remnant? The struggle of the people of Israel with this thought is inspiring for us today. For people involved in ministry, for those who should be guides on the way in life, this challenge can be painful. In deep spiritual turmoil they can get: "How can I guide people on their journey to God, if I am lost on my own way to Him?" (Tillard 1997).

The answer of the official churches on the crisis of religious experience tends towards a renewed and increased focus on the small group of core believers. In the Roman-Catholic and Protestant communities of Flanders (Belgium) and the Netherlands there is an apparent decrease in church support. Churches are confronted with the decline of resources and the necessity to establish priorities. A tendency towards conservatism can be discerned, a development that is expressed in a definite stressing of the distinctive features of ones' identity and hence certain pastoral policies. But it most certainly continues worldwide also. The largest religious research on youth and spirituality in the USA indicates that the mainstream churches have dozed off when it comes to handing over the faith to the coming generations and that precisely the smaller and more conservative denominations, predominantly of evangelical and charismatic origin, are popular among young adults (Smith & Lundquist Denton 2005). And one cannot deny that mainstream churches, when having read the research reports, feel tempted to pursue a mode of internal doctrinal and disciplinary concord.

This development cannot but effect living and learning in the church. A church who withdraws itself, who doesn't risk or dare itself to be scorched by the dynamics of the world and its future generations, will lose her correlative power, her vision on how faith and life relate, and on how God wants to exceed himself in this world. It needs no say that the theological reflection will also suffer the consequences. Some scholars choose the safe rationality of *religious studies*, others that of an explicit church theology. The presence of social and cultural theological representatives in the public debate and their feedback towards ecclesial theology subsides. The internal diversity within theology decreases, the official correction increases. Not much has been left of the initial enthusiasm that accompanied the theological projects during the twilight of Vatican II. We are at a great loss. Our theological reading glasses have been steamed-up and we don't know how to get them clean again.

## 2. Living in dedication

*The powerful testimony of open and empty hands*

Suppose that faith to our contemporaries no longer is a matter of concern, then what about that other component of the correlation, life itself? In my encounters with young and young adult people I discern that underneath the material and relational needs hides a deep longing for unconditional love. The most intimate question is as old as the hills itself, but it is asked passionately today: "Is there someone who loves me unconditionally, so that I dare trust and thrust myself in the arms of my own existence which so often is both adrift as well as full of longing?" I have found that many people do not have the courage to listen to their own biographical narrative and instead would rather like to run away from their destiny. The small story seems to be too insignificant for them and therefore they mindlessly log into the big scripts of the market and media. Today, we are for the greater part defined and determined by a lifeless secularism and aggressive consumer anthropology. Many fall a victim to this destructive plot, emotionally and mentally. Unfortunately, there are also people in our cultures who literally break down and become physically ruined. Not to mention the fates of our contemporaries on the southern part of the hemisphere.

Sometimes the thought occurs that "this ain't no living": in moments of contrast-experience ("This can't go on"), in experiences of sudden insight ("Now I see"), or in a situation of zest and engagement ("I care") (Stachel & Mieth 1978, 28-29). Through the cracks and holes of the consumer-society then dawns the insight that we forgot something essential, to life with empty hands, in susceptibility and dedication. During those precious moments we are aware of the fact that we do not have to manage on our own, that we in our struggle to organize and direct life, already are accepted and acknowledged. And with this we come close to the heart of what faith is about. According to Schillebeeckx, faith is about trusting oneself to the ultimate foundation of our existence, in the hope that this will not be in vain, that a human being cannot end up in complete meaninglessness. He adds that this act of humanity can be expressed in a religious language game with a transcendent origin. But it doesn't have to be necessarily so, he continues, for one's attitude can also be described from a secular perspective. As long as one is willing to accept the spiritual dimension of our existence, in the sense of: "I already have been noticed, I do not have to expose myself in order to be seen. I am already found, I do not have to root myself. In all of my searching, I already have been found. And if I fall, I will not fall into ultimate meaninglessness." (Schillebeeckx 1978). This culture-critical interpretation of Christianity, in fellowship with new secular developments for sustainable life, is becoming slowly but surely a new and viable 'Gestalt' of Christianity in Western-Europe. The leading question is: "How can churches be present and transparent with their rich traditions of openness to postmodern societies?" Scholars such as Erik Borgman (2006) in the Netherlands and Hans Joas (2004) in Germany are responding to such crucial questions.

This type of *faith* is no *submission;* this living in dedication is not the same as living in surrender. In contrary, those who have learnt to accept their human identity as a 'bestowed identity' (in German: ‚Identität-aus-Gratuität', see Chapter 8 § 3), dare to live life with an open approach and fight for more humanity, exactly in those areas where life itself is threatened. In this approach shimmers a twenty-first century spirituality: learning to let go of oneself as a human being, *amidst* all of the complexity, and yet not losing oneself as human being *because of* the same complexity – in concordance with many others who share the same belief in humanity. Empty hands turn into open and offering hands, once one has learned to share them.

*The unheard calling*

In consideration of future generations, this testimony of empty hands is a task that cannot be disregarded. Whether in my personal encounters with young and young adult people, or in meetings with youth workers in church and society, teachers and school administrators, there is always the resonation of: "Tell us about the ultimate ground of existence that encourages us to embrace our strength and that inspires us to anticipate the future with faith and hope." Young adults long for inspiration, understood as the encouragement of a passion that is already present within them (Dean 2004). They hope for acknowledgement, for someone who perceives and honors their potential and who lets them participate in the general project of 'humanity' (see also Chapter 2). To me, this is a 'calling' – an urgent assignment for our society that has been lulled to sleep, a project for our sedated schools and churches. A lot of the social discomfort stems from the given that people are no longer asked to perform altruistic acts of engagement. Underneath hides a more severe complaint: the fact that there does not resound a calling from the heart of that same society. The calling is no longer being stated explicitly, she has fallen silent. And it could as well be that we no longer are able to understand the calling of our youth as a call at all…

In order to discern this calling, our churches need to dare to open up, to free themselves of burden and to focus on what really matters. An act of faith does not end, according to Thomas Aquinas with a correct testimony of faith but in the act itself ("Actus credentis non terminatur ad enuntiabile, sed ad rem" – S.Th. IIa IIae, 1, 2, ad 2), or with Schillebeeckx: in the courage to entrust the ultimate ground of existence. Do we learn to understand how our youth today expresses their vulnerable faith in the future, with their own language and symbols? Do we dare trust that this new spiritual language also generates new experiences of faith? And in addition: are we, in our encounters with young adults, able to represent an open and mature faith? Is our trust in God visible in our own lives? Do we represent and resemble his solidarity with the world, recognizable and always surprisingly new, amidst the complexity of our existence, even through our own adult desperation and bewilderment? Do we dare show that we have faith in the future even though we don't know exactly what the ground of that faith is? Or do we keep up the façade, entrenched in our vestiges of faith with our gates closed, counting on the invincibility of our concrete answers?

*Soul food*

Our youth keep knocking on our door, asking for attention and seeking authenticity. They do not take on the excess baggage of religious systems and are not charged with the adult question of "how, for

God's sake, faith and church should evolve." Youth have taught me to leave questions like "How can we *possibly*...?" on the backburner and to focus myself with a steady faith on the future. They take care of their own business. At school they are educated to critically perceive moral and religious phenomena and also to practice and implement these critical skills by confronting the dynamics of philosophical and theological traditions. These reflective skills are an asset for the ability to critically position oneself in future society. The question however is, whether adolescents learn to discern and appreciate the specific character of the religious experience? Is there a place where they can display the answers they have found and place them in line with or in contrast with the narratives and figures of our tradition, as if these discovered answers are a 'new' tradition? For those who are hungry, a simple explanation of the digestive system will not be satisfying. What vocabulary do adults practice when they encounter yearning youth? What kind of 'soul food' can they offer? Young people challenge adults to show their true colors. They compel them to open their sight and tell them where they are at – even if their insights are provisional. Remaining silent is giving a statement too.

## 3. Prolegomena for a theology of youth ministry

This chapter asserts the generative power of the field of youth ministry. Inherent in working with the youth, is the creation of a new theology. Anyone who looks closely to the *human resources* that lie stored in adolescents will eventually change his perspective on the potential of theology. It is within the field of tension between light and dark, the *clair and obscur*, that young adults 'live to tell'. They articulate the contrasting experience of the intense yearning of our time versus the disillusionment of unfulfilled needs. Young adults who are on the verge of mature life (age 16 to 25 years), in particular, feel what it means to be poised between hope and fear. They have to form their identity in the context of a society that, once confronted with this central breach, hesitates in what strategy to follow. This is exactly the reason why young adults with ideals remain attractive for adult people: they function as a mirror for what is at stake in 'real life' and present an image of how to cope with these circumstances with creative vigor). In what follows I want to critically observe these developments.

To be young is to look with expectation to the future; 'progress' is the keyword, because life lies ahead of you. The horizon winks, you are permanently ready to leave and would rather not waste any time. You want to make a difference, and do a better job than your predecessors, catching on to the new 'vibrations' that can be sensed on the street. Adults are allowed to speak, sure, but their voice has to carry an undertone of hope. Young people are fed up with adults who 'sin against the Spirit': who desperately count their own blessings and fear for what dreams may come. It is exactly this type of adult who will send off youth none the wiser, telling them 'to sort it out themselves' or 'wait until later'.

According to the research of the Belgian sociologists Mark Elchardus et al., titled 'Zonder Masker' [Unmasked] (1999), a certain unease towards the future can be discerned among Belgian youth. Ten to twenty percent of the eighteen year olds have, to a greater or lesser extent, a rather gloomy view of their own future. Twenty percent worry about their chances on the labor market. Fear creeps up on these adolescents during their studies, especially when their course of study goes anything but smoothly. These experiences are even more strongly present in youth that participate in vocational training. More than their peers they feel that they will miss out on a great future. The right of every young individual with prospects for the future passes them by. Our society's answer to this is to work harder and so improve your achievements. Immortality can be realized, even if you run out of luck. You can have some difficulties, but you can also overcome your personal demons by challenging them with ferocity - as long as you try hard and do your best. The myth of self-sacrifice is persistent and ruins many lives. Those who do not succeed in facing a difficult time are proved to be losers. A lot of our pedagogical efforts don't do justice to the fundamental right of our youth to realize their interests. We try to lure them in getting their lives back on track, but forget that they yearn for authentic *involvement*. This means being with them, standing next to them and seeing them, in all their vulnerability and brokenness and in their desire for growth.

Shame, for not being able to live up to the tacit norms imposed by market and media, is a painful experience for today's young contemporaries. The sense of falling short vis-à-vis these internal standards while one thought to be autonomous at the same time (which is actually the paradox of post modern existence), bears deep; deeper even than the guilt experience that refers to a violation of external rules. North-American practical theologian, Evelyn Parker (2003), claims that young individuals look for a hideout in violent urban gangs because they are driven by their overwhelming sense of shame. In her ethnographic research she asked the following question: 'What do you want to safeguard with your violent behavior?' Often the answer was: 'In this gang I at least experience some sense of pride, dignity and respect'. Young people act in destructive behavior against themselves and others out of fear of not being noticed anymore, of not being included, of failing to exist. Random violence often is an ultimate reaction to this threat of annihilation.

## 4. Creating space for new light of day

Involvement is the keyword. An educator, who will give young people the opportunity to show their vulnerable 'social capital', is assured of an audience that is willing to listen. Those who understand the art of *maieutics* in their encounter with youth, those who, as 'midwives', are able to give birth to the deep insights that young individuals already bear within themselves and are willing to reveal, can count on respect. Revelation then happens in the deeper sense of the word. New life is born. New light of day is dawning. Life without consciousness is no life at all, as the ancient Greeks already knew. To be reborn is the fundamental destiny of a religious human being, Jesus says to Nicodemus in the gospel of John (John 3:1-21). Proper assistance is needed in this rebirth. According to the qualified hermeneutic tradition of West-European Roman-Catholic pastoral theology this learning process in assistance can be described in three stages: perception, judgment and action. In the following paragraph these three stages will also be theologically interpreted. It would be an interesting research to compare this European concept with the 'sharing faith' approach of Thomas Groome in the United States (1991), how it also deals with action and reason informed by faith through communication, and how it also generates new theological reflection.

*Seeing*

Youth ministers need to be finely tuned and equipped to perceive the experiences of the youth involved. They particularly must learn to adapt to the modes of expression that young people have developed themselves, in being able to capture their unstable position between light and dark, hope and fear and translate them into new images. It requires an almost ascetic attitude on the part of the pastor to really let the youth express themselves in their music, language and images. Instead of creating opportunities in which young people can define themselves and the context they are in, the pastor is often too eager in giving his own interpretation of the given situation. In too many cases youth work is a mental recovery for a distressed childhood of the adult. Many adults, being a casualty of a childhood gone awry, want to redeem themselves in their profession as a youth worker. But by doing this, they deprive young people the opportunity of being an independent and creative sign of hope for the future.

*Judging*

What professional attitude fits the pastor best? I would say an attitude of being present rather than eliminating deficiencies, an attitude of involvement rather than creating issues. The theory of presence developed by the Dutch practical theologian Andries Baart (2001) is a welcome source of inspiration that renders the notion 'that it is better to let something appear, namely human dignity, than to let something disappear, namely a problem'. The critical approach towards the life of adolescents then does not depart from the idea of 'crisis' (of something that belonged to the past and ceased to exist), but from a notion of *kairos,* an act of grace to see yourself and others with new eyes and to be 'moved' again (see Chapter 3).

*Acting*

Finally, there is the perspective of action. A dynamic youth worker will create space for new insights to (en)lighten the realm of human existence. He offers adolescents the chance of opportunity and stimulates them to become the agents of their own actions. And by doing this, he contributes to a 'life in abundance' (John 10:10). Too much of young life seems to be hammered shut, and left without any future expectations. A couple of years ago German public opinion ran a campaign to offer adolescents more opportunities for the future under the motto: *So jung und schon am Ende!* [So young and already over the edge!]. Quality youth work offers space for new light, as in a *Lichtung* (Martin Heidegger), an open space in the wood. Amidst the density of everyday life new rays of hopeful light illumine our existence. This light helps to see the wood for the trees and creates the clarity to enable youth to make a conscious choice in the multitude of life perspectives. It also helps them to catch better sight of drawbacks. Without light there cannot be shade, only indefiniteness and ignorance – like the night in which all the cattle is colored black. Quality leadership empowers youth by letting them make the difference without feeling ashamed about it.

## 5. Towards a theology of embrace

Within the whirling interaction of light and dark, between the fine line of hope and fear, young people are balancing on the cutting edge. They reinforce the dynamics of the desires present in our culture. 'Joie de vivre' alternates with dread. Instead of backing away from these confusing conditions, youth must take up the quest to face life in all its complexity and make a difference. As adults we can learn from the passion of these adolescents. To live a life in shades, literally means calling complexity into *existence*, in a sense of enduring and/or tolerating the internal dynamics of the human condition. It means refining a sense of meaning out of chaos, reconstructing life. It also means: contemplating in seclusion, awaiting new light of life. Those who do ministry with adolescents must be sensitive to the cravings of their own soul in their own search for the meaning of life. They must be inspired. Only then will 'mental support' become 'spiritual guidance' (van Knippenberg 2002). Only then will 'youth work' be-come 'youth ministry'. Again three stages can be discerned.

*Seeing*

The youth minister has steeped himself in practice, gaining the capacity to discern the biography of adolescents. He knows that his interest in their narratives is a risky investment and that his sincerity towards their experiences may eventually lead to a deeper sense of meaning. From a religious point of view, the minister knows that the living God manifests and reveals himself in the vulnerable stories of young people. The success of street kids priest Father Guy Gilbert (2003) in Paris for example, lies exactly in his spiritual capacity to trust on a God who presents himself among the children on the street. He can look at them in their own uniqueness and approach them because he deeply believes that "God created the human being because He loves stories" (Elie Wiesel), that He has created them in their specific narrative condition.

*Judging*

This looking through the lens of faith offers also a particular judgment: the judgment of 'noble casuistics' (Emmanuel Levinas, quoted in Burggraeve 1990, 160-165). This means that an adolescent is not measured, for instance, by his problematic participation in a gang or subculture, but as an independent and respected person in his own value. A person is not interesting because his case represents a particularization of a more general principle or problem, and thus is found to be of interest to the care giver, but because of the fact that he is a unique person himself. Presence towards the narrative of a single adolescent therefore is often more valuable than having solved a problem for a group of young people that has not been approached with sincere interest. This brings me to a 'theology of embrace': the living God qualifies himself in a fully qualitative encounter with people who long for a 'life in abundance' and who are willing to share this in community. Theology can be distant and cerebral. It can develop categories of faith and substantiate them with well-chosen cases of faith. It can also touch the more physical modes of humanity like engagement, struggle, ritual, friendship, art, and bring about new insight. It can be wholeheartedly and efficient. With this down to earth strategy, theology can create space for the new coming of the living God.

*Acting*

Of course, this incarnational approach requires a lot from the youth minister: spiritual stamina, theological wit, and a willingness to undertake action. Concerning the latter: it really is all about *maieutics*, about the vocation of the pastor to give birth to new life, who reveals unexpected capacities and opportunities in the life of the adolescent, who supports a broadening of perspective and who sometimes challenges the other to change or radically adjust his perspective. A pastor who accompanies adolescents in solidarity, will be 'contaminated' with their perspective on life. He exceeds in a risky kind of solidarity (he helps to restructure shame into respect), in the hope that this path will prove to be fruitful. In the hope also that this path will be compatible with the coming of the living God, who always goes 'outside' and 'off road' incarnationally in the life of His people. Revelation is always risky revelation.

This 'youth theology' is not a one-man business, but always rooted in and orientated to a discourse community. Therefore a fourth dimension needs to be added to seeing, judging and acting, according to the North-American religious educationalist David White. This is the 'spiritual-imaginative modus': the soul needs soul food to remain vital, resilient and critical in the process of discernment between what is and what could be. Young people need living and learning communities in which they can sharpen their perception, practice discernment and learn to act accordingly. In these communities prayer *(remembering)* and theological reflection *(dreaming)* are central activities (White 2005, 74-77). Without these lived and learned images, metaphors, stories and experiences, there can be no spiritual growth. Schematically this 'grounded' learning process of young adults within communities would go as follows (White 2005, 89-200):

| The Heart | The Mind | *The Soul* | The Body |
|---|---|---|---|
| Affective-Intuitive Modus | Reflective Modus | *Spiritual-Imaginative Modus* | Practical Modus |
| Seeing | Judging | *Remembering and dreaming* | Acting |

David White created this approach to youth theology on the basis of his wide experience with youth camps, youth academies and youth work at universities in the United States (for a European experience, see Chapter 13). His ideas remind us that every theology should focus on grass roots experiences and lived faith, in order to become a real living theology. This work is permanently under construction in the field of youth ministry, but not only there. In my opinion there is still a lot of work to be done in general pastoral ministry!

**Conclusion**

Many times I have been given the opportunity to experience that this view on God 'in the hands of human beings' really can appeal to adolescents. They have an aversion to immense theological projects in which God can be found somewhere *out there*. For them the fountain of life is immanent, hidden in daily acts of brother- and sisterhood, in the desire for a more humane world and in the surprising ingenuity of human minds and souls to bring this into realization. God is *in here*, within the whirling undercurrent of a life that asks for animated storytellers. This divine experience requires new religious educators and theologians who dare to submerge themselves into reality, in order to receive themselves a-new from that same reality (Borgman 2006, 86-87). It goes without saying, that a new theological vocabulary and new pastoral strategies will evolve out of this process, and that new religious experiences will, in the long term, contribute to the formation of new theological contents, even to the development of new Christian doctrine.

The gospel itself elucidates how this process takes place. There, you will not find any prophetic oracle or subtle apologetic arguments for the existence of God, but the narrative of a human being, Jesus of Nazareth. He is a loyal friend, companion, and guest at the table. He tells stories, but most of the time he listens. In his listening he becomes authoritative, because he radically places his fellow human beings in the middle. This man will not let adolescents be unmoved. I have learned from them that out of this fundamental experience of vulnerable self-offering (with and like Jesus), Christianity can be re-imaged and re-lived. Not out of the motive to conform or adapt the

Gospel to our present culture, but to bring the Gospel closer to itself, where it belongs, namely into the realm of friendship where God happens.

Hopefully adolescents will be granted the opportunity to generate such new religious experiences and language. And hopefully there will be enough resilient educators and ministers around who can unlock the wealth of our tradition and make it transparent in this quest. Finally, we can only hope that the church will continue to invest in this valuable project: as the 'backing vocals' of youth- and young adult ministry, a helping hand, to complete the chord, consonant or dissonant, but always with dedication.

# Chapter 13

# The Mirror Effect
# Youth Ministry and Theological Education

Contemporary theological education is facing a serious crisis of plausibility, mirroring the crisis of plausibility in contemporary religious experience, language and thought. In this chapter I will defend the idea that vital theological education must be daring to be involved seriously in these shifting grounds of post-modern religion. The education of future theologians in the field of religious education and pastoral ministry with youth and young adults will not only imply the development of new theological concepts for responding adequately to the unpredictability of new religious knowledge, but also new ways of 'responsive' behavior of the qualified theologian. In this chapter I will deal with this topic in the realm of youth ministry. On other occasions I have been discussing this topic in the framework of the 'Tilburg Summer Academies' with professionals in youth and young adult ministry. The theological outcomes of this work, in terms of 'emerging youth theology', are promising and ask for further research (see Roebben & Zondervan 2008; Zondervan 2008). In this chapter I present the explorative research preceding the summer academies.

The mirror effect mentioned in the title of the chapter is referring to the reflective power of 'good' theological education: it should be mirroring or dis-covering what it observes, but it should also be reflecting upon these findings. Reflection means portraying, but also consideration. The data on religious experience, language and thought gathered in the world of religious education and youth/young adult ministry should be in a permanent mode of re-consideration within theological reflection (see also Chapter 9). Post-modern social mobility is compelling contemporary theological institutions and faculties to reformulate their educational projects – within new complex frame-works of both acceleration and contemplation. In this chapter I will report on my own experience as theologian in the field, mirroring what I see and hear in the world of young adult culture – and reflecting upon theses findings from a theological point of view. This chapter offers at the same time an illustration and concretization of the pastoral and theological dimensions of post-modern youth ministry, respectively in the Chapters 11 and 12. I will report on two summer camps for young adults, organized by a Roman-Catholic service centre, and in which I was involved both as group leader and as participatory researcher. I will specifically have a closer look at religious leadership and at youth theology, both evolving out of this approach to young adult ministry. I will be concluding with the idea that 'risky solidarity' with the quest for meaning in future generations is radically stirring up our ideas on religious knowledge and theological education.

## 1. Survival in youth culture

Most adolescents manage to survive in these hectic times. Because they seem to have an innate talent to be socially flexible, adolescents are called the 'flex-generation' (Alma & Janssen 2000). They experiment with the dazzling supply of an affluent society and fully enjoy all the good things of these times that are geared exclusively towards children and adolescents. Their identity is a so-called 'balancing identity'. They maintain themselves in the complexity and haze of the supply. They are equipped to give meaning to what they encounter and try to stay motivated. This attitude towards life and modern society doesn't hold for all adolescents and this is exactly where the shoe pinches. There are many who have fallen a victim to the individualization scenario of today. Flexibility can lead to fragility, a requiring of the self can lead to an over-requiring of the self. In principle nobody is spared from over-requiring because flexibility is such a structural fact. For the trend to *be* somebody, proud and stubbornly post-modern, affects all contemporaries, both young and old.

The complex of questions that many young contemporaries are wrestling with, however, is this: 'Has anyone ever seen me in all my plainness, vulnerability, mortality?' And most of all: 'Is there anyone who will listen to me in all my loneliness, my struggling? With all the possibilities in communication, young people remain asking questions such as: 'Where do I find a *communio*, a community of human concern? Is there anyone who will listen to my yearning, my desire for an authentic life, and who will not immediately stuff my brain with cheap filling?' If we want to explore the contours of this era, we need only to watch the advertising commercials on television, where people's yearnings (the yearning for wholeness, true community, authentic spirituality, and so on) are intensely represented, where their questions are magnificently evoked. But the answers to these questions belong to the realm of commerce and saleability or non-saleability, and must therefore be critically looked at. The question is, who can – and dares to – represent this concrete situation of young people today and give voice to it?

So in their pursuit of their true selves many young people encounter a deeper yearning. I do not think this yearning is dead, but it does seem to have been hammered shut, hidden behind the wall of post-modern greed. People of today are greedy, not just with regard to food and drink, but also with regard to relaxation and work, relationships and life styles and/or life views. We are confronted with our lack of ascesis through the adolescent who, at first sight, seems uncommitted (refusing to enter into any relationship, old or new). Some young people express their protest by becoming fundamentalists ('at least that gives us something to hold on to in a hazy field of meanings'), others retreat to meaninglessness and indifference ('what difference does it make whether I differentiate myself by giving meaning; it's all the same anyway'). Fundamentalism and relativism are sources of cynicism. And these sources are utterly unwholesome for the raising, formation and education of young adults.

Evelyn Parker has demonstrated clearly how children in violent youth gangs are subjugated to experiences of overwhelming shame (Parker 2001; 2003). They permanently have the feeling not to be able to respond to the tacit norms of a demanding society. Parker is referring to ethnographic research in youth gangs in inner city areas in the US. One of the central interview questions that she and others adopt in their research is: 'What do you want so badly that you would sacrifice everything else in order to get it?' In many of the cases the answer was: 'Pride, dignity, self-esteem…'. They are exposed to destructive behavior to others and themselves, because they consider themselves null and void. Shame, dishonor and the feeling of not being counted can result in 'the fear that one will cease to exist, the prospect of psychic annihiliation', according to James Gabarino (Parker 2001, 156). Violent actions are part of the ultimate 're-action' to this situation, 'boosted' answers to the lack of existential interest in the lives and hopes of young people.

## 2. The summer camp as an event of resilience

In the first week of July 2002 I attended the summer camp, organized by the Catholic youth service of the Vlaams-Brabant and Mechelen diocese. Every year this youth service organizes a weeklong trip for young people aged sixteen to twenty five, to exchange thoughts, play games and work together. Several adults and/or young adults come along as guides, giving impulses within the various subgroups and during moments that are spent with the group as a whole. The atmosphere is pleasant: working sessions alternate with singing, eating and dancing sessions. There is room for silence as well: Each day contains 'oasis moments' of prayer or celebration, there is a silent area, there are creative workshops, et cetera. The central camp theme is approached from different angles: playful, creative, social, relational, and religiously deepening. The entire experience is resting upon three pillars: to be there as you are, dialogue with all participants and responsibility for your own words and actions.

The main theme in 2002 was: 'What are we waiting for? Changes in society!' The assignment was to reflect on social processes that hold people in their grasp, preventing them from being or becoming their true selves. The tension between honesty towards yourself and being defined by tacit norms of how to be honest to society was expressed aptly in the *Leitbild* or model of the summer camp: the surfer. The surfer will wait for the right wave before taking action, but his decision to ride the wave or not also depends on other circumstances, on the swell of the sea. The discussion about individualization and its risks (see paragraph 1), about freedom and limits, about surfing the waves of social context, turned out to be a recognizable subject matter to young people. The theme song, in a hip hop rendering, sounded something like this in English (translation BR):

'The Right are coming into power and Palestine is pining, people being exploited.
The rich are getting richer, the poor are getting poorer, injustice must be eliminated.
I am conservative or frightened like a child, I remain standing on the sidelines.
What is the meaning of all this, and if I started now, what good would that do?
Violence is unnecessary, change is necessary, peace is our dream.
The world is fighting, where is the revolution, we are standing in this stream.
Things can be different, things can be better. I feel powerless and very small.
Am I waiting for that one wave? Am I waiting for that perfect wave?
I will not remain standing on the beach, I want to go into the water now.
I will not wait for the perfect wave, somewhere there must be abundant life
(John 10:10)'

The expectations with regard to change tend to be quite modest nowadays, so it seems in the theme song. It is not the system itself that can be changed (you cannot adapt the sea to your own needs) but we *can* expect changes *within* the system (you can decide which waves to ride). The Dutch practical theologian Tjeu van Knippenberg discusses two modes of change: change within the system and change by breaking open the system itself. The second mode is not evident in a modern, high-tech culture that forces people permanently into system-immanency and system-obedience (van Knippenberg 2002, 88-92).

However, surprisingly and occasionally, while camping together, the light of a completely new insight broke through even with the initial assumption that the system was unruly and unchangeable. Now and then a clearing, a *Lichtung*, appeared in the dark forest of feasibility and obviousness, to use the words of Martin Heidegger, when the very rules of the game were repositioned and re-imagined while playing. This open-minded attitude seems to be characteristic of working with young people: Let's experiment and see where we will end up if we adopt an alternative attitude towards the facts. Nowadays such audacity is a sign of vulnerability rather than a sign of obviousness.

For the generation of the author of this essay (the so-called *Generation X*, whose members were born in the 1960s and 1970s and grew up in the 1980s and 1990s), it was common sense to get involved together with peers in radical perspective changes. The desire to change the world was deeply ingrained in activities and discussions. Today one can find more diffidence among young people: Rather than wanting to change the world, they are doing all they can just to keep their footing. It is quite something if they manage to do so. Moreover, many young people bear the additional weight of the frustrations of their parents who feel they have failed the emancipation project of the 1960s.

I have found three basic shifts with respect to the 'generational' appreciation of change: (i) the basic-democratic movement of the 1970s and 1980s has changed; today, young people ask for clarity: 'Tell us what needs to be done'. They don't like long disputes about different positions on the same topic. They want clarity and action. (ii) the relational-sexual experience has changed profoundly; nowadays, young people call for a realistic perspective of love and friendship instead of lifelong fidelity; mostly, they want to enjoy themselves without having to worry about break-ups. They want honesty in their subsequent vibrant relationships rather than 'keeping up appearances' in one continuing but inanimate relationship. (iii) finally, the experience of faith has changed radically; young people do not want to hear an adjusted, unemotional message of faith in their own language; what they do want is to be taken seriously in their own search for meaning, which is often a far cry from what religious leaders preach.

These young adults are aware of their position in a changing world and of their moderate abilities to change the world. They learn to live with these uncertainties. They are taught to react appropriately to these ambiguities. (Continuing) education serves to a large extent to cope more or less successfully with this situation. Churches however are uneasy with these developments. They do not know how to respond to the flexibility and provisionality of the young adult learning position (see Chapter 3 and 9). For them religious learning must be about what is fixed and unambiguous. With reference to the research of Robert Wuthnow, Rick Osmer and Friedrich Schweitzer qualify this to be the 'education gap'. 'The more people participate in education, the less likely they are to be involved in the church. Yet the church seems to be more dependent on education than ever for the maintenance of its membership in line of the ever higher degree of religious diversity and the general weakening of ascriptive ties to the church. In other words, the church needs an educated membership, yet education distances people from the church.' (Osmer and Schweitzer 2003, xvi).

Most of the young people of the summer camp have no connection with the church and its rigid learning community. They have been asked to come by their local youth minister – to think and play along, or simply to be there. It is good that the church offers young people such space for a confrontation with the questions and desires of a particular era. There is no hidden agenda whatsoever, to make converts, to bring them to a profession of faith, or whatever. The basic inspiration however does ring through at all times. The biblical notion of abundant life (John 10:10), which can be found in the camp song and which is the *Leitmotiv* of the pastoral plan of the diocese involved, is the ultimate perspective at which the summer camp is aiming overtly.

## 3. Religious re-imagination of the quest for meaning

In the summer of 2003 we prepared an explicitly religious workshop for the participants with the theme 'Home on the road: coming home in your own life story'. Fourteen young adults between nineteen and twenty five years old attended the workshop; we had to refuse five candidates. We were not the only ones who were successful with this approach. Two other groups gathered large numbers of interested youngsters with their meditation and spirituality materials. Almost one third of the older group of summer camp participants joined in a spirituality related workshop. The main theme was: 'Dreams, hopes, beliefs'.

Again, most of these people are not regular churchgoers. Most of them will not even consider themselves believers, let alone Christian believers. They experience a deep longing in their lives, when they are confronted with issues such as future, despair, loneliness, vocation, life style, relationships, etc. The astonishing thing is that they are accessible for images and stories of the good life – even for biblical language games – if they are related to these 'movements of the soul' – to their marginal experiences of hunger for orientation and meaning. We invited this year's participants directly to jump into the water and to swim without reserve. As leaders of the group we brought in our own narrative struggles with the ultimate ground of our lives. We gave them permanently the chance to interfere with our words and gestures, prayers and rituals, by using challenging discourse and play techniques. And we gave them ample opportunity to discuss their thoughts with their fellow human beings 'home on the road'. In the coming section I will tell the story of the summer camp.

The key word was journey. The four days were build around four basic elements in the life of the pilgrim: stone, rope, angel and walking-stick. The first day was organized as a long journey through the woods and the fields in the South of Leuven. The participants went two by two and were asked to reflect upon key stones of change and continuity in their lives. After lunch we stopped talking and every participant was invited to write down some ideas on these milestones in a sort of spiritual diary. We continued and arrived in one of the small Roman churches in the area (namely Tourinnes-la-Grosse), where we invited the participants to search for shelter and fresh air, and to flee for a moment from the heat outside. In the tower there was an inscription, almost saying this: 'Let your life speak' (Palmer 2000), take your time to reflect and to reshape your journey, and be confident that this is a valuable place to do so. We continued our trip and arrived finally in the middle of the fields, in a small chapel. On that spot every one was asked to write a letter to oneself, on possible inspirational key stones or embarrassing stones in the own journey. These letters were posted and arrived a couple of days later at the summer camp. At the end of the first day a spontaneous conversation about God started in the group. Most of the members said they felt connected in friendship with each other and in this coherence there was a deep spiritual embeddedness. But most of them refused to name this experience 'God' because this concept referred too much to an objective otherness, outside the real experience of human interconnectedness and solidarity.

The second day we organized a sort of labyrinth walk through the cellars of the old school building in which we were housed. After an introduction with a text of the medieval mysticist Jan Ruusbroec on 'emptying oneself to encounter the other as a new self' the participants went two by two in the dark, using the rope of Ariadne, in order to unveil their past experiences of despair and fear – and to connect to new ways of coping with them. This was a remarkable experience for most of the participants. For moments of self-awareness of one's own shadows in life can be very confronting and discomforting – and therefore the reliance on the walking partner is a thoughtful and overwhelming experience. Afterwards we were discussing the journey through the 'cellars of life' also from another, surprising angle. We collected our thoughts on blindness and discussed them with one of the participants who actually is a blind person. The key word appeared to be 'trust': how much trust or faith do you have in others and in yourself, when you loose the thread of your life or when you are looking for support and clarity to take up the thread again?

The next step in the spiritual journey of the summer camp was to explore the world of angels in our lives. We read the text of the encounter and the struggle of Jacob with the angel at the Jabbok river (Genesis 32: 23-33) and we were defining all sorts of situations in which we felt both challenged and sheltered by a guardian angel. The ideas of the German Benedictin monk Anselm Grün were very inspiring for this *exercitio* (Grün 2002). Participants were invited to design and to fabrique their own coat of shelter.

The final day was explicitly oriented towards a religious re-imagination of the journey. There was plenty of meditation time – and time for writing and talking one's path through questions such as: 'What gives you the ultimate ground under your feet? Where do you trust in ultimately? Where does your walking-stick comes from? Where can you find solidity and resilience? When do you experience yourself most deeply loved?' We read Psalm 23, we contextualized its words in the exile of the Jewish people, and we referred to other key words in religious traditions to explicate this experience of ultimate trust and love. Finally we provided the participants with a mission (Matthew 10 – 'Feel home on the road') and with a blessing.

Many of these people are carrying heavy burdens. They are often confronted with the failures of their parents and with the pain of loosing faith in their lives. But they do continue to revitalize small experiences of hope, in community, discourse and action. And they don't stop thinking about what keeps them running. One of the things they don't like however is to identify this struggle for the good life with a definitive reference to an ultimate transcendent being. For them the source of life is immanent, it is rooted in their daily lives and narratives of friendship and commitment. If they are offered a safe environment, they are eager to talk about their spiritual resources. Safe means safe from the social pressure of uninterested peers or from the educational pressure of adults who expect particular faith answers.

### 4. Young adult ministry as the 'art of maieutics'

What is the key to the success of the summer camp? It can be found on two different levels: on a community level and on a story level. This is no new notion. Responsible people in churches do know what is important in young adult work. What is regrettable however is that this inspiration tends to get pushed into the background in favor of 'youth work technology' and a guidance model that is as functional and anemic as the social technology of the adult world. Young people want involvement, they want to be 'fascinated' – which is not the same as being subject to great old stories that are not their own, and not the same as being absorbed by great new stories that steamroller their own small stories of hope.

Nobody can live without a narrative. People tell themselves and each other stories, they reconstruct their existence while telling. They link up the major events of their lives in the telling, portraying these events as if they constituted a perpetual umbilical cord that keeps them connected with the life dynamism of humanity. This is common sense. Nobody has to start at the very beginning when telling his story. People grow up in philosophical traditions, circles of explicitly meaningful life, with a characteristic vision of the good life, of friendship, desire, love and death. Such traditions offer insight into the individual's story, helping him to gain clarity as to who he is and who he wants to be. In such traditions values and meaning are personified, represented by concrete people of flesh and blood, who pass the narratives on while blending in their personal experiences of love and death (Miedema & Roebben 2008). Such people are not sacrosanct, they too have their struggles and their doubts. But they *are* explicit: They can be called to account for their convictions, they make themselves accessible.

The young adults who attend the summer camp are no snobs. They rather represent and amplify what remains easily unsaid among their peers. I want to present the following thoughts for consideration that I have distilled from their stories. Young people are in search of warm involvement in the adult world. They proceed, so to speak, to the place from where (they think that) adults should lead. They 'pro-voke' (from the Latin verb 'pro-vocare', to call forward) adults to show their true colors, to move away from indifference and to make a real difference. Again, in the present boom of values education it is not the authoritarian enforcement of common decency and socially well-adjusted behavior of young people – whether or not cleverly presented in attractive methodologies – that is important. Rather it is this question that is at the heart of it: Do adults still have faith in their children?

(Roebben 1995c). Do they have the courage to exert leadership in vulnerability and modesty while showing persuasiveness and insight? Do they show themselves in their greatness *and* in their plainness, in sum in their mature coping with the complexity of life?

In my opinion, young people are twice as vulnerable nowadays. All through their personal growth struggle runs today's social lack of clarity as to what is really worth living for. They lack biographical advice. In the 1970s the famous moral psychologists Kohlberg and Gilligan described this phenomenon as follows: "The adolescent is a philosopher by nature, and if not by nature, by counter-cultural pressure" (Kohlberg and Gilligan 1971). But how much rudderlessness can the young philosopher handle? Where are the bounds of his flexibility? How much irretrievability can one take before becoming irretrievably lost? Judging by our culture's perspective we should embrace change, according to Van Knippenberg (2002, 82-87). After all, this era likes to flirt with anything new and original. The first thing we look for when surfing the Internet, is the 'What's new?' column. But many contemporaries are in fact scared of losing themselves and becoming completely meaningless and thus valueless. This is why Van Knippenberg recommends spiritual leaders to continually assess the foundation of stability on which people stand in their dealings with plurality in a pluralistic culture (2002, 115-116).

The resilience of young adults to remain authentic to themselves in a confusing multitude of meanings (cfr. the surfer-metaphor used in the 2002 summer camp) can be strengthened by the exemplary conduct of resilient educators. They do not use words redundantly nor do they have program explanations ready. Instead they show the courage to express their convictions, fresh and original, animated and deliberate. Their walk is an indication of their talk. Franz Rosenzweig once said: 'Truth is not *proven* in the reality of the existence, it is *tested*; true is what can be tested. To believe a truth implies to bear witness to it' (quoted in Kirsch 2001, 92, translation BR). In a nutshell, this is the essence of this chapter.

The old Socratic image of the educator as a *maieuticus*, as a midwife, still appeals to one's imagination. She helps in the birth of new life. She reveals a new meaning to that specific person. In Dutch the word for 'to reveal' is 'open-baren'. This compound word can literally be translated as: 'to open for giving birth'. This form of leadership is a source of profound joy for those who stand amazed at what is happening. Because it might as well have been different. To lead young people in the pursuit of meaning, all of a sudden realizing that things go exactly in line with *or* exactly opposite to what had been pedagogically anticipated is one of the most powerful experiences of professional satisfaction of an educator, according to the philosopher of education Hanan Alexander (2001, 193-198).

**Conclusion**

This risky business of solidarity with future generations – the radical openness to their spiritual resources – has also its consequences for future theology. It will shed new light on the religious words and gestures of people who educate and on their theological justification of these words and gestures. This is so because risky solidarity is leading to the idea of risky revelation. Who actually listens carefully to the lives and hopes of future generations, could not only get involved in new patterns of faith, but also in new experiences and therefore in new contents of faith. Perhaps, then, it *can* actually happen: that a new insight suddenly breaks through within the given frameworks – an insight that makes the existing system burst open, creating room for what was completely unanticipated. Should this no longer be possible, which is what some culture pessimists claim, then future generations would be in for a rough time. If that were the case, then it would be impossible to educate at all.

# Chapter 14

# International Developments in Youth Ministry Research
# A Comparative Review

Conducting international comparative research in practical theology is far from evident. For the very concept of praxis is connected to the idea of the local community, with its own understanding, enactment and assessment of religious practices. Engaging in practical theology, and by extension in every form of praxis-sensible theology (Veling 1998), is engaging in a contextualized reflection on how human beings are dealing with the 'slow questions' in their life journeys, questions that do not endure 'fast food answers', and how they create in the midst of that process and in relationship with institutionalized forms of religion their own 'auto-*theo*-biographies' (Ward 2008). After many years of international collaboration in the fields of religious education (RE) and youth ministry (YM), two important access routes to practical theological research, I am becoming more and more aware of the structural difficulty of comparative research in these fields.

In the recent past I had many chances to network between researchers of different language groups, different local settings and theologies in Europe and abroad, as the president of the 'International Association for the Study of Youth Ministry', as an expert in the Council of Europe, as a regular contributor to the conferences of the 'European Forum of Teachers in Religious Education' and to the Dutch, German and North-American RE associations. However, even within one and the same language group, the differences were often huge and difficult to master. Belgium and the Netherlands, for instance, are neighboring countries, they use (partly) the same language, but still are so completely different in school and parish life culture. Hard to believe, but driving 120 kilometers from Leuven in Belgium to Tilburg University in the north and crossing the Dutch border often meant for me something like a culture shock!

Nevertheless there is one important element that forces us gently into a worldwide collegial and comparative reflection on practical theology in our work with young people in RE and YM, namely the issue of globalization. It is my contention that local theologies in RE and YM are in one way or another responding to this global issue. The dynamics of the globe (such as the international market, the social media, migration movements, common ecological concerns, etc.) are affecting the embodied lives of people living locally on that globe. The world is literally at our doorstep, or even more intimate, at our finger tips. We are universally connected in our vulnerable particularities. In this chapter I focus on research in YM, on the practices of local congregations and institutions in their work with young people and young adults, vis-à-vis these developments.

This chapter contains three parts: after a presentation of four organizational *con-texts* of international YM research, I will briefly discuss four central themes or *texts* in YM research. In the third part I will look deeper into the *textures* of these themes in order to unravel four challenges for future research in practical theology. The lens that I am using is the scholarly writing of colleagues in the field, in which I sense a deep commitment to local practices and reflections. My endeavor here is an exercise in modesty: gathering respectfully – as far as I can see with my subjective lens – the richness of the fruits of this research, inviting the readership to reflect on the different positions and offering building blocks for something of which I hope that can become a new and strong 'revelatory fellowship' (Paul Tillich) in practical theology.

## 1. Contexts for YM research: giving young people a real voice

Youth ministry (in German *Jugendseelsorge*, in French *pastorale des jeunes*, in Spanish *pastoral de juventud*, in Dutch *jongerenpastoraal*) relates to the activities of churches and faith communities to support young people and young adults in their moral and religious identity development. Worldwide there is a huge interest in research in this part of church work, but not always free from the instrumental concerns of adults. Or young people are the future and this is precisely what is often lacking in traditional communities and mainstream churches. In order to get a glimpse of the seismographic function of young people, the ways in which they mirror the global dynamics in contemporary societies, and in order to respond adequately to these dynamics with 'purpose driven' ministry, huge amounts of money are spent to conduct (both quantitative and qualitative) empirical youth research. Adults want to know and to be sure about how young people and young adults organize their lives, witness to their values, norms and ultimate meanings and rely on official providers of spirituality and religion in congregations and communities.

It goes without saying that it is important to know where the juvenile addressees of pastoral ministry can be found and how they can be nurtured. It remains however a difficult task to adapt empirical research methods to the complex and flexible life worlds of youth. At the one hand data gathering is often blind for new and creative developments in youth cultures. At the other hand data are often overestimated with regard to possible ways of attracting (or even forcing) youth into the official church and its ministry. As far as I am concerned it seems necessary to develop new ways of looking carefully and empathetically to the world of young people and their religiosity. Predominantly the voices of young people themselves should be heard in all stages of youth and YM research: in the perception of the topic, in the definition of the problem, in the actual gathering of data and in the discussion and implementation afterwards.

Giving young people a real voice, this means listening to their longings and dreams in a comprehensive way, relates to another problem: the ignorance and omission of humanities in general and youth studies in particular to deal with religious and spiritual topics (Lechner and Gabriel 2009). For instance, the so called *Shell Jugendstudie* in Germany, a regular state of the art report on youth cultures, did not include a topic on religiosity until the survey of 2006, mainly because the instrument to measure new forms of de-institutionalized and individualized religion was lacking. Yet other research circles have registered the need to open up their secular methods for the spiritual dimension of the lives of young people in a post-secular era (Benson et al. 2008). This ambiguity can, as far as I am concerned, only be solved if the *peer dimension*, so crucial in YM, namely that young people minister to each other, is also used for research means. Again, in order to understand what young people really believe, hope and love, they should be invited to become the real agents of perception, interpretation and change (see, judge, act), in other words, to become real researchers themselves! Educational research on inclusion could be helpful here, research in which "the involvement of children and young people and their families in identifying the kinds of questions which need to be asked about inclusion and exclusion could be an important first step towards providing the kind of knowledge that will be of use" (Allan 2008, 146).

In what follows I describe in a non-exhaustive way four *loci* where voices of young people can be heard, thanks to the explicit religious youth and YM research that has been giving a floor to these voices. The list of initiatives is definitely much longer and a good inventory is lacking. My intention is not to give an exhaustive overview. This short list should rather be seen as an invitation to the international research community to cooperate more intensively in gathering, exchanging and interpreting relevant data on this relevant topic. The relevance is global, but the presence of the entire globe in the research is painfully a non-presence. I come back to this later. The description of the four categories follows the line from the macro-perspective (society), via the meso-perspective (church and school) to the micro-perspective (the individual).

First of all large scale data sets are available in the Western world on youth and religion, religiosity and spirituality, just to mention a few: 'Youth in Europe' (Ziebertz and Kay 2005, 2006 and 2009), 'Soul Searching' in the USA (Smith and Lundquist Denton 2005; Dean 2010), 'Visualising hope' in Eastern Europe (Dunlop 2008), 'Generation Y' in the UK (Savage et al. 2006) and youth spirituality research in Australia (McQuillan 2007). Country reports can be found on the desks of local research entities. Regional and local congregations investigate on a regular basis the position of their children with regard to churches, congregations, faith communities and sects, like was argued before.

A second stream of research activities can be found on the meso-level, in ecclesiology and ministry studies. They relate to the world of youth churches, alternative worship, emerging churches, religious events, pastoral care and youth catechesis. Just to mention a few initiatives in this respect: research on community building in the UK (Baker 2011; Ward 2002), on youth liturgy (Sonnenberg and Barnard 2008; Stams 2008), on confirmation in European protestant churches (Schweitzer et al. 2010), on religious learning in church contexts (Afdal 2011), on the motivations of youth to participate in large religious events such as the World Youth Day (Scharnberg 2010), on the impact of ecumenical and interreligious gatherings on juvenile spirituality (Santos 2008), on the professionalization of youth leaders (Roebben & Zondervan 2008), on outreach activities (Warren 2002) and summer camps (see Chapter 13), etc. Central to these findings is the idea that young people with their creativity and openness are reinventing and revitalizing the complex inner dynamic of mystics and politics within churches.

Thirdly, there is a growing interest in YM and young adult ministry studies, mostly related to the life world of the school campus. Historically the origins of YM can be found in the presence of representatives of the church in the world of the school. The relational approach of 'Young Life' in the USA for instance was in the first part of the 20th century intentionally focused on entering "the foreign world of the high school adolescent to save it for Christ" (Root 2009, 22). Later the relationship became framed in a more open and inviting rather than in persuasive way and focused also on the college campus where young adults are gathering with their "big questions and worthy dreams" (Daloz Parks 2000). This idea of ministry with adolescents and young adults, understood as creating personal relationships (the so called *personales Angebot* in German), was and still is the paradigmatic option for YM in Europe. The Roman-Catholic and Protestant churches are still vividly present in the world of schools in Europe, specifically through their (confessional) RE courses in primary and secondary schools, but also through their pastoral presence. Affiliations of church and school (in German: *Schule in kirchlicher Trägerschaft*) are still high on the agenda, although the secularization has changed much of the content. A shift can be observed from institutional religious belonging to individual moral consultancy of youth, from the school as faith community to the school as a community of values (in Dutch: *waardegemeenschap*) (Geurts 2008; Schweitzer and Scheilke 1999). The newest research in this respect describes the ways in which young adults can be introduced in the world of religious practices, e.g. in the religious life of monasteries (Smeets 2007) and in reflections on the relationship between profession and vocation, e.g. as future teachers (Banning 2007; Van Aalsum 2011; Roebben 2011). Interesting to see how this field of attention has an equivalent in the USA with the movement of "linking social identity to community practices" (Dean 2004, 152, with extensive bibliography; Mahan et al. 2008).

And finally the whole body of research on spirituality of children (Hay and Nye 1998) and young people (Yust et al. 2005) in the Anglo-Saxon world and on theologizing with children and young people in the German, Dutch and Scandinavian discourse (Büttner 2007; Schlag and Schweitzer 2011; Yde Iversen et al. 2009; see also Chapter 6) needs to be mentioned here. The impact of this research stream, in which the traditional idea of handing over faith is replaced by an organic idea of raising the spiritual awareness of children and educating the critical reflection of young people and young adults, is huge and developing in a steady pace.

The description of the context of YM in these four research tracks – data on religious youth cultures, on explicit YM initiatives, on the presence of faith communities in the public realm and on the spiritual and theological voices of young people – seems to me of central value for any researcher in the field. In a context of globalization there is an urgent need to compare these findings internationally and to exchange educational methods in order to improve perceptions of and responses to the spiritual voices of youth. Moreover there is an urgent need to include voices from the Southern Hemisphere. Globalization is affecting youth and young adults 'all over the place', but we do not have a clue of what really is happening 'on the spot' in the South. The many voices of youth there and the vulnerable responses of local churches to these voices are not even heard, let alone scholarly registered. As far as I can see only two books deal explicitly with international findings, including the South: 'Global Youth Ministry' (Linhart & Livermore 2011) and 'Youth, Religion and Globalization' (Osmer & Dean 2006). The 'slow questions' that young people raise in a context of 'fast living' are comparable on a global scale. The material circumstances of poverty, oppression and migration however to deal with these questions differ radically between the continents of our globe. The awareness is growing in global institutions such as *Unicef*, *Unesco* and the *United Nations' Alliance of Civilizations* that the spiritual awareness of youth and the contribution of religions need to be considered as an integral dimension of the wellbeing of youth worldwide.

## 2. Thematic scripts in YM research: analyzing emerging problem fields

After the presentation of the major contexts in which YM can be discerned as a research topic, I now analyze four themes that shape the practical theological discussion on YM worldwide. One of the major observations in a context of growing globalization is that young people (but not only they!) are desperately looking for orientation in the midst of an overwhelming market place of life styles, values, norms and meaning giving systems. In psychotherapy and pastoral ministry sessions young people often express their feelings of permanently jumping into the void, into a vacuum 'full of meaninglessness'. They lack the points of reference to name and tame what they see and experience. Old master stories or dogmatic answers do not work anymore in everyday life. But also the 'terrorism' of 'anything goes', combined with the obsessive power of a hyper-personalized narration, remains unsatisfying. On the contrary, it is sometimes literally 'killing' people. The moral and spiritual compass in the heart of the postmodern self is running wild. Moreover young people are struggling with the feeling that they are left alone by adults (Champagne 2009, 3; Metz 2011, 205; Moore and Right 2007). Deep down however, in the stomach of society, there is a longing to overcome individualism and egocentrism by compassion, commitment, communication, communion – values that all begin with the prefix 'com' (which means: together with, connected to). Connection, dealing with diversity and complexity in a connected way – living and learning as "receiving the gift of friendship" (Reinders 2008) – seems to me a key challenge for the future. In the heart of the post-secular society new and vital spiritual connections are sought for and crafted by young contemporaries. This is a hopeful development. What now can be considered as four dimensions of this process? How do they trigger the attention of faith communities and research centers?

A second consideration relates to the vulnerability of young people. In their personal search for meaning solid orientations are often absent. Even the very grounds for existence and co-existence with others are sometimes lacking. Young people are then caught up in the tension between apathy and extremism. In a YM perspective this can be translated in the tension between an indifferent but "benign whateverism" or a radical "living and dying for God" (Smith & Lundquist Denton 2005; Dean 2010). There is comparative evidence that this dichotomy can be found transculturally, not only in the Christian tradition and not only in the United States of America (Van Dijk-Groeneboer 2010). On a global scale the need for a more holistic YM is expressed, especially in circumstances of mental distress, such as family breakdown, HIV-Aids, poverty and corruption. People are craving for a solid message in the midst of the "mess-age" in which they try to survive (Nuwoe-James Kiamu 2011). New connections of the churches' YM to community work, street corner and peer ministry, schools and other networks are urgently needed (Leys 2011). How can the dimension of liberation and hope be stimulated in YM (Parker 2003; Moore and Right 2007)? What are the relationships between globalization, religion, human flourishing and deeply embodied situations of distress? Where and how can churches be helpful in this respect?

The third script relates to the previous ones. Every form of YM and by extension YM research has a political dimension. The choices that are made in perceiving and recording the voices of youth are based on the socio-ethical presuppositions of the listening churches and the recording research institute. In a marvelous book three YM specialists in the US write: "When religious educators, youth ministers, and others encourage youth to claim *early and easy transcendence* over cultural distortions, they are playing directly into the hands of distorted elements of the culture. It is precisely the compensatory character of such early denials of the power of social scripts that sponsors later suspicion of the efficacy of faith to resist cultural distortions of being and doing" (Mahan et al. 2008, 85). And they continue: "Society, for its part, is more than happy to complement our tendencies toward intellectual, moral, and spiritual sloth by providing prefab answers to life's most enduring and complex problems, challenges, and dilemmas. (…) This is especially true about the turning points of life, those *kairos* moments when we start anew, when we are invited to take a different direction or to confirm one we already travel. There are no scripts for such occasions. There are, however, thank God, fellow travellers (…). We need to talk about these things openly, prayerfully" (Mahan et al. 2008, 102-103). One of the authors of the above mentioned book, David White, develops in this respect his religio-political framework for "practicing discernment with youth". He therefore uses the triad 'see-judge-act' (complemented with prayer and imagination), a powerful hermeneutic tool which has its equivalent in the European 'Catholic Action with Youth' of Jozef Cardijn in the middle of the 20$^{th}$ century (White 2005, 89-200).

The final observation to be made here is how religious diversity is interfering with globalization and the ongoing need for orientation. The expertise of interreligious learning in European schools, in the framework of 'learning in the presence of the other', with a view on "re-defining and re-dignifying" oneself can be helpful here (see Chapter 7 § 7). The "Interfaith Youth Core" of the American Muslim educationalist Eboo Patel has developed concrete ways of 'doing' this encounter through service learning, in order "to identify what is common between religions", but also to create safe space "where each can articulate its distinct path to that place" (Patel 2007, 167). Where can such space, safe for diversity, be installed? What is the contribution of faith communities in this respect?

## 3. Deep textures of YM research: chances and challenges for practical theology

The local contexts of YM research are offering us the main texts and thematic scripts for further discussion and cooperation. On the basis of our common concerns and passion for youth, I believe that we are able to develop a common research language that helps us to understand better the differences and communalities. Living on the same globe, confronted with the same questions, young people (ánd their researchers) develop different answers, because they are members of different local faith (ánd research) communities. Their contexts and texts are deeply textured by the pedagogical and theological discourses in which they are embedded.

Let me clarify my argument with an example. After many years of encountering American scholars and discussing European approaches to religion and education with them, the central difference between the two continents seems to be an educational one, with historical roots in society and politics. In the US it is unconstitutional to teach the inner dynamic of religion at school. Church and state are formally separated. Religion belongs to the private sphere of the family and the congregation and the nurturing and accompanying programs there. In Europe the intentional and spontaneous relationships between young people and religions are discussed publicly in all its complexity and diversity in the RE classroom. The education of future RE teachers is mainly organized by faculties and institutes of theology and religious studies. There is an internal link between theological discourse, religious experience and critical education. This is not the case in the US, although some scholars are pleading for training in religious literacy (interpreted as teaching *about* religion), integrated in school subjects such as history, literature and social sciences (AAR 2010; Moore 2007).

As far as I can see this situation has an influence on the status of theology in public life. In the United States theological reflection takes mainly place within the congregation. In Europe it can be executed in the open space of public life. This involves two different kinds of theology in the context of youth. In the US churches work mainly with YM, they deepen affirmatively the theological competence of youth through the participation at practices within one faith tradition, visualized in the congregation, initiated *into* religious nurture and inner conversion by convincing youth ministers. In Europe churches work more through their presence in RE in the public and private school system, they interfere critically with the religious convictions of youth through knowledge *about* and reflective learning *from* each other's practices, sometimes heavily discussed in the classroom, mainly through a critical appropriation of diversity in the personal stance *(Bildung)*, prepared and moderated by an authentic and self-critical teacher. Two different *rationales* are beyond the same practice: introducing young people in the world of religion(s). Two different *rationales* are beyond the same research topic: reflecting on young people when they are introduced in the world of religion(s)!

Nevertheless, anchored in a positive idea of comparative research, I now briefly present four textures for the further development of practical theology. The first encompasses the need for new research designs. Actual youth ministry offers not only a great deal of valuable research questions but also interesting concrete routes of dealing with these questions. As I argued in the introduction of this chapter new forms of 'peer related' research in the world of youth need to be stimulated. Thomas Schlag and Friedrich Schweitzer (2011) offer an interesting threefold framework for this cooperation, in the way that they are convinced that the implicit and personal "theologies of youth" should be the starting point for educational (read: explicit and reflected) processes of "theology with youth" and "theology for youth". This first step however is a difficult one: it radically demands a conversion of the researcher. The American practical theologian Tom Beaudoin is very (self-)critical in this respect to 'Soul Searching' and its underlying moralizing discourse: "The simplest evidence for this moralizing is that Soul Searching never considers that contemporary teen belief may have something substantially spiritually constructive and new, not just alarming, to teach the larger church" (Beaudoin 2008, 85). Critical studies through sustainable, longitudinal and interdisciplinary approaches are urgently needed, but not only in practical theology!

A second line of thought could be the relationship between ministry, community and leadership. The American YM researcher Andrew Root (2009) deepens the strategy of relational and missional YM into a theology of incarnational and even kenotic YM. In 'place sharing' with young people the minister engages in "participating in the living presence of God together with them right now" (Root 2009, 113). The English practical theologian Pete Ward (2008) argues: "When one is working in the field of the proclamation of the gospel with youth, theology needs not to be adapted to this situation. One is already participating in the expression and circulation of theology" (Ward 2008, 48). Here again the theological ánd political conversion of the youth minister is at stake. His task is "setting up contexts where the vital questions affecting young adults can be asked as part of a prayerful communal search for wisdom. Lacking such contexts some people may say later, 'We asked for bread and you gave us stone'" (Michael Warren, in Mahan 2008, 57-58). This place sharing is fundamentally an act of conversion.

The third consideration is about learning processes in the church. The irreverent quest for meaning is a right to be observed by every human being, included children and youth. Every human being has the right to develop his or her personal catechism (Karl Rahner), to undertake his or her own journey in faith, to create his/her own intensive communion with God and fellow believers. The Spirit is moving in this learning process of young people; it is the locomotive power "that transcend(s) their daily fragmentation and make(s) them feel whole"

(Dean 2004, 101). Will churches be able to respond to the movements of the Spirit in the lives of young people? For Dean a new "curriculum of passion" (2004, 161-172) is needed. The elaboration of it reminds me strongly of the spiritual theology of Meister Eckhart (14th century) and the mystagogical theology of Karl Rahner (20th century) – two German scholars who have lost nothing of their theological relevance for today. Once again, for this form of religious and theological education (and related research) a deep conversion and humility are needed. It all boils down to "lowering the bar of transcendence" (Dean 2004, 111).

And finally, these observations have strong implications for the textured relationship between practical and systematic theology. The tension between 'theology of youth' and 'theology for youth', between 'théologie forte' (in the academy and the church) and 'théologie faible' or 'lay theology' (Schlag and Schweitzer 2011, 22-24 and 47-51) are challenging. This tension should be productive and creative, rather than destructive. I believe that practical and systematic theologians can encounter each other on a deeper level in their public presence, when they engage together in a globalizing society and try to read the signs of the times in the light of the gospel. Once again, conversion is the key word.

## Conclusion

The incarnational dynamic of YM challenges practical theological research. In a context of globalization and radical vulnerability theological research is critically called to open the ears of the world for the voices of the coming generations. In this process we are all learners and even always absolute beginners. "What we share with our students, uncomfortably, is the complicated and obscure travail of intimacy with God, the uncanny concrete individual knowledge of the divine whose logic Rahner insurgently encouraged us to respect, the mysterious gift of desolation and consolation that not even the holiest among us can predict, our now passionate, now resigned, now outraged orientation to the uncontainable, the life of grace" (Beaudoin 2008, 74). Practical theological research is an exercise in modesty. So was the comparative endeavor of this chapter.

# Epilogue

In this book I took the reader on a journey through recent developments in religious education and youth ministry theory and practice, all over Europe. Hopefully he has learned a lot with regard to the great changes in this area of concern. Perhaps he is now able to recognize somewhat better facts and figures, possibilities and boundaries, history and future vision of moral and religious education. The world of contemporary education however remains complex, whether one is a teacher of religious education, parish catechist, youth minister, religious counselor or parent. It is not only the ongoing task to develop oneself as a young person which demands flexibility of educators, but also the fact that this process nowadays takes place in a complex environment. Becoming a responsible and spiritually sensible adult is a permanent interactive learning process. The life story of an adolescent or young adult is constantly 'under construction' and always in a tense relation with the environment. There is no reason to panic when one has understood this book correctly: this belongs to the journey or the way in which young people live and develop. Bumping and hurting, but also polishing themselves at an environment which is hopefully rich in impulses.

There is a huge need for human wholesomeness these days. We live our lives in a fragmented universe. Educators ask themselves the question: what is good for our children, what will we pass on as being of value? In everyday life, at work, in relationships and even in leisure time, many contemporaries experience an ongoing turbulence. We loose touch with ourselves and with the many traditional language games that we used so eagerly to describe what drives us. European religious institutions are loosing meaning, the churches are getting empty. The Christian frame of reference seems to be out of date. Yet still the need for wholesomeness keeps arising. Out of societal experiences of contrast – "this cannot go on any longer" – people come into motion. They experience that they themselves cannot be the ground of their own existence, that there are boundaries with regard to the self-directed life and that there can come cracks in a life which is merely self-centered.

Departing from a narthical perspective on religious education I stated the case to maximize the learning space and bring young people to 'green pastures', as to invoke their longing for knowledge and insight. This means that we have to involve them into journeys of longing and perspective, let them experience what it is like to have hunger and thirst, what it means to endure when one is on his way, what it means to look forward to getting home in the life of a pilgrim. We will have to feed them with impelling life and knowledge perspectives, but especially with our own struggle as educators when we bare witness to those perspectives ourselves. Faith cannot be taught, it can only be caught. It is learned 'ex auditu', on authority of hearsay: someone thought it meaningful and started living accordingly. This appealed to the imagination and inspired others. Good general education is radically spiritually laden (Alexander 2001; Jeanrond 2002; Koerrenz 1997; Roebben 2011). The main focus of education is letting go and expect (almost) everything from the dynamics of hope. The educator has to surrender himself to the learning abilities of the student or the group: he hopes the 'click' occurs. Learning is a permanent process of relearning, rearranging, renewal because everything can change constantly. The young person and the educator dare to see the complexity and endure the contingency. It is there that their little stories arise and become great stories. They let themselves not be swallowed up by the big, amazing stories of market and media, but quench themselves to the traditions of wisdom that are grand in their accessibility and humbleness and that inspire them to go on with their everyday quest.

Last but not least. One could expect from churches that they dwell meaningfully in the tension between longing and perspective, between what people nowadays seek to find in their vulnerable existence and the religious traditions of wisdom that teach people how to deal with this vulnerability. The churches must take well care of their *narthex*, their entrance, the passageway between outside and inside, between the longing of contemporaries and the fragmented answers that are handed over from tradition. This narthical acquaintance is, as stated, a pedagogical one, but also a theological one: I learn to know myself better in relation to religious cultures and movements, but also in my relationship with transcendence, the 'holy ground' of my existence that is always bigger than me. In this common quest a lot of voices can be heard. New communities should be build with others who also strive for a new humanity, in which the human person cannot and may not be reduced to his buying behavior or working capacity. In this cooperation with others, hopefully a movement of new Christian thinkers and practictioners can arise. They could give witness to the surprising transformations and metamorphoses of God today (Schillebeeckx 2005; Borgman 2006; Van den Bosch 2006). Their 'appreciative intellect' testifies of this quest: they experience their situation as a challenge to thoroughly contemplate and discuss, to see themselves as part of a long tradition chain of 'granted' humanity. They don't stand alone. But they feel called upon to take a stand.

# References

ADORNO, T.W. (1970), *Erziehung zur Mündigkeit. Vorträge und Gespräche mit Helmut Becker 1959–1969,* Frankfurt-am-Main.
AFDAL, G. (2011), *Researching Religious Education as Social Practice* (Religious Diversity and Education in Europe 20), Münster/New York/München/Berlin.
ALEXANDER, H.A. (1995), *Religion and Multiculturalism in Education,* in *Religious Education 90* (3-4), 377-387.
ALEXANDER, H.A. (2001), *Reclaiming Goodness. Education and the Spiritual Quest,* Notre Dame.
ALLAN, J. (2008), *Rethinking Inclusive Education. The Philosophers of Difference in Practice,* Dordrecht.
ALMA, H.A. & JANSSEN, J. (2000), *Jeugd en zingeving: een open vraag,* in H.A. Alma et al., *Zin op school. Zingeving in het voortgezet onderwijs,* Nijmegen, 9-25.
American Academy of Religion (2010), *Guidelines for Teaching About Religion in K-12 Public Schools in the United States.*
APEL, K.O. (1986), *Die transzendentalpragmatische Begründung der Kommunikationsethik und das Problem der höchsten Stufe einer Entwicklungslogik des moralischen Bewußtseins,* in *Archivio di Filosofia 54,* 107-157.
ASTLEY, J. (2002), *Ordinary Theology. Looking, Listening and Learning in Theology,* Burlington.
BAART, A. (2001), *Een theorie van de presentie,* Utrecht.
BAKER, J. (2011), *Youth Ministry Changes More than You Know,* in T. Linhart & D. Livermore (eds.), *Global Youth Ministry. Reaching Adolescents around the World,* Grand Rapids (MI), 43-55.
BAKKER, C. (2007), *Interreligious Learning. Teachers in Tension? Teachers between 'The Formal Christian Identity of the School' and 'Religious Diversity',* in D. Pollefeyt (ed.), *Interreligious Learning,* 291-308.
BALDERMANN, I. (1996), *Einführung in die biblische Didaktik,* Darmstadt.
BANNING, B. (2007), *Onderwijsdier in hart en nieren. Een persoonlijke visie op groei, professionaliteit en pedagogisch vermogen,* Budel.
BAUMAN, Z. (1996), *From Pilgrim to Tourist – or a Short History of Identity,* in S. Hall & P. Du Gay (eds.), *Questions of Cultural Identity,* London, 18-35.
BEAUDOIN, T. (1998), *Virtual Faith: the Irreverent Spiritual Quest of Generation X,* San Francisco.
BEAUDOIN, T. (2008), *Witness to Dispossession: The Vocation of the Postmodern Theologian,* Maryknoll (NY).
BENEZET, B. (2006), *Wij, Franse jongeren, zijn ons zelfvertrouwen kwijt,* in *De Standaard,* 22 maart 2006.

BENSON, P.L. et al. (eds.) (2008), *Spiritual Development* (Series New Directions for Youth Development), San Francisco.
BERG, H.-K. (1991), *Lebenspraxis als Ausgangs- und Zielperspektive der Bibellektüre*, in *Jahrbuch für Religionspädagogik 8,* 139-154.
BIERINGER, R. (1997), *The Normativity of the Future. The Authority of the Bible for Theology*, in *Bulletin ET 8*, 52-67.
BITTER, G. (1996), *Plädoyer für eine zeitgemäße Korrelationsdidaktik*, in *Lebendige Katechese 18* (1), 1-8.
BITTER, G. (1998), *Religionsunterricht als eine sozialhygienische Dringlichkeit*, in *Lebendige Seelsorge 49* (2/3), 135-138.
BLUYSSEN, J. (1989), *De vele wegen en de ene weg*, Baarn.
BONNET, M. (1986), *Personal Authenticity and Public Standards. Towards the Transcendence of a Dualism*, in D.E. Cooper (ed.), *Education, Values and Mind. Essays for R.S. Peters*, London, 111-133.
BOPP, K. (1995), *Wozu kirchliche Jugendarbeit? Überlegungen zu einer lebensweltbezogenen Jugendarbeit*, in *Stimmen der Zeit 120,* 401-411.
BORGMAN, E. (1994), *Alexamenos aanbidt zijn God. Theologische essays voor sceptische lezers*, Zoetermeer.
BORGMAN, E. (2000), *Zoeken naar het zelf of wachten op God?*, in *De Bazuin*, 10 november 2000.
BORGMAN, E. (2002), *Identiteit verwachten: van theologische antropologie naar cultuurtheologie*, in *Tijdschrift voor Theologie 42,* 174-196.
BORGMAN, E. (2006), *Metamorfosen. Over religie en moderne cultuur*, Kampen/Kapellen.
BOSCHKI, R. (1998), *Dialogisch-kreative Religionsdidaktik. Eine Weiterentwicklung der korrelativen Hermeneutik und Praxis*, in *Katechetische Blätter 123*, 13-23.
BOSCHKI, R. (2003), *„Beziehung" als Leitbegriff der Religionspädagogik*, Ostfildern.
BOWMAN, L. (2006), *Understanding the Study of Religion in Undergraduate Programs of Religious Studies as Religious Education*, in *Religious Education 101*, 143-146.
BOYS, M. (1997a), *Authenticity, not Demonization: An Education for Paradox*, in *Journal of Ecumenical Studies 34*, 350-355.
BOYS, M. (1997b), *Jewish-Christian Dialogue. One Woman's Experience*, New York.
BOYS, M. (2000), *Has God Only One Blessing? Judaism as a Source of Christian Self-Understanding*, New York/Mahwah (NJ).
BOYS, M. (2008), *Learning in the presence of the other*, in *Religious Education 103*, 502-506.

BUCHER, A. (1995), *Die Moraltheorie von Lawrence Kohlberg als Paradigma fur Moraltheologie und religiös-sittliche Erziehung*, in V. Eid, A. Elsasser & G.W. Hunold (ed.), *Moralische Kompetenz*, Mainz, 37-75.
BUCHER, A. (1999), *Stimmt die Entkoppelungsthese? Zum Verhältnis allgemeiner und kirchlicher Religiosität in einer Stichprobe von 2700 Schuljugendlichen in Österreich*, in C. Friesl & R. Polak (ed.), *Die Suche nach der religiösen Aura*, Graz, 224-230.
BUCHER, A. (2002), *Kindertheologie: Provokation? Romantizismus? Neues Paradigma?*, in *Jahrbuch für Kindertheologie 1*, 9-27.
BURGGRAEVE, R. (1990), *Levinas over vrede en mensenrechten*, Leuven/Amersfoort.
BURGGRAEVE, R. (1991), *De bijbel geeft te denken. Schepping, milieu, lijden, roeping, Gods passie en de ander, vergeving, bevrijding van de ethiek. In gesprek met Levinas*, Leuven/Amersfoort.
BÜTTNER, G. (2007), *Kinder – Theologie*, in *Evangelische Theologie 67*, 216-229.
BÜTTNER, G. (2009), *Children's Concepts of Contingency as a Subject of Philosophizing*, in G. Yde Iversen, G. Mitchell & G. Pollard (eds.), *Hovering over the Face of the Deep*, 25-36.
CARR, D. (1996), *The Moral Role of the Teacher. Perspectives on Values 3*, Edinburgh.
CHAMPAGNE, E. (2009), *Together on the journey of plurality*, in *International Journal of Children's Spirituality 14*, 1-3.
COHEN, E.H. (2006), *Research in Religious Education. Content en Methods for the Postmodern and Global Era*, in *Religious Education 101* (2), 147-152.
COPLEY, T. (2005), *Indoctrination, Education and God. The Struggle for the Mind*, London.
CRAWFORD, M. & G. ROSSITER (2006), *Reasons for Living. Education and young people's search for meaning, identity and spirituality. A handbook*, Camberwell.
DALOZ PARKS, S. (2000), *Big Questions, Worthy Dreams. Mentoring Young Adults in Their Search for Meaning, Purpose, and Faith*, San Francisco.
DAMON, W. & GREGORY A. (1997), *The Youth Charter. Towards the Formation of Adolescent Moral Identity, Journal of Moral Education 26* (2), 117-130.
DASBERG, L. (1980), *Wat is er terechtgekomen van de 'eeuw van het kind'?*, in A.G.M. van Melsen et al., *Wie ben ik, wie zijn jullie? Een waardenvaste opvoeding in een waardeloze wereld?*, Baarn.
DEAN, K.C. (2004), *Practicing Passion. Youth and the Quest for a Passionate Church*, Grand Rapids (MI).
DEAN, K.C. (2010), *Almost Christian: What the Faith of Our Teenagers Is Telling the American Church*, New York.

DEKKER, G., DE HART, J. & PETERS, J. (1997), *God in Nederland. 1966-1996*, Amsterdam.
DELEU, P. (1988), *De kinderen zijn vrij. Over gezin, kerk en geloofsopvoeding*, Tielt.
*Den Religiösen Hunger Stillen – in der Schule? (Streitgespräch zwischen Albert Biesinger und Jürgen Lott)*, in *Publik Forum*, 10 April 1998.
*De school staat niet alleen. Verslag van de commissie Samenleving-Onderwijs aan de Koning Boudewijnstichting* (1994), Tielt.
DE WILDT, K. (2012), *With all senses: something for body and mind. An empirical study of religious ritual in school* [unpublished doctoral dissertation], Dortmund.
DILLEN, A. (2006), *Geloof in het gezin. Ethiek, opvoeding en gezinnen vandaag*, Tielt.
DILLEN, A. (2007), *Religious participation of children as active subjects: toward a hermeneutical-communicative model of religious education in families with young children*, in *International Journal of Children's Spirituality 12*, 37-49.
DOBBELAERE, K., M. ELCHARDUS & J. KERKHOFS (2000), *Verloren zekerheid. De Belgen en hun waarden, overtuigingen en houdingen*, Tielt.
DOMMEL, C. (2007), *Religions-Bildung im Kindergarten in Deutschland und England: Vergleichende Bildungsforschung für frühkindliche Pädagogik aus religionswissenschaftlicher Perspektive*, Frankfurt.
DREHSEN, V. (1994), *Wie religionsfähig ist die Volkskirche? Sozialisationstheoretische Erkundungen neuzeitlicher Christentumspraxis*, Gütersloh.
DUFFY, S.J. (1995-96), *Christianity in Dialogue. Jesus at the Circumference or Center?*, in *The Living Light 32* (2), 61-72.
DUMESTRE, M.J. (1997), *A Church at Risk. The Challenge of Spiritually Hungry Adults*. New York.
DUNLOP, S. (2008), *Visualising Hope. Exploring the Spirituality of Young People in Central and Eastern Europe*, Haverhill.
EBERTZ, M.N. (1999), *Kirche im Gegenwind. Zum Umbruch der religiösen Gesellschaft*, Freiburg/Basel/Wien.
EID, V. (1995), *Moralerziehung in pluraler Lebenswelt - und 'christliche Moral'?*, in V. Eid, A. Elsasser & G.W. Hunold (ed.), *Moralische Kompetenz*, 143-174.
EID, V., ELSASSER, A. & HUNOLD G.W. (ed.) (1995), *Moralische Kompetenz*, Mainz.
ELCHARDUS, M. (ed.) (1999), *Zonder maskers. Een actueel portret van jongeren en hun leraren*, Gent.
ENGEDAL, L.G. (2006), *Homo Viator. The Search for Identity and Authentic Spirituality in a Post-modern Context*, in K. Tirri (ed.), *Religion, Spirituality and Identity*, Bern et al.
ENGLERT, R. (1992), *Religiösen Erwachsenenbildung: Situation, Probleme, Handlungsorientierung*, (Praktische Theologie Heute 7), Stuttgart.

ENGLERT, R. (1993), *Die Korrelationsdidaktik am Ausgang ihrer Epoche: Plädoyer für einen 'ehrenhaften' Abgang,* in G. Hilger & G. Reilly (ed.), *Religionsunterricht im Abseits? Das Spannungsfeld Jugend-Schule-Religion,* München, 97-110.
ENGLERT, R. (1998), *Der Religionsunterricht nach der Emigration des Glauben-Lernens,* in *Katechetische Blätter 123,* 4-12.
ENGLERT, R. (2007), *Die Krise pädagogischer Berufe und das Berufsethos des Religionslehrers,* in M. Langer & W. Verburg (Eds.), *Zum Leben führen. Handbuch religionspädagogischer Spiritualität.* München, 45-63.
ETSCHEID-STAMS, M. (2011), *Doppelte Diaspora: Ergebnisse der Shell-Jugendstudie 2010,* in *Katechetische Blätter 136,* 218-223.
EXELER, A. (1984), *Jungen Menschen leben helfen. Die alten und die neuen Werte,* Freiburg/Basel/Wien.
FEIFEL, E. (1995), *Didaktische Ansätze der Religionspädagogik,* in H.-G. Ziebertz & W. Simon (ed.), *Bilanz der Religionspädagogik,* Düsseldorf, 56-110.
FEIFEL, E. & KASPER, W. (1987), *Tradierungskrise des Glaubens,* München, Kösel.
FEININGER, B. (2000-2001), *Mit der Bibel das Leben erzählen,* in *Bibel und Kirche 56,* 148-155.
FRAAS, H.-J. (1989), *Gemeinschaft – Geschichte – Persönlichkeit. Dt 6,20 als Grundmodell religiöser Sozialisation,* in W. Homolka & O. Ziegelmeier (Eds.), *Von Wittenberg nach Memphis* (FS R. Schwarz), Göttingen, 21-37.
FREUDENBERGER-LÖTZ, P. (2009), *'I didn't know that God can speak...' Theological conversations with children. Chances and challenges for teacher training,* in G. Yde Iversen, G. Mitchell & G. Pollard (eds.), *Hovering over the Face of the Deep,* 85-93.
FUCHS-HEINRITZ, W. (1990), *Jeugd als statuspassage of geïndividualiseerde jeugdbiografie?,* in *Jeugd en Samenleving 20,* 451-473.
GABRIEL, K. (1991), *Tradition im Kontext enttraditionalisierter Gesellschaft,* in D. Wiederkehr (Ed.), *Wie geschieht Tradition? Überlieferung im Lebensprozeß der Kirche* (Quaestiones Disputatae 133), Freiburg-im-Breisgau.
GEERINCK, I. (2004), *God Embarrassed by the Pastor? A Search for New Practices in Religious Education,* in D. Nauer, R. Nauta & H. Witte (eds.), *Religious Leadership and Christian Identity,* Münster, 143-153.
GEERINCK, I. (2006), *Identiteit als toegevoegde waarde. Het kritische heden en verleden van het godsdienstonderwijs,* Leuven.
GEFFRE, C. (2000), *Le pluralisme religieux et l'indifférentisme, ou le vrai défi de la théologie chrétienne,* in *Revue théologique de Louvain 31,* 3-32.
GEURTS, T. (2003), *Het riskante leren: gevaar en kwetsbaarheid in waardegericht leren,* in *Narthex. Tijdschrift voor levensbeschouwing en educatie 3* (4), 12-19.
GEURTS, T. (2008), *Het team als pedagogische waardegemeenschap. Waardegericht leren en de toekomst van de school,* in *Narthex. Tijdschrift voor levensbeschouwing en educatie 8* (5), 42-47.

GILBERT, G. (2003), *Mijn kerk is de straat,* Tielt.
GIROUX, H.A. (1993), *Living Dangerously. Multiculturalism and the Politics of Difference,* New York.
GREINER, U. (2000), *Der Spur des Anderen folgen? Religionspädagogik zwischen Theologie und Humanwissenschaften,* Münster.
GREINER, U. (2005), *Junge Erwachsenen: Schlüsselfiguren religiöser Bildung,* in R. Englert & S. Leimgruber (ed.), *Erwachsenenbildung stellt sich Pluralität* (Religionspädagogik in pluraler Gesellschaft 6), Freiburg/Basel/Wien, 136-150.
GRIMMITT, M. (1987), *Religious Education and Human Development,* Great Wakering.
GROOME, T. (1991), *Sharing Faith. A Comprehensive Approach to Religious Education and Pastoral Ministry: the Way of Shared Praxis,* San Francisco.
GRÖZINGER, A. (1998), *Die Kirche – ist sie noch zu retten? Anstiftungen für das Christentum in postmoderner Gesellschaft,* Gütersloh.
GRÜMME, B. (2002*), Religionsförmigkeit als heimliche Pointe der Korrelationsdidaktik? Zum Begriff der Erfahrung in einer Zeit gottvergessener Religionsfreudigkeit, in Theologie der Gegenwart 45, 13-29.*
GRÜMME, B. (2007a), *Mystagogische Performanz. Der Religionsunterricht als Raum religiöser Praxis,* in *Theologie der Gegenwart 50,* 291-300.
GRÜMME, B. (2007b), *Vom Anderen eröffnete Erfahrung. Zur Neubestimmung des Erfahrungsbegriffs in der Religionsdidaktik,* Gütersloh/Freiburg-Basel-Wien.
GRÜMME, B. (2009), *Theologie der kleinen Leute,* in R. Miggelbrink, D. Sattler & E. Zenger (eds.), *Gotteswege. Für Herbert Vorgrimler,* Paderborn/München/Wien/ Zürich, 241-257.
GRÜN, A. (2002), *Vijftig engelen voor je ziel,* Tielt/Baarn.
HAAKEDAL, E. (2011), *Images of God and life attitudes in religious education workbooks. Interpreting some examples of 'theologizing' among Norwegian pupils in a changing school context,* in F. Kraft, H. Roose and G. Büttner (eds.), *Symmetrical Communication? Philosophy and Theology in Classrooms across Europe,* Loccum, 133-149.
HABERMAS, J. (1992), *Nachmetaphysisches Denken,* Frankfurt-am-Main.
HABERMAS, J. (2001), *Glauben und Wissen. Friedenspreis des Deutschen Buchhandels 2001,* Frankfurt-am-Main.
HAERS, J. (2004), *Religious Education as Conversation: Schools as Communities of Discernment,* in H. Lombaerts & D. Pollefeyt (eds.), *Hermeneutics and Religious Education* (BETL 180), Leuven, 313-336.
HALSALL, A. & ROEBBEN, B. (2006), *Intercultural and Interfaith Dialogue Through Education,* in *Religious Education 101* (4), 443-452.
HASTE, H. (1996), *Communitarianism and the Social Construction of Reality,* in *Journal of Moral Education 25,* 47-55.
HAY, D. & NYE, R. (1998), *The Spirit of the Child,* London.

HENDRIKS, J. (2000), *Gemeente als herberg. De kerk van 2000 – een concrete utopie*, Kampen.
HENS, T. (2001), *Eerst seks, dan God. Het lieve leven van Studio Brussel-man Lieven Vandenhaute*, in *De Standaard Magazine*, 9 november 2001.
HERMANS, C.A.M. (2003), *Participatory Learning. Religious Education in a Globalizing Society*, Leiden.
HERVIEU-LÉGER, D. (1990), *Religion and Modernity in the French Context. For a New Approach to Secularization*, in *Sociological Analysis 51*, 15-25.
HESS, M. (2003), *Practising Attention in Media Culture*, in J.P. Mitchell & S. Marriage (eds.), *Mediating Religion. Conversations in Media, Religion and Culture*, London/New York, 133-142.
HESS, M. (2005), *Engaging Technology in Theological Education: All That We Can't Leave Behind*, Lanham (MD).
HILGER, G., LEIMGRUBER, S. & H.-G. ZIEBERTZ (2002). *Religionsdidaktik. Ein Leitfaden für Studium, Bildung und Beruf*, München.
HUGGLER, J. (2009), *Religious Education as an Intellectual and Cultural Enterprise: Some Questions about 'Theologising with Children'*, in G. Yde Iversen, G. Mitchell & G. Pollard (eds.), *Hovering over the Face of the Deep*, 117-125.
HULL, J. (1996), *The Ambiguity of Spiritual Values*, in J.M. Halstead & M.J. Taylor (eds.). *Values in Education and Education in Values*, London, 33-44.
HUSSAIN, A. (2004), *Islamic Education: Why is there a Need for it?*, in *Journal of Beliefs and Values 25*, 319-323.
IPGRAVE, J. (2009a), *'My god and other people's gods'. Children's Theology in a Context of Plurality*, in G. Yde Iversen, G. Mitchell & G. Pollard (eds.), *Hovering over the Face of the Deep*, 54-69.
IPGRAVE, J. (2009b), *The language of friendship and identity. Children's communication choices in an interfaith exchange*, in *British Journal of Religious Education 31*, 213-225.
JACKSON, R. (1997), *Religious Education: An Interpretive Approach*, London.
JACKSON, R., MIEDEMA, S., WEISSE, W., WILLIAIME, J.-P. (eds.) (2007), *Religion and Education in Europe. Developments, Contexts and Debates* (Religious Diversity and Education 3), Münster/New York/München/Berlin.
JÄGGLE, M. et al. (2009), *Lebens – Werte – Schule. Religiöse Dimensionen in Schulkultur und Schulentwicklung*, Wien.
JANSSEN, J. & PRINS, M. (2000), *'Let's reinvent the Gods'. De religie van Nederlandse jongeren in een Europese context*, in *J\* Tijdschrift over jongeren 1* (4), 4-14.
JEANROND, W. (2002), *Geloof, vorming en vrijheid – categorieën van religieuze opvoeding in de kerk*, in *Concilium* (4), 65-74.
JOAS, H. (2004), *Braucht der Mensch Religion? Über Erfahrungen der Selbsttranszendenz*, Freiburg/Basel/Wien.

KAMMEYER, K. (2009), *„Lieber Gott, Amen!" Theologische und empirische Studien zum Gebet im Horizont theologischer Gespräche mit Vorschulkindern*, Stuttgart.
KIAMU, N.-J. (2011), *Message for a Mess-Age. Ministry to Youth in West-Africa*, in T. Linhart & D. Livermore (eds.), G*lobal Youth Ministry. Reaching Adolescents around the World*, Grand Rapids (MI), 95-104.
KIRSCH, H.-C. (2001), *Martin Buber. Biografie eines deutschen Juden,* Freiburg/ Basel/Wien.
KIRSCHENBAUM, H. (1991-92), *A Comprehensive Model for Values Education and Moral Education,* in *Phi Delta Kappan 73*, 771-776.
KLIE, T. (2003), *Performativer Religionsunterricht. Von der Notwendigkeit des Gestaltens und Handelns im Religionsunterricht*, in *Loccumer Pelikan 4,* 171-177.
KOERRENZ, R. (1997), *Hermeneutik des Lernens. Der anthropologische Wirklichkeitsbezug der biblischen Überlieferung,* in *Jahrbuch für biblische Theologie 12*, 221-242.
KOHLBERG, L. (1981), *The Philosophy of Moral Development. Moral Stages and the Idea of Justice*, San Francisco.
KOHLBERG, L. (1984), *The Psychology of Moral Development. The Nature and Validity of Moral Stages*, San Francisco.
KOHLBERG, L. & GILLIGAN, C. (1971), *The Adolescent as a philosopher. The discovery of the self in a postconventional world*, in *Daedalus 100,* 1051-1086.
KOHLER-SPIEGEL, H. (2007), *Wider das Vergessen – wider das Verstummen. Erfahrungen mit der Bibel,* in *Jahrbuch der Religionspädagogik 23,* 19-28.
KOZYREV, F. (2006), *The Roles of Dialogue in Religious Education. A Russian Perspective*, in D. Bates, G. Durka & F. Schweitzer (eds.), *Education, Religion and Society. Essays in Honour of John M. Hull,* London/New York, 215-227.
KUNDERA, M. (2007), *Die Weltliteratur*, in *The New Yorker*, 8 January, 28-35.
KUYK, E. et al. (2007), *Religious Education in Europe. Situation and Current Trends in Schools,* Oslo.
LECHNER, M. (1993), *Pädagogik des Jugendraumes. Neue Impulse für die kirchliche Jugendarbeit*, in *Trierer Theologische Zeitschrift 102,* 271-285.
LECHNER, M. & A. GABRIEL (eds.) (2009), *Religionssensible Erziehung. Impulse aus dem Forschungsprojekt „Religion in der Jugendhilfe" (2005-2008),* München.
LESCH, W. (1995), *Gesellschaft - Gemeinschaft – Gemeinwohl,* in V. Eid, A. Elsasser & G.W. Hunold (ed.), *Moralische Kompetenz*, Mainz, 117-142.
LEYS, L. (2011), The *New Latin America. From Renewal to Revolution*, in T. Linhart & D. Livermore (eds.), G*lobal Youth Ministry. Reaching Adolescents around the World*, Grand Rapids (MI), 105-114.
LICKONA, T. (1991), *Educating for Character. How Our Schools Can Teach Respect and Responsibility,* New York.

LINHART, T. and D. LIVERMORE (eds.) (2011), *Global Youth Ministry. Reaching Adolescents Around the World*, Grand Rapids (MI).
LOMBAERTS, H. (1997), *Religion, Society, and the Teaching of Religion in Schools*, in M. Warren (ed.), *Sourcebook for Modern Catechetics*, (Vol. 2), Winona, 306-329.
LOMBAERTS, H. & POLLEFEYT, D. (eds.) (2004), *Hermeneutics and Religious Education*, Leuven/Paris/Dudley (MA).
LOMBAERTS, H. & ROEBBEN, B. (eds.) (2000), *Godsdienst op school in de branding. Een tussentijdse balans* (Cahiers voor Didactiek 7), Deurne.
LUBARSKY, S. (1996), *Dialogue: "Holy Insecurity"*, in *Religious Education 91*.
LUTHER, H. (1992), *Religion und Alltag. Bausteine zu einer Praktischen Theologie des Subjekts*, Stuttgart.
MAAS, J. & ZIEBERTZ, H.-G. (1997), *Over breukvlakken en bruggenhoofden: religieuze opvoeding in het gezin*, in *Tijdschrift voor Theologie 37*, 384-404.
MAHAN, B.J., M. WARREN & D.F. WHITE (2008), *Awakening Youth Discipleship. Christian Resistance in a Consumer Culture*, Eugene (OR).
MALLON, M.C. (2004), *Globalization at large. Approaching the Ecclesial Question of Tradition in the Twenty-First Century*, T.W. Tilley (ed.), *New Horizons in Theology* (CTS Volume 50), Maryknoll (NY), 135-161.
MARTENS, E. (2009), *Children's Philosophy and Children's Theology – A Family Resemblance*, in G. Yde Iversen, G. Mitchell & G. Pollard (eds.), *Hovering over the Face of the Deep*, 97-115.
MCQUILLAN, P. (2007), *Youth Ministry in a World of Diversity. A Review of the International Research Project on Youth Spirituality*, in *Journal of Youth and Theology 6*, 70-91.
MEIJER, W.A.J. (1995), *The Plural Self. A Hermeneutical View on Identity and Plurality*, in *British Journal of Religious Education 17*, 92-99.
MEIJER, W.A.J. (2004), *Tradition and Reflexivity in Religious Education*, in H. Lombaerts & D. Pollefeyt (eds.), *Hermeneutics and Religious Education* (BETL 180), Leuven, 121-138.
METZ, J.B. (2011), *Mystik der offenen Augen. Wenn Spiritualität aufbricht*, Freiburg-Basel-Wien.
MEYER, H. (2009), *Was ist guter Unterricht?* Berlin (6th edition).
MERCER, J.A. (2005), *Welcoming Children. A Practical Theology of Childhood*, St. Louis (MO).
MERCER, J.A. & ROEBBEN, B. (2007), *Europe: just do it! Recent developments in European religious education research*, in *Religious Education 102*, 438-450.
METTE, N. (1994a), *Religionspädagogik* (Leitfaden Theologie 24), Düsseldorf.
METTE, N. (1994b), *Bildung und verbindliches Handeln. Identität in universaler Solidarität*, in *Stimmen der Zeit 119*, 453-464.

METTE, N. (2001), *Identity Before or Identity Through Familiarizing with Plurality? The Actual Discussion Concerning School Religious Education in Germany*, in B. Roebben & M. Warren (eds.), *Religious Education as practical Theology. Essays in Honour of Professor Herman Lombaerts*, Leuven/Paris/Sterling (VA), 217-244.
METTE, N. (2002), *Religieuze vorming op school – mogelijkheden en grenzen*, in *Concilium* # 4, 27-36.
METTE, N. (2005), *Einführung in die Katholische praktische Theologie*, Darmstadt.
METTE, N. (2007), *Praktisch-theologische Erkundungen 2*, Münster.
MICHIELS, R. & B. ROEBBEN (eds.) (1994), *Kerk op-nieuw. Variaties op het hedendaagse kerkgebeuren*, Leuven/Amersfoort.
MIEDEMA, S. (2000), *Levensbeschouwelijke vorming voor alle leerlingen op alle scholen*, in H. Alma et al., *Zin op school. Zingeving in het voortgezet onderwijs*, Nijmegen, 72-87.
MIEDEMA, S. (2007), *Contexts, Debates and Perspectives of Religion in Education in Europe. A Comparative Analysis*, in Jackson, R., Miedema, S., Weisse, W., Williaime, J.-P. (eds.) *Religion and Education in Europe. Developments, Contexts and Debates*, 267-283.
MIEDEMA, S. (2008), *Niederlände*, in F. Schweitzer, V. Elsenbast & Chr. Th. Scheilke (eds.), *Religionspädagogik und Zeitgeschichte im Spiegel der Rezeption von Karl Ernst Nipkow*, Gütersloh, 288-298.
MIEDEMA, S. & ROEBBEN, B. (2008), *The Two Contested Concepts of Culture and Tradition in Religious Education*, in *Religious Education 103*, 480-492.
MOKROSCH, R. (1999), *Brauchen Kinder und Jugendliche einen konfessionell geöffneten Religionsunterricht oder werden sie damit überfordert?*, in R. Frieling & C. Th. Scheilke (ed.), *Religionsunterricht und Konfessionen* (Bensheimer Hefte 88), Göttingen, 23-51.
MOLLENHAUER, K. & RITTELMEYER, C. (1978), *Einige Gründe für die Wiederaufnahme ethischer Argumentation in der Pädagogik*, in H. Blankertz, *Die Theorie-Praxis-Diskussion in der Erziehungswissenschaft*, Weinheim/Basel.
MOORE, D.L. (2007), *Overcoming Religious Illiteracy. A Cultural Studies Approach to the Study of Religion in Secondary Education*, New York.
MOORE, M.E.M. & A.M. RIGHT (2007), *Children, Youth, and Spirituality in a Troubling World*, Atlanta.
MOORE, S. (1993), *Four Steps Towards Making Sense of Theology*, in *Downside Review 111*, 79-100.
MÜLLER-FRIESE, A. (1996), *Miteinander der Verschiedenen. Theologische Überlegungen zu einem integrativen Bildungsverständnis*, Weinheim.
MUSTAKOVA-POSSARDT, E. (2004), *Education for critical moral consciousness*, in *Journal of Moral Education 33* (3), 245-269.
NADEAU, J.-G. (1994), *Evangelization and Youth Culture seen from French Canada*, in *Concilium* (2), 88-97.

NIJHUIS, H.G.M. (1996), *Waarde(n)vol leren. Analyse en evaluatie van waarden en normen in schoolboeken* (Opleiding en identiteit 4), Den Haag.
NIPKOW, K.E. (1994), *Ziele interreligiösen Lernens als mehrdimensionales Problem*, in J.A. van der Ven & H.-G. Ziebertz, *Religiöser Pluralismus und interreligiöses Lernen*, Kampen/Weinheim, 197-232.
NUSSBAUM, M. (1993), *La vertue rétablie. Habitude, passion et réflexion dans la tradition aristotélicienne*, in *Le Supplément # 186*, 171-187.
O'BRIEN, M. (1997), *How We Are Together: Educating for Group Self-Understanding in the Congregation*, in *Religious Education 92*, 315-331.
O'BRIEN, M. (2007), *A Study of Ministerial Identity and Theological reflection among Lay Ecclesial Ministers*, in *International Journal of Practical Theology 11*, 212-233.
OSEWSKA, E. (2011), *Catechesis with children in a Polish family – Empirical insights*, in F. Kraft, H. Roose and G. Büttner (eds.), *Symmetrical Communication? Philosophy and Theology in Classrooms across Europe*, Loccum, 35-48.
OSMER, R.R. & K.C. DEAN (eds.) (2006), *Youth, Religion and Globalization. New Research in Practical Theology,* Berlin.
OSMER, R.R. & SCHWEITZER, F. (2003), *Religious Education between Modernization and Globalization. New Perspectives on the US and Germany*, Grand Rapids.
OTT, R. (1995), *Lernen in der Begegnung mit der Bibel*, in H.-G. Ziebertz & W. Simon (ed.), *Bilanz der Religionspädagogik*, Düsseldorf, 291-304.
PALMER, P.J. (1983), *To Know as We Are Known. A Spirituality of Education*, San Francisco.
PALMER, P.J. (2000), *Let Your Life Speak. Listening for the Voice of Vocation,* San Francisco.
PANIKKAR, R. (1978), *The Intra-Religious Dialogue,* New York.
PARKER, E.L. (2001), *Hungry for honour: Children in violent youth gangs*, in *Interpretation. A Journal of Bible and Theology 55,* 148-160.
PARKER, E.L. (2003), *Trouble Don't Last Always. Emancipatory Hope Among African American Adolescents,* Cleveland.
PATEL, E. (2007), *Acts of Faith. The Story of an American Muslim, the Struggle for the Soul of a Generatio,* Boston.
PELLETIER, A.M. (2002), *Pour que la Bible reste un livre dangereux*, in *Etudes 397*, 335-345.
PETERMANN, H.-B. (2009), *'The story wants to make us think...' Opportunities for Theologising and Philosophising with Children*, in G. Yde Iversen, G. Mitchell & G. Pollard (eds.), *Hovering over the Face of the Deep*, 129-145.
PETERS, R.S. ($1978^5$), *Ethics and Education*, London ($1966^1$).
PETERS, R.S. (1980), *Education and the Education of Teachers,* London.
PEUKERT, H. (1984), *Über die Zukunft von Bildung*, in *Frankfurter Hefte 6,* 129-137.

PEUKERT, H. (1987), *Tradition und Transformation. Zu einer pädagogischen Theorie der Überlieferung*, in Religionspädagogische Beiträge *19*, 16-34.
PEUKERT, H. (2002), *Reflexionen über die Zukunft religiöser Bildung*, in Religionspädagogische Beiträge # 49, 49-66.
POLLEFEYT, D. (ed.) (2007), *Interreligious Learning*, Leuven-Paris-Dudley (MA).
POLLEFEYT, D., HUTSEBAUT, D., LOMBAERTS, H., DE VLIEGER, M., DILLEN, A., MAEX, J. & SMIT, W. (2004), *Godsdienstonderwijs uitgedaagd. Jongeren en (inter)levensbeschouwelijke vorming in gezin en onderwijs* (Instrumenta Theologica 26), Leuven.
POTOK, C. (1972), *My Name is Asher Lev*, New York.
POTOK, C. (1990), *The Gift of Asher Lev*, New York.
PROKOPF, A. & ZIEBERTZ, H.-G. (2000), *Abduktive Korrelation – eine Neuorientierung für die Korrelationsdidaktik?*, in Religionspädagogische Beiträge # 44, 19-50.
RAHNER, K. (1966), *Gedanken zu einer Theologie der Kindheit*, in Id., *Schriften zur Theologie* (Band VII), Einsiedeln/Zürich/Köln, 313-329.
REGAN, J. (2002), *Toward an Adult Church: A Vision of Faith Formation*, Chicago.
REINDERS, H. (2008), *Receiving the Gift of Friendship. Profound Disability, Theological Anthropology and Ethics,* Grand Rapids (MI).
RICKERS, F. (1998), *Interreligiöses Lernen. Die religionspädagogische Herausforderung unserer Zeit,* in F. Rickers & E. Gottwald (ed.), *Von religiösen zum interreligiösen Lernen: wie Angehörige verschiedener Religionen und Konfessionen lernen,* Neukirchen-Vluyn, 119-139.
RICOEUR, P. (1986), *Life: A Story in Search of a Narrator*, in M.C. Doeser & N. Kraaj (eds.), *Facts and Values. Philosophical Reflections from Western and Non-Western Perspectives,* Dordrecht, 121-132.
RIEDEL-SPANGENBERGER, I. (2004), *Art. Missio Canonica*, in S. Häring and H. Schmitz (eds.), *Lexikon des Kirchenrechts.* Freiburg, kol. 662-664.
RIEGEL, U. & ZIEBERTZ, H.-G., *Religious Education and Values*, in Journal of Empirical Theology *20*, 52-76.
RIEGGER, M. (2003), *Compassion: Learning and Doing. A Study on the Implementation of the Compassion Project at a State School in Germany*, in Journal of Empirical Theology 16 (2), 5-32.
ROEBBEN, B. (1995a), *Een tijd van opvoeden. Moraalpedagogiek in christelijk perspectief,* Leuven/Amersfoort.
ROEBBEN, B. (1995b), *Catching a Glimpse of the Palace of Reason. The Education of Moral Emotions,* in Journal of Moral Education *24*, 185-197.
ROEBBEN, B. (1995c), *Do We Still Have Faith in Young People? A West-European Answer to the Evangelization of Young People in a Postmodern World*, in Religious Education *90*, 327-345.
ROEBBEN, B. (1997), *Shaping a Playground for Transcendence. Postmodern Youth Ministry as a Radical Challenge,* in Religious Education *92*, 332-347.

ROEBBEN, B. (1999a), "*Middelpuntvliedende kracht*". *De interreligieuze dynamiek van het christelijk godsdienstonderwijs,* in J. Haers & T. Merrigan (eds.), *Christus in veelvoud.* Pluraliteit en de vraag naar eenheid in de hedendaagse christologie, Leuven/Amersfoort, 229-242.

ROEBBEN, B. (1999b), *Youth Ministry in and beyond the Church. The Sacrament of Confirmation in the Roman Catholic Church as a Testcase,* in *Journal of Beliefs and Values 20* (1), 51-59.

ROEBBEN, B. (1999c), *Spiritual and Moral Education in/and Cyberspace: Preliminary Reflections,* in *Journal of Education and Christian Belief 3,* 85-95.

ROEBBEN, B. (ed.) (2000), *Religieus opvoeden in een multiculturele samenleving,* Leuven.

ROEBBEN, B. (2001a), *Youth, Modernization and the Identity of the Catholic School. The Case of "Days of Reflection" in Flanders,* in H.-G. Ziebertz et al., *Religious Individualization and Christian Religious Semantics* (Empirische Theologie 8), Münster/Hamburg/London, 97-114.

ROEBBEN, B. (2001b), *The Vulnerability of the Postmodern Educator as Locus Theologicus. A Study in Practical Theology,* in *Religious Education 96,* 175-192.

ROEBBEN, B. (2001c), *Religious Education Through Times of Crisis. Reflections on the Future of a Vulnerable School Subject,* in B. Roebben & M. Warren (eds.), *Religious Education as Practical Theology. Essays in Honour of Professor Herman Lombaerts,* Leuven/Paris/Sterling, 245-272.

ROEBBEN, B. (2001d), *Moralpädagogische Überlegungen im Hinblick auf die Entwicklung christlicher Identität im Kulturwandel,* in T. Schreijäck (ed.), *Christwerden im Kulturwandel. Analysen, Themen und Optionen für Religionspädagogik und Praktische Theologie. Ein Handbuch,* Freiburg/Basel/Wien, 248-274.

ROEBBEN, B. (2003), *Bewogenheid in beweging. Een visie op de spiritualiteit van een christelijke school,* Brussel.

ROEBBEN, B. (2007), *Godsdienstpedagogiek van de hoop. Grondlijnen voor religieuze vorming,* Leuven.

ROEBBEN, B. (2009), *De speelruimte van het geloof. Getuigenis van een theoloog,* Leuven.

ROEBBEN, B. (2011), *Scholen voor het leven. Kleine didactiek van de hoop in zeven stappen,* Leuven.

ROEBBEN, B. (2012), *Living and learning in the presence of the other. Defining religious education inclusively,* in *International Journal of Inclusive Education 16,* 1175-1187.

ROEBBEN, B. & BURGGRAEVE, R. (1992), *Opvoeding als opvordering. Over de relatie tussen opvoeding en ethiek,* in G. Maertens & J. Verstraeten (eds.), *Ethische perspectieven op mens, maatschappij en milieu,* Tielt, 191-238.

ROEBBEN, B. & L. VAN DER TUIN (2004), *Mapping the Roads of Transcendence. Religious Education in a Multicultural Society,* in D. Nauer, R. Nauta & H.

Witte (eds.), *Religious Leadership and Christian Identity*, Münster, 130-142.
ROEBBEN, B. & T. ZONDERVAN (2008), *„Und wenn Gott unter uns wäre".*
*Praktische Kulturtheologie und die Lebenswelt junger Erwachsener*, in *International Journal of Practical Theology 12,* 256-273.
ROEBBEN, B. & K. DE WILDT (2010), *Religious Socialisation and Religious Education in the Netherlands. Developments and Perspectives,* in K. Tenfelde (Ed.), *Religiöse Sozialisationen im 20. Jahrhundert. Historische und vergleichende Perspektiven*, Essen, 219-230.
ROEBBEN, B. & C. DOMMEL (2013), *Education as Negotiation: Discovering New Patterns of Religious Identity Formation in Germany* [unpublished paper], Dortmund.
ROOSE, H. & C. BUTT (2009), *'God cannot always forgive'. Reading Mt 18:21-35 with children,* in G. Yde Iversen, G. Mitchell & G. Pollard (eds.), *Hovering over the Face of the Deep*, 37-51.
ROOT, A. (2009), *Relationships Unfiltered,* Grand Rapids (MI).
RUSTER, T. (2000), *Der verwechselbare Gott. Theologie nach der Entflechtung von Christentum und Religion.* Freiburg.
SANDER, H.J. (2005), *Theologischer Kommentar zur Pastoralkonstitution über die Kirche in der Welt von heute ‚Gaudium et spes',* in P. Hünermann and B.J. Hilberath (eds.), *Herders Theologischer Kommentar zum Zweiten Vatikanischen Konzil* (Volume 4), Freiburg, 581-886.
SANTOS, J.B. (2008), *A Community Called Taizé: A Story of Prayer, Worship and Reconciliation,* Nottingham.
SAVAGE, S., S. COLLINS-MAYO & B. MAYO (eds.) (2006), *Making Sense of Generation Y. The World of 15-25-year-olds*, London.
SCHAMBECK, M. (2006), *Mystagogisches Lernen. Zu einer Perspektive religiöser Bildung,* Würzburg.
SCHARNBERG, C. (2010), *Event – Jugend – Pastoral. Eine quantitativ-empirisch gestützte Theorie des religiösen Jugendevents am Beispiel des Weltjugendtages 2002,* Berlin.
SCHILLEBEECKX, E. (1977), *Gerechtigheid en liefde. Genade en bevrijding.* Bloemendaal.
SCHILLEBEECKX, E. (1978), *Glaube und Moral,* in D. Mieth & F. Compagnoni (ed.), *Ethik im Context des Glaubens. Probleme – Grundsätze – Methoden* (Studien zur theologischen Ethik 3), Freiburg/Wenen.
SCHILLEBEECKX, E. (2005), *Christelijke identiteit, uitdagend en uitgedaagd. Over de rakelingse nabijheid van de onervaarbare God*, in M. Kalsky, A. Lascaris, L. Oosterveen & I. Van Der Spek, *Ons rakelings nabij. Gedaanteveranderingen van God en geloof,* Nijmegen/Zoetermeer, 13-32.
SCHLAG, T. & F. SCHWEITZER (2011), *Brauchen Jugendliche Theologie? Jugendtheologie als Herausforderung und didaktische Perspektive,* Neukirchen-Vluyn.

SCHMIDT, P. (1993), *Verstaan we nog zelf wat we zeggen? Over de mededeelbaarheid van de geloofstaal*, in J. Claes & J. Kerkhofs (eds.), *Geloof en cultuur. Christen-zijn in het Europa van morgen*, Averbode/Apeldoorn, 87-103.
SCHNEIDERS, S. (2003), *Religion versus Spirituality: A Contemporary Conundrum*, in *Spiritus: A Journal of Christian Spirituality 3* (2), 163-185.
SCHOBERT, I. (2002), *Glauben-lernen heisst eine Sprache lernen*, in *Religionsunterricht an höheren Schulen 45* (1), 20-31.
SCHWARZ, E. (2003), *Philosophieren und Theologisieren mit Kindern. Ein Akademielehrgang besonderer Art*, in *Jahrbuch für Kindertheologie 2*, 203-206.
SCHWEITZER, F. (1993), *Der Wandel des Jugendalters und die Religionspädagogik*, in *Jahrbuch für Religionspädagogik 10*, 71-88.
SCHWEITZER, F. (1996), *Die Suche nach eigenem Glauben. Einführung in die Religionspädagogik des Jugendalters*, Gütersloh.
SCHWEITZER, F. (1998), *Schlüsselerfahrungen – ein neues religionpedägogisches Konzept?,* in *Jahrbuch für Religionspägogik 16*, 191-212.
SCHWEITZER, F. (1999), *"Identität und Verständigung" und "Bildende Kraft des Religionsunterrichts"*, in R. Frieling & C.Th. Scheilke (eds.), *Religionsunterricht und Konfessionen*, Göttingen, 71-86.
SCHWEITZER, F. (2000), *Das Recht des Kindes auf Religion. Ermutigungen für Eltern und Erzieher*, Gütersloh.
SCHWEITZER, F. (2003a), *Elementarisierung im Religionsunterricht. Erfahrungen, Perspektiven, Beispiele*, Neukirchen-Vluyn.
SCHWEITZER, F. (2003b), *Was ist und wozu Kindertheologie?,* in *Jahrbuch für Kindertheologie 2*, 9-18.
SCHWEITZER, F. (2004a), *Comparative Research in Religious Education: International-Interdenominational-Interreligious*, in R. Larsson & C. Gustavsson (eds.), *Towards a European Perspective on Religious Education*, Lund, 191-200.
SCHWEITZER, F. (2004b), *The Postmodern Life Cycle. Challenges for Church and Theology*, St. Louis (MO).
SCHWEITZER, F. (2006), *Religionspädagogik* (Lehrbuch Praktische Theologie Band 1), Gütersloh.
SCHWEITZER, F. (2007), *Religious individualization: new challenges to education for tolerance*, in *British Journal of Religious Education 29*, 89-100.
SCHWEITZER, F. & C.T. SCHEILKE (1999), *Religion, Ethik, Schule. Bildungspolitische Perspektiven in der pluralen Gesellschaft*, Münster/New York/München/Berlin.
SCHWEITZER, F., W. ILG & H. SIMOJOKI (eds.) (2010), *Confirmation Work in Europe: Empirical Results, Experiences and Challenges. A Comparative Study from Seven Countries*, Gütersloh.
SCHWENZER, A. (1996), *Unbegrenzte Möglichkeiten? Das Internet als Chance und Herausforderung*, in *Herder Korrespondenz 50*, 519-524.

SEDMAK, C. (2002), *Doing Local Theology. A Guide for Artisans of a New Humanity,* Maryknoll (NY).
SIMMONS, J.K. (2006), *Vanishing Boundaries: When Teaching About Religion Becomes Spiritual Guidance in the Classroom,* in *Teaching Theology and Religion 9* (1), 37-43.
SIMON, W. (2007), *Weltjugendtage: Orte der Präsenz von Religiosität Jugendlicher,* in *Christlich-Pädagogische Blätter 120,* 105-108.
SIMONS, M. & J. MASSCHELEIN (2009), *The Public and Its University: beyond learning for civic employability?,* in *European Educational Research Journal 8,* 204-217.
SJAH, J.M. (2002), *Axis mundi,* in *Narthex. Tijdschrift voor levensbeschouwing en educatie 2* (1), 26-29.
SMEETS, W. (2007), *Verleiden tot God. Jongeren inwijden tot christelijke spiritualiteit,* Tielt.
SMITH, C. & LUNDQUIST DENTON, M. (2005), *Soul Searching. The Religious and Spiritual Lives of American Teenagers,* Oxford.
SNIK, G. (1992-93), *Morele opvoeding in het licht van het liberalisme-communitarisme-debat,* in *Wijsgerig perspectief 33* (2), 36-43.
SONNENBERG, R. & BARNARD, M. (2008), *'God Talk between Beat and Silence. Presentatie van een PhD-project over youth worship in protestantse contexten,* in *Jaarboek voor liturgie-onderzoek 24,* 177-197.
STACHEL, G. & D. MIETH (1978), *Ethisch Handeln Lernen. Zu Konzeption und Inhalt ethischer Erziehung,* Zürich.
STAMS, E. (2008), *Das Experiment Jugendkirche. Die ersten Jahre der Jugendkirche TABGHA in Oberhausen. Eine exemplarische Fallstudie zur Problematik jugendpastorale Neuorientierung* (Praktische Theologie heute 94), Stuttgart.
STERKENS, C., HERMANS, C.A.M. & VAN DER VEN, J.A. (1999), *Theories About the Relationship Between Religions in Religious Education,* in A. Ploeger & C. Sterkens (eds.), *Search for Meaning. Education into Realms of Meaning in a Plural Society* (Theologie und Empirie 31), Kampen, 163-190.
STREIB, H. (1994), *Erzählte Zeit als Ermöglichung von Identität und seine Implikationen für die religionspädagogische Rede von Identität und Bildung,* in D. Georgi, H.-G. Heimbrock & M. Moxter (ed.), *Religion und die Gestaltung der Zeit,* Kampen, 181-198.
STREIB, H. (1998), *The Religious Educator as Story-Teller. Suggestions from Paul Ricoeur's Work,* in *Religious Education 93,* 314-331.
STREIB, H. (2001), *Inter-Religious Negotiations: Case Studies on Students' Perception of and Dealing with Religious Diversity,* in H.-G. Heimbrock, C.Th. Scheilke & P. Schreiner (eds.), *Towards Religious Competence. Diversity as a Challenge for Education in Europe,* Münster, 129-149.

TAPPAN, M.B. & BROWN, L.M. (1996), *Envisioning a Postmodern Moral Pedagogy,* in *Journal of Moral Education 25,* 101-109.
TAYLOR, C. (1996), *De politieke cultuur van de moderniteit,* Kampen/Kapellen.
THÉVENOT, X. (1991), *Rendre moral l'influence éducative,* in X. Thévenot & J. Joncheray et al., *Pour une éthique de la pratique éducative* (Relais-Etudes 9), Parijs, 261-286.
THEVENOT, X. (1993), *Une éthique au risque de l'évangile. Entretiens avec Yves de Gentil-Baichis,* Paris.
TIELEMAN, D. (1995), *Geloofscrisis als gezichtsbedrog. Spiritualiteit en pastoraat in een postmoderne cultuur,* Kampen.
TILLARD, J.-M. (1997), *Sommes-nous les derniers chrétiens?,* Québec.
TRACY, D. (1987), *Plurality and Ambiguity. Hermeneutics, Religion, Hope,* San Francisco.
VALADIER, P. (1990), *Identité chrétienne et morale,* in J. Doré, *Sur l'identité chrétienne,* Paris, 91-102.
VALSTAR, J. & H. KUINDERSMA (2008), *Verwonderen en ontdekken. Vakdidactiek godsdienst primair onderwijs,* Amersfoort.
VAN AALSUM, L. (2011), *Spiritualiteit in het onderwijs. Een handreiking,* Delft.
VAN DEN BERK, T. (1999), *Mystagogie. Inwijding in het symbolisch bewustzijn,* Zoetermeer.
VAN DEN BOSCH, H. (2006), *In het spoor van Gods gedaanteverandering. Praktische theologie als hermeneutiek van de cultuur,* in *Tijdschrift voor Theologie 46,* 33-57.
VAN DER VEN, J.A. (1985), *Vorming in waarden en normen,* Kampen.
VAN DER VEN, J.A. (1994), *Kontingenz und Religion in einer säkularisierten und multikulturellen Gesellschaft,* in J.A. van der Ven & H.-G. Ziebertz, *Religiöser Pluralismus und interreligiöses Lernen,* Kampen/Weinheim, 15-37.
VAN DER VEN, J.A. (1995), *Het religieus bewustzijn van jongeren en de crisis van het jongerenpastoraat,* in *Praktische Theologie 22,* 342-364.
VAN DER VEN, J.A. (1998), *Formation of the Moral Self* (Studies in Practical Theology 1), Grand Rapids/Cambridge.
VAN DER VEN, J.A. & ZIEBERTZ, H.-G. (1994), *Religiöser Pluralismus und interreligiöses Lernen,* Kampen/Weinheim.
VAN DIJK-GROENEBOER, M. (2010), *Handboek Jongeren en religie. Katholieke, Protestantse en Islamitische jongeren in Nederland,* Almere.
VAN GERWEN, J. (1995), *Ethiek als profiel, ethiek als koopwaar. Het Gentse communicatiebureau "Imagine",* in J. Taels (ed.), *De vis heeft geen weet van het water. Ethiek tussen berekening en zorg,* Kapellen, 71-90.

VAN HAAFTEN, A.W. (1986), *Over de rechtvaardiging van morele opvoeding,* in *Nederlands Tijdschrift voor Opvoeding, Vorming en Onderwijs 2,* 178-194.
VAN HARSKAMP, A. (2000), *Het nieuw-religieuze verlangen,* Kampen.
VAN KNIPPENBERG, T. (2002), *Toward religious identity. An exercise in spiritual guidance,* Assen.
VAN RIESSEN, R. (2007), *Man as Place of God. Levinas' Hermeneutics of Kenosis,* Dordrecht.
VELING, T. (1998), *"Practical Theology": a New Sensibility for Theological Education,* in *Pacifica* 11, 195-210.
*Visietekst van de Vlaamse bisschoppen 'Het vak RK godsdienst in de scholen van Vlaanderen'* (1996), Brussel.
VON STOSCH, K. (2012), *Ekklesiologische Konsequenzen der Inkarnation,* in *Rellis 1* (2), 4-6.
VOSSEN, E. (1986), *Religieuze vorming in een gerationaliseerde kultuur,* in *Praktische theologie 13,* 235-254.
VRIENS, L.J.A. (1998), *Niet het kind maar de cultuur is gewelddadig,* in *De Bazuin,* 6 februari 1998, p. 24-27.
VUIJSJE, H. (2002[6]), *Pelgrim zonder God,* Amsterdam/Antwerpen.
WARD, P. (2002), *Liquid Church,* Peabody (MA)/Carlisle (Cumbria).
WARD, P. (2008), *Participation and Mediation. A Practical Theology for the Liquid Church.* London.
WARD, P. (2012), *The hermeneutical and epistemological significance of our students,* in *International Journal of Practical Theology 16,* 55-65.
WARREN, M. (1982), *Youth and the Future of the Church: Ministry with Youth and Young Adults,* New York.
WARREN, M. (1987), *Readings and Resources in Youth Ministry,* Winona.
WARREN, M. (1994-95), *Judging the Electronic Communications Media,* in *The Living Light 31* (2), 54-64.
WARREN, M. (1998), *Youth, Gospel, Liberation,* Dublin.
WARREN, M. (2002), *Youth Ministry in an Inconvenient Church,* Princeton.
WHITE, D. (2005), *Practicing Discernment with Youth. A Transformative Youth Ministry Approach,* Cleveland (OH).
WINNICOT, D.W. (1963), *The Young Child at Home and at School,* in W.R. Niblett (ed.), *Moral Education in a Changing Society,* London, 96-111.
WRIGHT, A. (2009), *The Integrity of Students' Theological Discourse: Critical Realism and the Variation Theory of Learning,* in G. Yde Iversen, G. Mitchell & G. Pollard (eds.), *Hovering over the Face of the Deep,* 163-175.
YDE IVERSEN, G., G. MITCHELL & G. POLLARD (eds.) (2009), *Hovering over the Face of the Deep. Philosophy, Theology and Children,* Münster.
YUST, K.M. et al. (eds.) (2005), *Nurturing Child and Adolescent Spirituality: Perspectives from the World's Religious Traditions,* Lanham (MD).

ZIEBERTZ, H.-G. (1995), *Religious Socialisation and the Identification of Religion*, in E. Henau & R.J. Schreiter (eds.), *Religious Socialisation*, Weinheim/Kampen, 17-29.
ZIEBERTZ, H.-G. (2003), *Religious Education in a Plural Western Culture. Problems and Challenges,* Münster/Hamburg/London, Lit-Verlag.
ZIEBERTZ, H.-G. (2005), *Models of Inter-Religious Learning: an Empirical Study in Germany,* in L.J. Francis, M. Robbins & J. Astley (eds.), *Religion, Education and Adolescence. International Empirical Perspectives,* Cardiff, 204-221.
ZIEBERTZ, H.-G., HEIL, S. & PROKOPF, A. (2001), *Schülerorientierung und korrelative Professionalität. Konsequenzen einer abduktiven Korrelationsdidaktik*, in H. Mendl & M. Schiefer-Ferrari (ed.), *Tradition, Korrelation, Innovation. Trends der Religionsdidaktik in Vergangenheit und Gegenwart,* Donauwörth, 162-174.
ZIEBERTZ, H.-G. & W. K. KAY (eds.) (2005), *Youth in Europe I,* Berlin.
ZIEBERTZ, H.-G. & W. K. KAY (eds.) (2006), *Youth in Europe II,* Berlin.
ZIEBERTZ, H.-G. & W. K. KAY (eds.) (2009), *Youth in Europe III,* Berlin.
ZONDERVAN, T. (2004), *Forms of God. Meditation, Liturgy and Gregorian Chant in Religious Youth Work*, in *Tà Katoptrizomena. Magazin für Theologie und Ästhetik* # 27.
ZONDERVAN, T. (2006), *Faith in Networks. Religious Education of Dutch Young Adults in a 'Post-Ecclesial Era*, in *Journal of Youth and Theology* 5 (1), 52-67.
ZONDERVAN. T. (ed.) (2008), *Bricolage en bezieling. Over jongeren, cultuur en religie*, Averbode.

# Acknowledgments

Chapter 1 – [Previously published as] *To Initiate into a World of Difference: A Design for Dynamic-Integral Values Education*, in *Louvain Studies* 19 (1994) 4, 338-349.

Chapter 2 – Not published before.

Chapter 3 – [Previously published as] *Religious Communication in Modern Culture. The Case of Young Adults*, in B. Roebben & L. van der Tuin (eds.), *Practical Theology and the Interpretation of Crossing Boundaries. Essays in Honour of Professor M.P.J. van Knippenberg* (Theologie Band 52), Münster/Hamburg/London, Lit-Verlag, 2003, 165-186.

Chapter 4 – [New draft of] *The Vulnerability of the Postmodern Educator as Locus Theologicus. A Study in Practical Theology*, in *Religious Education* 96 (2001) 2, 175-192.

Chapter 5 – [Previously published as] *Narthical Religious Learning. Redefining Religious Education in Terms of Pilgrimage*, in *British Journal of Religious Education* 31 (2009) 1, 17-27.

Chapter 6 – [New draft of] *Children's Theology: Concepts and Contexts, Problems and Horizons,* in F. Kraft, H. Roose and G. Büttner (eds.), *Symmetrical Communication? Philosophy and Theology in Classrooms across Europe*, Loccum, RPI, 2011, 11-24.

Chapter 7 – [Previously published as] *Learning in difference. Interreligious learning in the secondary school,* in P. Kieran & A. Hession (eds), *Exploring Religious Education: Catholic Religious Education in an Intercultural Europe*, Dublin, Veritas, 2008, 124-140.

Chapter 8 – [Previoulsy published as] *Modern Narrative Identities and the Bible. Notes on a Subversive Concept of Religious Education*, in H. Lombaerts & D. Pollefeyt (eds.), *Hermeneutics and Religious Education* (Bibliotheca Ephemeridum Theologicarum Lovaniensium, 180), Leuven, Peeters, 2004, 215-231.

Chapter 9 – [Previously published as] *Young adults on the crossroads between professionalization and spirituality. Roman-Catholic theology and the education of teachers in religion in Western-Europe,* in *Journal of Adult Theological Education,* in *Journal of Adult Theological Education* 6 (2009) 1, 55-68.

Chapter 10 – Not published before.

Chapter 11 – [New draft of] *Shaping a Playground for Transcendence. Postmodern Youth Ministry as a Radical Challenge*, in *Religious Education* 92 (1997) 3, p. 332-347.

Chapter 12 – [Combination of previously published] *Witnessing on the Way. West-European Perspectives on the Roman-Catholic Church as a Learning Community*, in *Journal of Youth and Theology* 6 (2007) 2, 60-68, and *Light of Day. Scaffolding a Theology of Youth Ministry*, in *Journal of Youth and Theology* 4 (2005) 1, 23-32.

Chapter 13 – [Previously published as] *The Mirror effect: Reflective Theological Education and Religious Consciousness in Young Adult Ministry,* in R. Larsson & C. Gustavsson (eds.), *Towards a European Perspective on Religious Education* (Bibliotheca Theologiae Practicae 74), Lund, Artos, 2004, 332-343.

Chapter 14 – [Previously published as] *International Developments in Youth Ministry Research. A Comparative Review*, in *Religious Education* 107 (2012) 2, 192-206.

# Index

Adorno, T.W. 31
Afdal, G. 253
Alexander, H.A. 62, 104, 168, 171, 181, 206, 257, 276
Allan, J. 262
Alma, H.A. 246
Anselm of Canterbury 226
Apel, K.-O. 51
Arendt, H. 263
Astley, J. 132
Baart, A. 238
Baker, J. 253
Bakhtin, M. 203-204
Bakker, C. 161
Baldermann, I. 11, 174
Banning, B. 264
Barnard, M. 253
Beaudoin, T. 78, 271, 272-273
Benson, P.L. 262
Berg, H.-K. 173, 180
Bieringer, R. 177
Bitter, G. 170, 178
Bluyssen, J. 65-66
Bonnett, M. 100
Bopp, K. 220, 225
Borgman, E. 82, 177, 231, 242, 277
Boschki, R. 94, 203
Bowman, L. 160
Boys, M. 144, 159, 162-164
Buber, M. 203
Bucher, A. 47, 52-53,
58, 113, 133, 172
Burggraeve, R. 101, 181, 240
Büttner, G. 24, 130, 265
Butt, C. 132
Callahan, S. 46
Cardijn, J. 268
Carr, D. 47
Champagne, E. 266
Cohen, E.H. 126
Copley, T. 57, 179
Crawford, M. 146
Daelemans, A. 86
Dalferth, I. 130, 178
Daloz Parks, S. 12, 44, 130, 264
Dasberg, L. 39
Dean, K.C. 232, 253, 264, 265, 267, 272
Defois, G. 88
Dekker, G. 67, 75
Deleu, P. 69
Dewey, J. 203
De Wildt, K. 67, 128
Dillen, A. 45, 134
Dobbelaere, K. 67
Dommel, C. 128, 151
Drehsen, V. 69-70, 222-224
Duffy, S.J. 104
Dumestre, M.J. 93
Dunlop, S. 253
Ebertz, M.N. 72, 74, 79, 89
Eid, V. 57, 99

Elchardus, M. 235
Engedal, L.G. 126
Englert, R. 76-77, 93, 121, 171, 172, 191
Exeler, A. 33
Farley, E. 197
Feifel, E. 69, 171
Feininger, B. 174, 180
Fraas, H.-J. 181
Fuchs-Heinritz, W. 217
Gabriel, A. 262
Gabriel, K. 67, 69
Ganzevoort, R. 176
Geerinck, I. 165
Geffré, C. 104
Geurts, Th. 52
Gibran, K. 101
Gilbert, G. 239
Gilligan, C. 256
Giroux, H.A. 153
Greiner, U. 203, 208, 217
Grimmitt, M. 237
Groome, Th. 211
Grözinger, A. 95
Grümme, B. 121, 137, 175, 177, 178, 203
Grün, A. 253
Gutierrez, G. 228
Haakedal, E. 138
Habermas, J. 51, 226
Haers, J. 52
Halsall, A. 112, 163
Haste, H. 55
Hay, D. 113, 132, 135, 265

Heidegger, M. 238, 250
Heil, S. 172
Heimbrock, H.-G. 258
Hendriks, J. 83
Hermans, C. 111, 152
Hervieu-Léger, D. 73-74
Hess, M. 44, 214
Hilger, G. 190
Huggler, J. 130
Hull, J. 57
Hussain, A. 112
Ipgrave, J. 139
Jackson, R. 111, 113, 129, 147, 156
Jäggle, M. 128
Janssen, J. 77, 78, 81, 246
Jeanrond, W. 276
Joas, H. 60, 120, 203, 204, 231
Kammeyer, K. 134
Kant, I. 130
Kasper, W. 69
Kay, W.K. 253
Kiamu, N.-J. 267
Kirsch, H.C. 256-257
Kirschenbaum, H. 48
Klie, Th. 121
Koerrenz, R. 177-178, 205, 276
Kohlberg, L. 34, 36, 46, 52, 158, 256
Kohler-Spiegel, H. 199
Kozyrev, F. 203-204
Kuindersma, H. 136
Kundera, M. 19
Kuyk, E. 131
Lechner, M. 223, 262
Leimgruber, S. 190

Lesch, W. 49, 51
Levinas, E. 101, 203, 204, 240
Leys, L. 267
Lickona, Th. 46-47, 52
Linhart, T. 265
Lipmann, M. 129
Livermore, D. 265
Lombaerts, H. 111, 146, 148, 192
Lubarsky, S. 159
Lundquist Denton, M. 230, 253, 267
Luther, H. 87
Lutz, H. 24
Maas, J. 85
Mahan, B. 264, 268, 271
Mallon, M.C. 213-214
Marquez, G.G. 201, 217
Martens, E. 130, 135
Masschelein, J. 202
McQuillan, P. 253
Meijer, W.A.J. 149
Meister Eckhart 272
Mercer, J.A. 56, 107, 131
Mette, N. 56, 80, 111, 146, 147, 170, 178, 224
Metz J.-B. 266
Meyer, H. 207
Michiels, R. 65
Miedema, S. 143, 147, 255
Mieth, D. 231
Mokrosch, R. 151
Mollenhauer, K. 31

Moltmann, J. 228
Moore, D.L. 269
Moore, M.E.M. 266, 267
Moore, S. 93, 105
Müller-Friese, A. 203
Nadeau, J.-G. 194
Newman, J.H. 104
Nijhuis, H. 47, 50
Nipkow, K.E. 147, 155
Nussbaum, M. 96-97
Nye, R. 113, 132, 135, 265
Oakeshott, M. 201
O'Brien, M. 93, 198
Osewska, E. 138
Osmer, R.R. 70, 128, 251, 265
Ott, R. 174, 180
Panikkar, R. 162
Palmer, P.J. 208, 253
Parker, E. 236, 248, 267
Patel, E. 267
Pelletier, A.M. 175
Petermann, H.-B. 129-130, 131, 136
Peters, R.S. 35-36, 97
Peukert, H. 122, 178, 203
Pola, Th. 24
Pollefeyt, D. 111, 146, 152, 159, 192
Potok, C. 15-16
Prins, M. 77, 81
Prokopf, A. 172
Rahner, K. 131, 132, 228, 271, 272-273
Regan, J. 93
Reinders, H. 266
Rickers, F. 156

Ricoeur, P. 100, 116, 172, 177
Riedel-Spangenberger, I. 186
Riegel, U. 159
Riegger, M. 52
Right, A.M. 266, 267
Rittelmeyer, C. 31
Root, A. 264, 271
Rosenzweig, F. 256-257
Roose, H. 132
Rossiter, G. 146
Ruster, Th. 175-177
Sander, H.-J. 188
Santos, J.B. 253
Savage, S. 253
Schambeck, M. 121
Scharnberg, C. 253
Scheilke, C. Th. 264
Schillebeeckx, E. 103, 177, 228, 231, 233, 277
Schlag, Th. 265, 270, 272
Schmidt, P. 86
Schneiders, S. 60, 177
Schobert, I. 174, 182
Schreiter, R. 213-214
Schwarz, E. 135
Schweitzer, F. 70-72, 90, 111, 112, 118, 120, 127-128, 133, 136, 146, 151, 172, 178, 181-182, 217, 251, 253, 264, 265, 270, 272
Sedmak, C. 138
Segundo, J.-L. 177
Servotte, H. 14
Simmons, J.K. 160
Simon, W. 214

Simons, M. 202
Sjah, J.M. 144
Smeets. W. 264
Smith, C. 230, 253, 267
Snik, G. 49
Sölle, D. 226
Sonnenberg, R. 253
Stachel, G. 231
Stams, E. 253
Sterkens, C. 152
Streib, H. 116, 149, 158, 172
Taylor, Ch. 54-56, 203
Thévenot, X. 225
Thomas Aquinas 223
Tieleman, D. 75
Tillard, J.-M. 87, 229
Tillich, P. 260
Tracy, D. 207
Valadier, J. 148
Valstar, J. 136
Van Aalsum, L. 264
Van den Berk, T. 121
Van den Bosch, H. 235, 277
Van der Tuin, L. 159
Van der Ven, J.A. 35-37, 45, 98, 148, 152, 154, 156, 222
Van Dijk-Groeneboer, M. 267
Van Gerwen, J. 79
Van Haaften, W. 32
Van Harskamp, A. 74, 80, 81-82
Van Knippenberg, T. 172, 178, 216, 239, 249, 256
Van Riessen, R. 204

Veling, T. 259
Von Stoch, K. 204
Vuijsje, H. 126
Vossen, E. 84-85, 87
Ward, P. 138, 197, 214, 259, 271
Warren, M. 215, 220, 221, 223, 253, 271
White, D. 21, 56, 218, 241-242, 268
Wiesel, E. 240

Winnicott, D. 29
Wright, A. 129-130
Wuthnow, R. 251
Yde Iversen, 129-130, 265
Yust, K.-M. 265
Ziebertz, H.-G. 45, 72, 85, 95, 111, 159, 172, 190, 253
Zondervan, T. 197, 198, 214, 228, 245

**Dortmunder Beiträge zu Theologie und Religionspädagogik**
hrsg. von Prof. Dr. Michael Basse und Prof. Dr. Thomas Pola

Wai-Kwong Sun
**Der Idealmensch des Konfuzius in paulinischer Betrachtung**
China ist im Aufschwung. Warum? Wohin? Ist das ein Segen für die Welt? Oder ein Fluch? Wenn man China verstehen will, kommt man an Konfuzius nicht vorbei. Das vorliegende Buch ist eine historisch erarbeitete Chinakunde. In einem zweiten Schritt wird das Menschenverständnis von Konfuzius in das Licht der paulinischen Missionstheologie gestellt.
Bd. 9, 2011, 296 S., 34,90 €, br., ISBN 978-3-643-11448-8

**LIT** Verlag Berlin – Münster – Wien – Zürich – London
Auslieferung Deutschland / Österreich / Schweiz: siehe Impressumsseite

Ekkehard Graf
**Durch Leiden geprägt**
Die gegenwärtigen Leidenserfahrungen der indischen Nethanja-Kirche mit einem Blick auf die paulinischen Gemeinden
Die Christen der noch jungen Nethanja-Kirche in Indien erleiden Bedrängnis und Verfolgung wegen ihres Glaubens. Trotzdem oder gerade deswegen wächst diese Kirche ständig. Diese Situation scheint mit den ersten christlichen Gemeinden in neutestamentlicher Zeit vergleichbar zu sein, was mit einem Blick auf Paulus und die von ihm gegründeten Gemeinden überprüft wird. Nach Informationen über die indische Gesellschaft und die Nethanja-Kirche werden die in Interviews geschilderten Leiden der indischen Christen dargestellt und in Verhältnis zu denen der paulinischen Gemeinden gesetzt. Inwieweit die Leiden das Selbstverständnis der Nethanja-Kirche sowie ihr Leben und ihren Glauben prägen, wird abschließend erörtert und Folgerungen für die Kirchen westlicher Prägung gezogen.
Bd. 10, 2012, 344 S., 29,90 €, br., ISBN 978-3-643-11595-9

LIT Verlag Berlin – Münster – Wien – Zürich – London
Auslieferung Deutschland / Österreich / Schweiz: siehe Impressumsseite

Florian Förg
**Die Jahwe-König-Psalmen und die Apokalyptik**
Im biblischen Buch der Psalmen umfassen die Jahwe-König-Psalmen, auch Thronbesteigungspsalmen genannt, die Psalmen 47 und 93-99. Sie heben sich durch einen überwältigenden Grundton der Freude und des Jubels von ihren Nachbarpsalmen ab. Die Königsherrschaft Jahwes bildet den Anlass der Freude in dieser Psalmgruppe – zugleich ist sie auch das Kernthema von apokalyptischen Texten. Die vorliegende, exegetisch ausgerichtete Studie untersucht die vielfältigen Beziehungen zwischen den Jahwe-König-Psalmen und der Apokalyptik.
Bd. 11, 2012, 160 S., 19,90 €, br., ISBN 978-3-643-90276-4